THE TERRORISTS

THE

The story of
the forerunners of Stalin

TERRORISTS

Robert Payne

FUNK & WAGNALLS COMPANY · NEW YORK

For the Martyrs

. . . I will do such things,—
What they are yet I know not,—but they shall be
The terrors of the earth.

KING LEAR

You seem to think there was a good deal of clair-
voyance in my latest novel, The Brothers Karamazov, *but wait till you read its sequel. I am*
working on it now. I am taking Alyosha Karamazov
out of his holy retreat in the monastery and I am
making him join the Nihilists. My pure Alyosha
shall kill the Czar!

—DOSTOYEVSKY, JANUARY 1881,
in a letter to the Russian editor Suvorin.

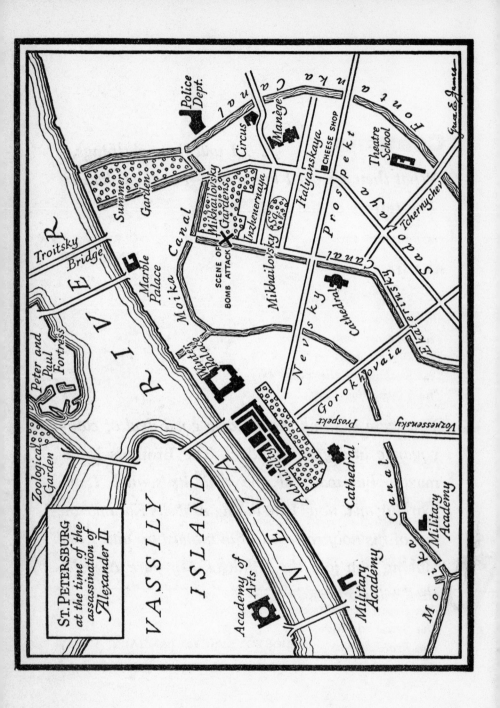

Police Dept.

Manège

Circus

Theatre School

CHEESE SHOP

Canal

Fontanka

Summer Garden

Mikhailovsky Gardens

Italyanskaya

Prospekt

Inzhenernaya

Mikhailovsky Sq.

Troitsky Bridge

R I V E R

Marble Palace

Moika Canal

SCENE OF
MIKHAILOVSKY
BOMB ATTACK

Mikhailovsky Canal

Nevsky

Kazan Cathedral

Tchernychev

Sadovaya

Ekaterinsky Canal

Peter and Paul Fortress

Winter Palace

Zoological Garden

Gorokhovaia Prospekt

Voznessensky

Admiralty

VASSILY

Cathedral

Canal

Moika

Military Academy

ISLAND

N E V A

Academy of Arts

Military Academy

Military Academy

ST. PETERSBURG
at the time of the
assassination of
Alexander II

Geo. E. James

Contents

KALIAYEV

Introduction

In one of those strange statements of purpose which the arch-terrorist Sergey Nechayev drew up, he wrote: "Our task is terrible, total, universal and merciless destruction."

When Nechayev wrote this, he meant exactly what he said, but the vision of terror exerted on a universal scale did not originate with him. It had its roots deep in Russian history, in the great blood-baths during the reign of Ivan the Terrible and in the violence of the schismatics who, quarreling over the interpretation of the scriptures, announced that all those who disagreed with them must suffer violent deaths. They were perfectly prepared to suffer violence upon themselves, for was it not written that all the world shall be cast into the flames? Deep within the Russian consciousness lay this tragic sense of the inevitability of doom.

No single incident in Russian history led to this strange desire for annihilation, which seemed to grow keener as the years passed. Men brooded in the endless plains of Russia; they saw visions, and fed on their own suffering. Slavery sharpened the misery of the peasants, and the landowners with their vast estates suffered from a sense of terrifying guilt. In the eighteenth and nineteenth centuries the autocratic rulers of Russia seemed determined to ruin the country, for they ruled by violence, and were incapable of coming to terms with the people. And many prophesied that out of the peasantry there would come a wave of terror which might destroy all Russia.

No one ever accused Ivan Turgenev, the sanest of Russian novelists, of a desire to embrace apocalyptic visions. He was a man of the world with a penetrating insight into the peasantry, whose virtues he was always celebrating. The peasants on his estate loved him. Yet he, too, was aware of the doom which awaited the rulers of Russia.

One day, while talking to his friend Leonid Polonsky, he fell into a brown study. Later Polonsky asked him what he had been dreaming about.

"I dreamed we were at my house in the country," Turgenev answered. "You and I—we were sitting on the terrace. Suddenly a crowd of peasants came up to us. They removed their hats and bowed low, and I remember saying: 'Well brothers, what can I do for you?' And they answered: 'Excuse us, please. Do not be angry with us. You are a good master, and we love you well. But all the same we must hang you, and this gentleman as well!' Then I said: 'What on earth are you talking about? Hang us?' They replied slowly and diffidently: 'Yes, master, it's all according to the law. A new order has been issued. We have brought the rope. Say your prayers. We can wait a little while.'"

The dream haunted Turgenev. He told it many times, and in many countries. Once he told Prosper Mérimée he believed that the Czar's decision to free the serfs would almost certainly end in "a frightful catastrophe," a general revolution and the hanging of all the landowners. He said he expected his own gamekeeper would probably hang him, if there was a revolution.

The Russian peasants had good reason to murder their masters, and all through the nineteenth century an exasperated peasantry was ripe for rebellion. Reforms came, but they were bitterly slow in coming. There were great peasant revolts in the seventeenth and eighteenth centuries: they

were put down with such violence that the peasants feared
further rebellion, but their lives were so intolerable that
rebellion was inevitable.* The revolt could come in many
forms. It could come in the form of an anarchic explosion, or
it could come slowly, spasmodically, the heat welling in the
boiler until at last it exploded with a momentum so great
that it destroyed everything around it. It could come in the
form of a peasant march on the capital, or in the formation
of a peasant army in the forests bordering the Volga. In the
age-old battle between the village and the town, the vil-
lagers have the advantage of numbers: they could build a
ring around Moscow and St. Petersburg, and starve out the
inhabitants. And if none of these things happened, there was
still the terrifying possibility that out of the peasantry there
would emerge cohorts of men dedicated to the destruction of
their adversaries.

Of the four terrorists whose lives are related in this book,
three did come out of the peasantry. The fourth, a young
poet, grew up in Warsaw and became a terrorist out of an
instinctive sympathy with the peasants.

The terrorists who emerged in Russia in the second half
of the last century were men who saw that the dynasty
could be overthrown only by terror. They terrorized the
Czar and the ruling bureaucracy, but they did not succeed
in their aim of making Russia better for the peasants. They
were the proud amateurs of revolt, who prepared the way
for the professionals. Their importance in history lies in the

---

* As late as 1857 the Russian peasant was bound by the law which stated:
"The landowner may impose upon his serfs any kind of labor, may take
from them money dues and demand from them personal service, with this
one restriction that they shall not thereby be ruined." The landowner could
at will take his peasants into his house and make them work as domestic
servants. He was legally allowed to punish them without trial: he could administer corporal punishment not exceeding forty lashes of the birch-rod or
fifteen blows with a stout stick. In fact, he punished as he pleased. The
emancipation of the serfs in 1861 barely changed the situation. See *Russia*,
by Sir Donald Mackenzie Wallace. New York: 1905. Pp. 421-2.

fact that they weakened the Russian state to an extent which helped to bring the Bolsheviks to power. And it is impossible to understand the rise of Russian Communism without an understanding of the terrorist movement. In the place of individual acts of terror, the Communists introduced mass terror. It is significant that they employed mass terror first against the terrorists, the men they feared most deeply.

In the eighties of the last century the terrorists were at the height of their power. They killed the Czar and threatened the bureaucracy. They had their own spies in the government, and even in the aristocracy. Ironically, their very success led to their eventual defeat; and their lack of a program which could be translated into a call to arms made them vulnerable to the Communists. They produced great leaders, but no rank and file. The peasants watched them admiringly from a distance, applauded, and then went back to work in the fields. When Lenin came to power, he destroyed the Social Revolutionaries, who had inherited the mantle of the terrorists, and he did this deliberately, quietly, without compunction, with the same calm with which he would have killed a fly.

He did not, however, destroy the legend which accompanied those early revolutionaries in their wayward lives, and long afterward. They were colorful men, of astonishing courage and relentless purpose. For years they worked secretly, always in danger of arrest, always at the mercy of spies. They knew, or half-guessed, that their individual acts of terrorism would soon be forgotten. The names of Nechayev, Zhelyabov, Sazonov, and Kaliayev are rarely mentioned now; yet each of them represented an important facet of the Russian character, which changes only a little over the centuries. Nechayev, shackled in his cell, dominated his guards and was able to send messages out of the Peter and Paul Fortress to the revolutionaries who regarded him as a living legend. Zhelyabov, a peasant who resembled a judge, dominated the audience at his trial and seemed even then to be invoking judgment upon Russia. The brilliant, headstrong Sazonov lived out his prison years under the weight of a sense of guilt and deliberately committed suicide to summon people's attention to the misery of the Russian prison system. The young and ardent Kaliayev assassinated a Grand Duke with the same careless delight with which he wrote his poetry. These men are worth studying for their own sake, but their importance lies in history. We shall understand Russian Communism better by examining the ground from which it sprang.

The tragedy of the terrorists lay in their beliefs, for they believed in nothing except science. They believed that only the scientists held the keys of the future: their spiritual forefathers were the Englishmen Darwin, Buckle, and Herbert Spencer. With this total belief in science went a total belief in asceticism, and in this they descended from the Russian hermits who lived passionately in caves and wandered carefree over the length and breadth of Russia. These young revolutionaries asserted: "A pair of boots is more important than all your Madonnas and all your refined talk about Shakespeare." Their tragedy was that they possessed no philosophy except their simple faith in science and their repudiation of existing conventions, and while attempting to create a morality of their own, they were trapped into an extreme form of asceticism which could have no popular appeal. Turgenev gave them the name "nihilists," but he did not mean that they believed in nothing: he meant that they believed in the destruction of the existing state. One day, when he was walking along the shores of the Isle of Wight in England, he had another waking dream. Mysteriously there appeared in front of him "a giant, huge, wild and melancholy, deeply rooted in the soil, strong, bitter, honest to a fault, and doomed to destruction because for all his elemental force he was merely standing at the gate of the future." This man, arising out of Turgenev's stored memories of the Russian peasantry, became Bazarov, the nihilist leader of *Fathers and Children*. Bazarov went out among the peasants to heal their wounds and died inevitably of blood-poisoning, careless of his own life and posssesed of a bitter scorn against the ruling aristocracy.

The terrorists never accepted the term "nihilists." They believed like Nechayev, the most redoubtable of them all, that a new society would arise fully fledged from the ashes of the old. They made no blueprints for the future: they were concerned only with the immediate present. Like Lenin, who came to power without any plans for the state he had captured with such singular ease, they were incapable of visualizing the future. Walking the tortuous path between the letter and the spirit, they invented a workable philosophy for themselves, a simple philosophy based upon loyalty to friends, implacable hatred of autocracy and an overwhelming sympathy for the oppressed. In their letters and in the casual remarks they dropped at moments of intense excitement we can see them attempting to hammer out a way of life, and sometimes we can watch them wrestling with problems which can never be solved, because they lie at the heart of the mystery. Has a man a right to kill his oppressor? Are men their brothers' keepers? Can we ever lift the burden of guilt from ourselves? Can we expiate our crimes?

These terrorists did not enjoy terrorism. They resorted to terrorism because they were outnumbered, and in the hope of opening the way for a peasant revolt. If they had succeeded in their aim, there would have been no Communist Revolution. If we can compare them with any other people, we should look to the Puritans of New England with their strict codes, their icy belief in Messianic revelations and their determination to put the witches and unbelievers, "those enemies of the Most High God," out of existence.

They committed their murders without enjoyment, and in this they differed from the mechanical political murderers of our own time.

These terrorists fought against appalling odds, and sometimes they were very human. When Kaliayev saw the Grand Duke's carriage, he held the bomb until he could see clearly who was in it, and when he saw that the Grand Duchess and two children were in the carriage, he refused to throw the bomb. After killing the Minister of the Interior, Sazonov under torture gave his own name away, against the terrorists' code; his grief over killing a man fought with his grief over jeopardizing his associates. When Nechayev's body was rotting away and the shackles were biting into his flesh and all writing implements were refused to him, he wrote a savage attack on the prison warden with a nail dipped in his own blood. Zhelyabov, disguised as the prospective owner of a tannery, joked with the townspeople, while preparing to lay the bomb which would derail the Czar's train. They were men to be respected. Of the arch-terrorist Nechayev Lenin wrote: "People completely forget he possessed unique organizational talent, an ability to establish the special techniques of conspiratorial work everywhere, an ability to give his thoughts such startling formulations that they were forever imprinted on one's memory." He admired Nechayev and Zhelyabov without stint: one the visionary of destruction, the other the superb destructive agent. And if he had nothing but contempt for Sazonov and Kaliayev, it was because the sense of guilt and the poetic temper were foreign to him.

Nechayev is the giant, and it is odd that he is so little known. I discussed him briefly in two chapters of *Zero* (John Day, 1950), but he deserves a more extended treatment, if only because his influence has been so vast. Even today his shadow falls across the Kremlin. More and more as we seek to penetrate the heart of the mystery of Russian

Communism, we see his living presence. There was a time when Gorky declared flatly that Lenin was the servant of Nechayev. Before an official gathering of representatives of Communism from all over the world, Stalin once was moved to declare that he was not a follower of Nechayev; but after Stalin's death it became only too evident that Nechayev's ghost had been wandering free over Russia, pitiless as ever, and it was Stalin who had given him full rein—the denial was no more than a salute to the implacable founder of a religion of destruction and despair. Millions who had never been born when Nechayev was alive died because *The Revolutionary Catechism* had been followed to the letter. And like that mysterious giant who rose before Turgenev's imagination as he wandered by the seashore, Nechayev has power to haunt us still. In our own time we can hardly hope to know whether his ghost will ever be laid.

The three other terrorists were lesser men. But all of them possessed gifts that were lacking in Nechayev. There are moments when Nechayev seems almost inhuman, no more than a pure nerve of destruction, a disembodied idea, the face of terror coming across a room. He belonged to the dark places of the heart, and was at home in the landscape of treachery. He knew men's faults, and how easily they can be made to destroy themselves. He had no sense of the dignity of the human creature created in the image of God. It is significant that the three other terrorists were constantly aware of human dignity. They lacked Nechayev's power, as they lacked his ruthlessness, and they do not haunt us. It is possible to forgive them, but it is doubtful whether Nechayev and his followers can ever be forgiven. There are evils which go beyond forgiveness. There are men who leave a stain on the earth which can never be washed away.

Here, then, are four terrorists who staked their lives to bring about the downfall of the Czars. I have endeavored to show them against the background of their time, as individuals whose motives and decisions were sometimes obscure, but whose lives shone with a particular kind of clarity. I am aware that at times their story reads like a novel. It should be remembered that on some occasions we have accounts by many eyewitnesses, and from these it has been possible to re-create the scene with details carefully observed and recorded at the time. After the Revolution of 1917 the Bolsheviks opened the archives of the secret police. We have the terrorists' letters from prison, and sometimes a day-by-day account of their behavior under their prison guards. There exist at least ten separate and authentic accounts of the assassination of Alexander II. The terrorists themselves wrote extensively, to justify their actions or to terrify their enemies. In Russia a vast literature has grown up around them. I have relied largely on original Russian sources, and owe a special debt to *Literatura Narodnoi Voli,* a compilation of the documents issued by the secret printing presses of the terrorists from 1879 to 1884, published in 1905. This huge volume—it extends to nearly a thousand closely-printed pages—gives the day-by-day thoughts of the revolutionaries as they went about their work, prints their correspondence, their poems, their essays and manifestoes. From it we can learn week by week how many terrorists were arrested in distant parts of Russia, how many were executed, and what they said, or were thought to have said, on their way to the scaffold. In these fading pages we see the terrorists face to face.

Finally, there is a moral to the story. Nietzsche wrote once: "Violence, slavery, danger in the street and in the heart, everything evil and terrible in man serves as well for the elevation of the human species as its opposite." The history of the terrorists proves the statement untrue. Violence, slavery, danger and evil only breed greater violence, greater slavery, greater danger, and more evil than men can tolerate. Though the terrorists sometimes acted from the most humble motives, they served only to bring a greater and more enduring evil to their country. Yet some honor is due to those who wielded the infernal weapon single-handed. These murderers and assassins should not be forgotten. With flaming swords they stand at the gate of the future, and we must pass beyond them before we enjoy peace in the world.

Robert Payne

NECHAYEV   as he appeared at the time of his trial

NECHAYEV

*Our task is total, terrible, universal
and merciless destruction.*

The Young Tiger

Nechayev stands at the threshold of the modern world—the dedicated terrorist determined to put the world to the flames. But in the rare photographs that survive, there is no hint of the terror he caused. A mass of thick, dark, curly hair, a broad forehead, veiled eyes under level eyebrows, a flat nose, lips that are almost feminine. In one of these photographs he wears the wide-lapelled coat of a dandy, and gazes out of the oval frame with the insolence of an aristocrat. To the end there was something of the aristocrat in him: he disdained danger, spoke on familiar terms with the aristocracy and regarded himself as one born to lead.

He was small and frail, dark-skinned, nearly always hungry. Those who knew him say he was always slovenly in appearance, his shirt falling to ruins, his hair tousled and his beard uncombed. They speak of his strange, quick walk, his broad accent, his habit of biting his finger-nails. Men were in awe of his courage. Obstinate, never accepting defeat, forever dreaming of destroying the autocracy, always wandering restlessly, he was like a mad ghost let loose upon the world, a ghost breathing fire and murder. From the beginning he seems to have hated the world, not only the world of the Czar, but the peasant world from which he sprang. He set himself up against the vast power of the Czarist police, and continually slipped from their clutches. He was a blackmailer, a murderer, a seducer, and a thief—these were his lesser crimes. His greatest crime was that he lived with a pure thirst for destruction and in different ways influenced both Lenin and Hitler, for the theses he stated were adopted directly by one and indirectly by the other. In his own time he was so important that the conspirators plotting the assassination of Alexander II debated whether the rescue of the legendary revolutionary Nechayev was more necessary than the destruction of the Czar. In his life he committed only one murder, but he may be responsible for millions of murders; and the single murder he committed seems to have been an act of gratuitous bravado, but there were few such acts. His life was a dogged, interminable struggle against the autocracy; and when he was shackled to the wall and there was almost no strength in him, he continued to fight. He was everything that was evil, but even in his evil he possessed a raw, human courage.

Sergey Gennadievich Nechayev was born at Ivanovo, near Vladimir, a hundred miles to the northeast of Moscow, on September 20, 1847. Ivanovo was then a small textile town, hardly more than an overgrown village: it had not yet blossomed into the great manufacturing city of Ivanovo-Voznessensk. His father was an innkeeper, sometime small merchant, artisan, and factotum, who married the daughter of a house-painter from Kostroma. After the marriage he followed his father-in-law's trade, became a house-painter and was on good terms with the local gentry, attending weddings and putting up the decorations. He was a good worker and much sought after. His wife helped out with dressmaking. She had been a serf and her husband had bought her freedom.

Nechayev spent some of his early years with his maternal grandparents in Kostroma, a city of medieval splendor. Here in the year 1313 the Tartar Prince Chet, the commander of the Golden Horde, saw a vision of the Virgin, was converted to Christianity, and built a Cathedral in her honor. Here too the young Mikhail Feodorovich Romanov, the first of his line, took refuge from a marauding Polish army and received the submission of the boyars. Somewhere on the outskirts of Kostroma the peasant Ivan Sussanin was captured by Polish cavalry and ordered to reveal the Czar's hiding-place. Because he refused, he was tortured to death. Glinka wrote the opera *A Life for the Czar* to celebrate the peasant's heroism.

When Nechayev was four years old there was erected on the main square of Kostroma a huge granite column in memory of the Czar and the peasant. At the top of the column stood a gigantic bronze bust of the Czar. Leaning against the column, in the attitude of a slave mourning his master, was a bronze of the murdered peasant. The day of unveiling was a holiday. The bands played the tumultuous choruses from Glinka's opera. A Grand Duke officiated and received the messages of humble loyalty which were duly transmitted to the Czar; and on the cobblestones the serfs from a hundred miles around knelt to receive the blessings of the Metropolitan. It was a day which people remembered for many years to come. Somewhere in the Cathedral, no one knew exactly where, the peasant had been buried. In no Russian town were the Czars worshipped with greater devotion.

But Kostroma was dying. It had been dying for a very long time. The old battle-flags hung in the Cathedral of the Assumption, which faced north because it was in the north that the Grand Duke Vassily Kostromsky had seen another vision of the Virgin. The flags were falling to dusty ribbons, and the paint was flaking off the great cupolas. Early in the sixties a royal commission was despatched to Kostroma to inquire into the general decay threatening the palaces and cathedrals of the city, but little was done except to restore the secret chamber where the Czar had hidden from the Poles. Kostroma lived on with its memories. From the fever of decay, from the hallucinations of the medieval past, Nechayev may have drawn a part of his strength.

When Nechayev came to St. Petersburg, he rarely spoke about his youth. We know little about his childhood. He was fourteen when he heard the town-crier reading the Act of Emancipation on a cold, blustery morning in the town square of Ivanovo. That night there was a banquet in the town hall, followed by prayers for the safety of the royal family in the churches; and he may have remembered the long procession of ex-serfs making their way through the town with lanterns, singing hymns. Within a week the ex-serfs were wondering what the Act of Emancipation amounted to, for there was no immediate change in their social position.

From being a house-painter Nechayev's father became a builder, and Sergey, after an unprofitable period spent serving behind the counter of a local shop, became his father's errand-boy. Once he was sent out on an errand during a snowstorm with a letter for an important client. The letter was lost. Sergey floundered about in the snow, trying to find the letter, which probably was blown out of his hands. It was very late when he returned home. Asked about the letter, he confessed he had lost it. His father turned on him and cursed him for a good-for-nothing. Much depended on the letter, and the old man was almost out of his wits with hate. He had never inflicted corporal punishment on his son before. For the first and last time his father took down a birch-rod and flogged him. Long afterwards one of Nechayev's childhood friends remembered the incident as a turning-point: from that moment there was a core of bitterness in him.

He learned to play the flute and he played with cardboard soldiers, a game which boys played in Russia well into their teens. The soldiers were painted crudely, red for the Russians, blue for the Turks. Then they were shot down with peas. When he was younger he played the game of "banker" with the gold and silver foil from the tops of wine-bottles representing coins and scribbled bits of paper representing paper money. He learned a little French and German, accompanied his father into the houses of the wealthy merchants, became an expert floor-polisher, and learned how to paint signs passably well. There is a story that he drank heavily for a while and then gave it up. He was restless and sought out the company of the educated and he despised the merchants. One day he announced that he was determined to be a student. An obscure writer of *feuilletons* named Nefedov gave him some letters of introduction to students in St. Petersburg. A few days later Nechayev left Ivanovo for ever. He was twenty-one, and he had wasted the whole of his youth.

For the next four years he lived at an astonishing level of intensity. Within a few months of his arrival in St. Petersburg he was in single-handed control of a vast network of conspiracy. Superbly confident in his own insolence, plotting destruction, he dominated the Russian revolutionary scene until he disappeared in the underground cells of the Peter and Paul Fortress; but even then, like a dark ghost, he terrorized from behind the prison bars. It was as though he was determined to make up for lost time.

Small and thin, with a long dark face and piercing blue eyes, with no experience of revolutionary activity and almost no schooling—he only learned to read when he was sixteen—Nechayev seems to have arrived in St. Petersburg with his plans already made. From the beginning he talked about overthrowing the dynasty. Was it boredom, poverty, hatred of the merchants of Ivanovo, the memory of Ivan Sussanin, the ancient medieval lusts burning in him? No one knows.

From those who survived his revolutionary activities we have brief glimpses of him walking the streets in a threadbare coat, wearing boots too large for him. It is autumn, the snow already falling. He has a job as teacher of religious instruction in a day-school. At night he attends lectures at the University. He lives in a small dark room off a court-yard, almost without furniture. There are portraits of Ro-bespierre, Saint-Just and Herzen on the walls, and books everywhere—Carlyle's *French Revolution* in a Russian trans-lation, the works of Blanqui, Robert Owen, and Babeuf, histories of the Decembrists. He is taking lessons in French and he knows Chemchugnikov's poem on the death of Dmitri Karakozov by heart. In April, 1866, Karakozov, a young student, saw the Czar walking outside the Winter Palace, pulled out a revolver and fired. He missed his aim, was arrested immediately and hanged. Whenever the dis-cussions among the young revolutionaries were floundering, Nechayev would look up sharply and say: "Remember Kar-akozov!"

He lived in a student hostel, an old house boarded up into a number of small rooms which resembled caves. The winter damp came through the walls. A small group met in the apartment of Yenisherlov, a rich student who could afford comfortable sofas, bookcases, delicate chairs. There were even two immense tables strewn with books. In the group were Vladimir Orlov, and the two brothers Amethystov: Ivan was a student at the University, Evlampy a student at the Medico-Chirurgical Academy. They were joined a lit-tle later by Zemphyr Arbore-Ralli and Prince Cherkessov, the owner of a celebrated bookshop much frequented by students. There were perhaps twenty others. They were dedicated revolutionaries, prepared to sacrifice their lives in the struggle against autocracy, but in need of leadership. Nechayev provided the leadership. He had a simple solu-tion for all problems. Bring the students out on strike, take over the arsenals, destroy the Emperor. Orlov was put in charge of a scheme for organizing the student movement, while Nechayev maintained over-all control. In December, 1868, as head of the "Secret Revolutionary Committee," Nechayev drew up a brief outline of his plans for the coming months:

> Up to the month of May, 1869, the activity of our best men should be concentrated in Petersburg, Moscow and all other cities where there are universities. We must prepare for a student protest movement in all universities and high-schools. We must demand the right of assembly. At the same time propaganda must be immediately begun among the proletariat, and there should be further propaganda in all cities and towns where the poorer classes are concentrated.

This was not especially illuminating, but Nechayev was merely warming up. In January and February he was sending delegates to Moscow, Kiev, and Kharkov, and he had received the oath of allegiance from ninety-seven students who signed their names to a sheet of paper—the list turned up mysteriously sixty years later in the police archives. Early in February overtures were made to the revolutionary Peter Tkachev, whose pamphlet called *To the Public* was being widely read among the students. It was Tkachev who had first announced the possibility of a technique of revolt, and suggested that the revolution should begin from within the universities: Nechayev provided the date, the sense of overwhelming urgency, and the conception of a simultaneous uprising of students and workmen. Nechayev also provided the iron discipline and the threat of the death penalty to anyone who refused to obey the commands of the Central Committee. The movement was growing. It now included Vladimir Cherkezov,* who had been implicated in the Karakozov affair, and a host of serious-minded and determined students. They possessed their own printing press, borrowed from a certain Semeon Serebrennikov who was to play a

* Not to be confused with Prince Cherkessov.

strange role in Nechayev's life later. The secret printing press was operated by Alexandra Dementieva, the eighteen-year-old daughter of a staff-captain, who later became the wife of Tkachev. On the press immense quantities of the pamphlet *To the Public* were printed for distribution during the uprising. Everything was ready. The colleges were seething, but there was still some opposition to united action. Suddenly, toward the end of February, the police pounced on two or three of the emissaries Nechayev had sent to the universities, and Nechayev himself was summoned to the police station. He succeeded in throwing the police off the scent, but he knew he was a marked man and would be arrested at the moment of the outbreak. He decided to leave St. Petersburg and seek the safety of Moscow.

Two days later Vera Zasulich, then a young college student at St. Petersburg, received a letter in the ordinary mail. There were two enclosures. One read:

> I was walking in the Vasilievsky Island this morning and I passed the police cart used for the transport of prisoners. As it went by a hand appeared at the window and I heard the voice of a dear friend: "If you are a student send this to the address given." I feel it is my duty to fulfill what is demanded of me. Destroy this note, in case the handwriting is recognized.
>
> A Student.

The other note, scribbled in pencil, was in Nechayev's handwriting:

> They are taking me to the fortress. Do not lose heart, beloved comrades. Continue to have faith in me, and let us hope we meet again.

Nechayev's message was in fact a brilliant piece of deception, but there was nothing wildly improbable in the story. He was already a legend, and because the message portrayed him as a revolutionary hero, he was merely reinforcing a portrait that already existed in the minds of many students. Vera Zasulich believed in the message implicitly. She immediately informed Anna Grigorievna, Nechayev's sister, who was also studying at the University, and soon all the young revolutionaries knew about Nechayev's arrest. If Nechayev was in the Peter and Paul Fortress on a small island facing St. Petersburg—for his reference to "the fortress" could hardly mean anything else—then he was the first martyr of the student revolt, and a mass meeting was called to demand his release. The police were puzzled. They knew he was not in the fortress, but they could find no trace of him. In fact while the police were frantically searching for him and the students were demanding his release, Nechayev was living quietly in Moscow under one of his many aliases. He remained in Moscow for two weeks, and then with the passport of his friend Nikolayev slipped out of the country and made his way to Switzerland.

No one knows why he left St. Petersburg so abruptly. It is possible that he lost his nerve. It is also possible that he intended his bogus arrest as a method of retaining power over the students: though he had failed to lead the revolt, the story of the arrest, and the subsequent stories of his escape, would help him to consolidate his authority. In later years, living under another name, he would tell the story of how he had escaped, pause dramatically and say: "And do you know where this mysterious Nechayev is now? He is standing in front of you. No, I am not Pavlov. I am Nechayev." It is also possible that Nechayev left Russia because he was convinced that the outbreak in the universities would be ingloriously stamped out by the Russian police, and needed the prestige of someone greater than himself to lead it to success. Leaving Russia, he went straight to Geneva, where the old anarchist Mikhail Bakunin received him with open arms. He had come, he said, as a delegate of the

Russian Revolutionary Committee, with its headquarters at St. Petersburg, to seek the advice and protection of the greatest of all living revolutionaries. Bakunin was overjoyed. He took Nechayev into his house and listened with rapt attention while Nechayev spoke of how he had scaled the fortress walls and made his way from St. Petersburg to the Rumanian border with the police hot on his trail. He had outwitted them; he would always outwit them; and now he demanded only the blessing of Bakunin before returning to Russia and leading the revolt.

If the students had known the real circumstances of Nechayev's escape, they might have torn him limb from limb. The revolt, so carefully planned, broke out on March 19. There were wild speeches, and a good deal of waving of the revolutionary flag. The students refused to attend lectures and marched with banners in the streets. But to the students' dismay the police paid very little attention to them until nightfall; then they swooped down and arrested the ringleaders with the help of student-spies. The first arrests took place in the Medico-Chirurgical Academy. These were followed by arrests in the Technological Institute and the Institute of Engineering. The revolt had sputtered out. Even the police refused to treat it seriously, and most of the arrested students were sent home in a few days.

Early in March Nechayev sent a letter to Vera Zasulich explaining in detail how he had escaped from the fortress. It was all very easy. He had simply put on the coat of a general, and slipped out. He went on to explain that the journey to the border was far more dangerous: he was arrested in southern Russia, and it had been necessary for him to fight one of the guards and one of the officials put in charge of him. He had pushed them out of his way, and then started running, and these Russian policemen were far too slow—he had outdistanced them. These stories, with their circumstantial details, were relayed to the students who were beginning to wonder whether Nechayev had really escaped from the fortress. In veiled language Nechayev promised to return and this time lead the revolt to success.

In those days Bakunin was already losing his powers. He was fifty-four, enormously stout, toothless, and suffering from asthma. A giant of a man, resembling an elephant, with small, watery blue eyes and a great mane of iron-gray hair, he had all the born aristocrat's charm, the large gestures, the contempt for danger. A former artillery officer and the descendant of a long line of landed gentry, he had once been arrested by the Russian police and confined in the dreaded Alexis Ravelin of the Peter and Paul Fortress. Since then he had been in many prisons and taken part in many ineffectual revolutions. Though he was old and shabby and lived from hand to mouth, he was still a name to be reckoned with. His wife was unfaithful to him. His friends sometimes refused to take him seriously. He made converts with surprising ease, and lost them as easily. He was always about to embark on some new revolutionary activity, but something nearly always happened to shatter his plans at the last moment. He had only a handful of followers. Yet he remained the supreme optimist of revolution, the only revolutionary whose name was a legend.

The relations between Bakunin and Nechayev were soon intimate. In these early days Bakunin never seems to have distrusted Nechayev's motives. Bakunin had a curious habit of looking in silence at people when he first met them, holding his head quizzically, frowning, muttering to himself, attempting to absorb them into his own stream of consciousness. First impressions counted. And the impression produced by Nechayev was evidently one of considerable force. Here was the ideal young Russian, the born revolutionary leader, who had come to Geneva just at the time when the old revolutionary was losing all hope of witnessing even the faintest spark of the revolutionary fervor. A few years earlier he had dismissed Russia as a byzantino-tartaro-germanic empire. Nothing could be done with it. The people were too stupid. And here was Nechayev with news of daily revolts springing out of the Russian colleges and universities. Nechayev became his guest. He called Nechayev "Boy," remembering the English he had learned during his brief stay in London. Nechayev called him "Matrena," a diminutive for Maria.* Bakunin seems not to have cared; he seems even to have delighted in the new name; and there is some evidence that the twenty-two-year-old Nechayev seduced the old revolutionary. They were always together. They swore oaths of eternal loyalty to one another. The dead weight of revolutionary frustration lifted from Bakunin's shoulders; he grew visibly younger in the presence of the dangerous and seductive revolutionary who brought him a breath of his native land. Nechayev was introduced to Bakunin's friends. Nikolai Ogaryov was living in Geneva. A poet and a revolutionary, with a curious history of tragic love-affairs, a man of immense charm, suffering from epilepsy and given to frequent bouts of drunkenness, he was introduced to Nechayev, and immediately fell under his sway. Ogaryov was so ravished by his new acquaintance that he sat down to write a poem in his honor. It is not a good poem. It was probably the worst poem he ever wrote, but in the original Russian it is recognizably Ogaryov's and moves with considerable passion:

THE STUDENT

To my young friend Nechayev

He was born to a wretched fate,
And was taught in a hard school,
And suffered interminable torments

---

* This was not the first time Bakunin received a feminine name. Three-year-old Liza Herzen called him 'Big Liza' when he stayed with the Herzens in London.

In years of unceasing labor.
But as the years swept by
His love for the people grew stronger,
And fiercer his thirst for the common good,
The thirst to improve man's fate.

There were two more verses, celebrating the great future opening out before the young revolutionary. Nechayev prized the verses nearly as much as he prized a document dated May 12, 1869, which marked his entry into the World Revolutionary Alliance, and ran as follows:

The bearer of this certificate is one of the accredited representatives of the Russian Section of the World Revolutionary Alliance.   No. 2771.

Mikhail Bakunin

This certificate was a wonderful invention, with its seal and flamboyant signature and the suggestion that there were at least 2770 other members. In fact, Nechayev was the only member of a revolutionary organization which seems to have been invented on the spur of the moment. The seal affixed to the certificate bore the words "European Revolutionary Alliance, Central Committee." No one had ever heard of the European or World Revolutionary Alliance, and no one was ever to hear of it again; but it satisfied Nechayev's desire for documentation, and Nechayev could henceforth prove to any doubting Thomases in Russia that he had received the blessing of two famous revolutionaries whose names were known throughout Europe and who were reverenced by Russian students. And just as Bakunin was impressed by Nechayev, so Nechayev was impressed by the constant coming and going of revolutionaries who made their way to Bakunin's disorderly study, with its books piled all over the chairs and the samovar half hidden under monstrous mountains of paper. Nechayev listened to their discussions, which often lasted all night. He was impressed by the perpetual activity. New life was springing in Bakunin. He was losing weight. By dieting he had lost fifty pounds of fat, but he was still eating gargantuan amounts of beef and drinking by the bucket, and seeming never to be drunk. Herzen, who came to visit him in May, wrote that he was "charging forward like a locomotive which has got too much steam up and has run off the rails." Bakunin would have denied that he had run off the rails, but there was no doubt that he was going full steam ahead; and Nechayev was able to write to friends in St. Petersburg that "our work is seething here: a soup is brewing such as all Europe will be unable to gulp down." Very calmly and happily the conspirators were talking of fanning the flames of Europe from end to end.

Nechayev's letters to St. Petersburg were a source of annoyance to many of the recipients. Nechayev, intoxicated by the prospects of world-wide revolution as seen through the failing eyes of Bakunin, had forgotten to take even elementary precautions. Bakunin wrote openly through the mails. He would use initials or numbers instead of names, but he took no further precautions, arguing that the police were altogether too stupid to understand what he was talking about. In this he was wrong. The police of six or seven nations were trailing him closely, while the Russian police were keeping close watch on the vast correspondence Nechayev was conducting with Russia. Every letter Nechayev wrote seems to have been opened, copied, and carefully weighed as evidence to be brought against Nechayev later. Between March and August, 1869, the authorities seized 560 letters and pamphlets written by Nechayev, involving 387 persons in St. Petersburg alone. A rather smaller number of letters and documents sent to Moscow were also seized. If Nechayev received no reply to letters which were being held up for examination by the secret police, he would write abusive letters accusing his friends of cowardice or treason or, worse still, indifference to the revolution. It has been argued that he did this in order to compromise the recipients, but this is doubtful. He was puzzled and annoyed by their silence, and deeply hurt, and like Bakunin he refused to believe that the police were sufficiently intelligent to see through his thin disguises. On July 22, 1869, he sent an open telegram to his friend Uspensky, which read:

Monsieur Uspensky, Moscou, Loubianka, Librairie Tscherkezoff

Pour retourner Pavloff envoyez argent, écrivez vite, télégraphiez réponse Genève, quai Seudet, 15.

Monschal

Even if this were the only communication to fall into their hands, the police would have learned matters of considerable interest to them. They knew already most of Nechayev's pseudonyms—he called himself at various times Ivan Petrov, Ivan Pavlov, Dmitri Feodorovich and Captain Panin. The telegram informed them that he was about to return to Russia, was in need of money and had an easily accessible accommodation address. They could have sent their special agents in Switzerland to the address, but apparently no special watch was taken at this time, and the copies of the letters were simply filed and temporarily forgotten.

Nechayev's need of money, vast sums of money, was growing urgent. He was determined to return to Russia and bring the revolution about, and revolutions are expensive. As usual, Bakunin himself was in dire straits. He remembered, however, that the sum of eight hundred pounds sterling had been deposited in 1858 in a London bank in the name of the revolutionary Alexander Herzen. Herzen had spent a few weeks with him in Geneva in May, and taken a violent dislike to Nechayev. The money had been placed in

Herzen's hands by a certain Bakhmatiev, an eccentric Russian landowner who had passed through London on his way to found a communist paradise in the Marquesas. Pausing only long enough for some brief discussions with Herzen, he had disappeared forever into the Pacific. The capital was still intact. Ogaryov had a presumptive claim on half of it. Working through Ogaryov, Bakunin suggested that the money could be profitably used in encouraging the Russian revolution which he and "Boy" were about to launch. Ogaryov was soon sold on the idea. He was slowly drinking himself to death, and hardly cared what happened to the money, though he received from time to time little trickles which represented his share of the interest: this was employed to finance the publication of his poems and pamphlets. Under the combined pressure of Bakunin and Nechayev, Ogaryov began a series of begging letters to Herzen in London. At first he asked for the entire sum. Later he begged for half. The correspondence lasted several weeks, and it was not until the end of July that Herzen agreed to surrender one half of the Bakhmatiev fund, amounting to 10,000 francs. Herzen suggested that the money be spent on establishing a revolutionary printing press in Geneva, adding that Bakunin would be better employed superintending a printing press than pursuing nebulous adventures in Russia. The money was solemnly received by Ogaryov, who in turn handed it to Bakunin. Most of it was then transferred to Nechayev.

With the money, Ogaryov's poem, and the slip of paper which announced his admission into the World Revolutionary Alliance, Nechayev was now prepared to return to Russia. He had not been lazy. He had thought out some of the revolutionary problems which would face him when he returned, and with the help of Ogaryov and Bakunin had written a number of manifestoes, projects, and encyclicals. Altogether eight pamphlets were produced. These were:

Some Words to our Young Brothers in Russia
To the Students of the University
Two articles contained in *The People's Vengeance,* No. 1,
  which appeared in the summer of 1869
On the Russian Nobility
The Student (Ogaryov's poem, also called *Enlightened Person-
  ality*)
How the Revolutionary Question Presents Itself
Principles of Revolution
The Revolutionary Catechism

Of these only the first two and Ogaryov's poem were
signed. Nechayev's open letter to the students was written
in a form somewhat reminiscent of an imperial rescript. He
spoke of having scaled the frozen walls of the Peter and Paul
Fortress by the grace of divine providence. He had thwarted
the dark forces of the Czardom, and now promised to lead
the students in a fight to the death against the evils of reaction. *Some Words to our Young Brothers in Russia* was a
muddled plea to young students to assume the role of mid-
wives to the revolution:

> Dear brethren, I urge you with all my heart to abandon the
> doomed world of academies, schools and universities, from
> which you are now being expelled and where you were con-
> tinually taught to stand at a distance from the people. Go
> among the people! There you will find your true campus, your
> wisdom and your lives! Learn from the people how to serve
> them, and how to help them to their best advantage. Remem-
> ber above all that young educated people should not be the
> teachers, benefactors, and dictatorial leaders of the people,
> but should act as midwives helping to bring about the self-
> emancipation of the peasants, concentrating their forces and
> assisting them to employ their true energies.

The pamphlet *On the Russian Nobility* has no particular
interest, and the articles in *The People's Vengeance,* al-

most certainly by Nechayev, covered ground more expertly covered in *Principles of Revolution*, which appears to have been written by Nechayev and Bakunin in tandem, for there are passages which have all the diffused grandeur of Bakunin's style at its best and other passages as incisive as anything Nechayev ever wrote. "We recognize," says the author of *Principles of Revolution*, "no other activity except the work of utter destruction, but we admit that the form of this activity may assume varied forms—poison, the knife, rope, etc. In this struggle the revolutionary sacrifices everything." This sounds like vintage Nechayev, while the following passage seems to contain both hands:

> Brigandage has always been one of the most honored forms of Russian national life. The brigand is the hero, the defender, the popular avenger, the irreconcilable enemy of the state, and of all social and civil order established by the state. He is the wrestler in life and in death against all this civilization of officials, nobles, priests, and kings . . . He who does not understand brigands cannot understand the history of the Russian masses. He who is not sympathetic with them cannot sympathize with the lives of the people, and lacks the strength to avenge the ancient, interminable wrongs suffered by the people: he belongs to the camp of the enemy, the partisans of the state . . . It is only through brigandage that the vitality, ardor and strength of the people can be established indisputably . . . The brigand in Russia is the true and unique revolutionary . . . He who desires to make a serious revolution in Russia must enter their world. The season is at hand. The anniversaries of Stenka Razin and Pugachov are approaching, and it is time to celebrate these warriors of the people. Let us all prepare for the feast.*

The last and the most deservedly famous of the revolutionary essays composed between March and August, 1869

* Stenka Razin's rebellion was crushed in 1671, Pugachov's rebellion in 1773.

shows all the signs of having been composed by Nechayev, though a few easily identifiable phrases may have been inserted by Bakunin. This is *The Revolutionary Catechism*. In all that has gone before, we are aware that the revolutionaries are playing with revolution: now at last we encounter the gaunt and haggard face of the real thing. In the original Russian it moves at the slow and steady pace of a funeral march—a funeral march over an entire civilization.

The Revolutionary Catechism consists of twenty-six formal articles on the nature of the revolution of destruction. In cold blood, without ever hinting at mercy, Nechayev demonstrates how a handful of men can destroy a whole civilization. Total destruction is the aim: he does not care if anything survives the flames, and if nothing survives this is a matter of total indifference to the revolutionary. Those who take part in the revolution and those who oppose it are placed in their precise categories. There are ominous underscorings, hints of undisclosed powers, moments when the pen seems about to falter, but Nechayev goes on to the end, depicting with the utmost calm the portrait of the terrorist at the height of his powers.

THE REVOLUTIONARY CATECHISM

The Duties of the Revolutionary toward Himself

1. The revolutionary is a dedicated man. He has no personal inclinations, no business affairs, no emotions, no attachments, no property and no name. Everything in him is subordinated towards a single exclusive attachment, a single thought and a single passion—the revolution.
2. In the very depths of his being, not only in words but also in deeds, he has torn himself away from the bonds which tie him to the social order and to the cultivated world, with all its laws, moralities and customs and with all its generally accepted conventions. He is their implacable enemy, and if he

continues to live with them it is only in order to destroy them more quickly.

3. The revolutionary despises all dogmas and refuses to accept the mundane sciences, leaving them for future generations. He knows only one science: the science of destruction. For this reason, and only for this reason, he will study mechanics, physics, chemistry, and perhaps medicine. But all day and night he studies the living science of peoples, their characteristics and circumstances, and all the phenomena of the present social order. The object is the same: the prompt destruction of this filthy order.

4. The revolutionary despises public opinion. He despises and hates the existing social order in all its manifestations. For him, morality is everything which contributes to the triumph of the revolution. Immoral and criminal is everything that stands in his way.

5. The revolutionary is a dedicated man, merciless toward the state and altogether merciless toward the educated classes; and he can expect no mercy from them. Between him and them there exists, declared or concealed, a continual and irreconcilable war "for life or for death." He must accustom himself to enduring torture.

6. Tyrannical toward himself, he must be tyrannical toward others. All the soft and tender affections arising from kinship, friendship and love, all gratitude and even all honor must be obliterated, and in their place there must be the cold and single-minded passion for the work of revolution. For him there exists only one pleasure, one consolation, one reward, one satisfaction—the success of the revolution. Night and day he must have but one thought, one aim—merciless destruction. Aiming cold-bloodedly and indefatigably toward this end, he must be ready to destroy himself and destroy with his own hands everyone who stands in his way.

7. The nature of the true revolutionary excludes all romanticism, all sensitivity, all exaltations and enthusiasms. He must also exclude private vendettas and personal hatred. The revolutionary passion, practiced at every moment of the day until it becomes a habit, is to be employed with cold calculation.

At all times and in all places the revolutionary must refuse to allow himself to be guided by his personal impulses, but only by the total submergence of himself in the revolution.

Relationship of the Revolutionary toward the
Revolutionary Comrades

8. The revolutionary can have no friendly feeling to anyone unless, like him, the other is dedicated to revolutionary affairs. His degree of friendship, devotion, and obligation towards a comrade must be determined only by the degree of the comrade's usefulness in the practical work of complete and destructive revolution.

9. It is superfluous to speak of solidarity among revolutionaries. The whole strength of the revolutionary work lies in this. Comrades who possess the same revolutionary passion should, as much as possible, deliberate all important matters together and come to unanimous conclusions. But the revolutionary, in accomplishing whatever plan is finally decided upon, must rely altogether on himself. The contract of revolutionary destruction demands that no comrades should come running up with advice and assistance if this detracts from the success of the plan.

10. Each comrade should have under him several revolutionaries of the second or third rank, i.e. comrades who are not completely dedicated. These should be regarded as portions of a common fund of revolutionary capital, to be expended as he thinks fit. He should expend them as economically as possible, always attempting to derive the utmost possible use from them. He should regard himself as capital consecrated to the triumph of the revolution; and he must not be regarded as expendable without the entire agreement of the fully initiated comrades.

11. When a comrade is caught in a dangerous extremity and the question arises whether he should be rescued or not rescued, the revolutionary must make his decision without recourse to personal feelings, but only in terms of the eventual success of the revolution. Therefore it is necessary to balance carefully the usefulness of the comrade in so far as it is a ques-

tion of revolutionary strength, and the most careful consideration should be made to decide whether he is worth rescuing.

Relationship of the Revolutionary toward Society

12. Whether a new member, after giving proof of loyalty by word and deed, should be accepted is a matter to be decided only by unanimous agreement.

13. The revolutionary enters the world of the state, of the classes and of so-called culture, and he lives in this world only because he has faith in its speedy and total destruction. He is not a revolutionary if he feels any sympathy for this world. He must not hesitate to destroy any position, any place, or any man in this world—all must be equally detested by him. All the worse for him if he has parents, friends and loved ones; he is no longer a revolutionary if they can stay his hand.

14. Aiming at implacable destruction the revolutionary can and sometimes must live within society while pretending to be other than what he is. A revolutionary must penetrate everywhere, among the lowest and the middle classes and in the houses of commerce, in the churches, in the palaces of the aristocracy. He must know the world of the bureaucrats and of the military and of literature, and he must enter into the Third Division [secret police] and even into the Winter Palace.

15. All the members of this filthy society can be split up into several categories: the first category comprises those to be condemned to death without delay. The comrades should compile a list of those to be condemned, weighing the relative gravity of their crimes against their value to the revolution; and the executions should be carried out according to the prepared order.

16. In the preparation of these lists and in placing the condemned according to the prepared order, no private sense of outrage should be considered, nor is it necessary to pay attention to the hatred provoked by these people among the comrades or the people. But hatred and the sense of outrage must to some extent be made use of, because these things help to incite rebellion among the people. It is necessary to

be guided only by the relative usefulness of these executions for the sake of the revolution. Above all those who are especially inimical to the revolutionary organization must be destroyed; their violent and sudden deaths will produce the utmost panic in the government, it will shake the foundations of government and deprive it of the services of its most intelligent and energetic agents.

17. The second group consists of those to whom we concede life provisionally in order that their bestial behavior shall drive the people to inevitable revolt.

18. The third category consists of a multitude of personages or animals distinguished neither for intelligence nor for energy: those who enjoy wealth, connections, influence, and power. These must be exploited in every possible way; they must be implicated and confused; as far as possible their dirty secrets should be found out, so that we can make them our slaves. Their power, influence, and connections, their riches and energy will form an inexhaustible treasure and a precious help in our various undertakings.

19. The fourth category is composed of ambitious people and liberals of various shades. We shall pretend we are following their ideas and give them cause to think we are blindly conspiring with them, while in fact we take them under our own control. We shall root out all their secrets and compromise them to the uttermost, so that there will be no way out for them and they can be used to create disorder in the state.

20. The fifth category consists of doctrinaires, conspirators, revolutionaries: all idle word-spillers who orate before meetings or in front of a piece of paper. They must be constantly driven forward to make violent declarations carefully arranged to agree with our purpose. The majority of these will leave nothing behind but a vast ruin; from a few of them we shall attain real revolutionary gains.

21. The sixth category is especially important: women. They should be divided into three chief divisions. First: those frivolous, thoughtless and vapid women, whom we shall use as we use the third and fourth category of men. Second: women who are ardent, gifted and devoted, but do not be-

long to us because they have not yet achieved a passionless and austere revolutionary understanding: these must be used like the men of the fifth category. Finally there are the women who are completely on our side, i.e. those who are wholly dedicated and who have accepted our program in its entirety. We should regard these women as the most valuable of our treasures; without their help it would be impossible to succeed.

The Duties of our Society toward the People

22. The aims of our Society are none other than the entire emancipation and happiness of the people, i.e. the common laborers. Convinced that their emancipation and the achievement of this happiness is brought about only by means of an all-destroying popular revolt, we shall see that society will employ all its power, all its resources towards increasing and intensifying the calamities and evils until their patience is exhausted and they will break out in a *levée-en-masse.*

23. By a popular revolution, the Society does not mean a revolution tailored according to the classic western model, a pattern which is fundamentally restrained by the existence of property and the traditional social orders of so-called civilization and morality. Until now such a civilization has cast down one political form only to substitute another, thereby attempting to bring about a so-called revolutionary state. The only salutary form of revolution is one which destroys the entire state to the roots and exterminates all imperial traditions, the whole social order and all the existing classes in Russia.

24. With this end in view the Society refuses to impose any new organization from above. Any future organization will doubtless work its way through the movement and life of the people: but this is a matter for future generations to decide. Our task is terrible, total, universal, and merciless destruction. (. . . *strashnoe, polnoe, povsemestnoe i bezposhchadnoe razrusheniye.*)

25. Therefore, in drawing closer to the people, we must above all unite with those elements of popular life which, from the

very beginning of the imperial power of Muscovy, have never ceased to protest, not only in words but in deeds, against everything directly or indirectly connected with the State: against the nobility, against the bureaucracy, against the priests, against business, and against the tight fist of the extortioner. We must unite with the adventurous tribes of brigands, who are the only true revolutionaries of Russia.

26. To knit the people into a single force which is wholly destructive and wholly invincible—such is our organization, our conspiracy, and our task.

Such is *The Revolutionary Catechism*, which was to have important consequences for the world, since it was read by Lenin and influenced the course of the Bolshevik Revolution. This cold and ascetic document, which demanded of the revolutionary such extraordinary qualities of detachment and heroism and a complete self-effacement, was Nechayev's masterpiece. With this he threw down his gantlet. One of the characters of Dostoyevsky's novel *The Possessed* is made to say: "To level the hills is a good idea." In *The Revolutionary Catechism* Nechayev shows succinctly, clearly and almost without emotion how the leveling process can be carried out.

Nechayev was not the first revolutionary to demand extremes of violence. In 1862 the young revolutionary Zaichnevsky called for the murder of all the members of the Czar's party. He wrote:

Kill them in the squares, if they dare to show themselves in the squares. Kill them in the narrow alleyways of the provincial towns, and in the broad streets of Moscow. Hack them to pieces in the villages. Remember, those who are not with us are against us!

Zaichnevsky's astonishing call to arms derived from the intellectual abstractions of the philosopher Pisarev and was directed against the group around the Czar and against no other group. Nechayev's blue-print was directed against all groups except one, the people he calls *cherno-rabochiyi lyudi,* the "black working people," peasants and laborers, and it would seem from the *Catechism* that he was not too greatly concerned about them. If they perished in the conflagration, there would still be a handful of people left to create the new society he only vaguely dreamed about, for according to Nechayev the destruction of the outworn society was the immediate task: somehow, by some means unknown, the new society would arise phoenix-like from the ashes. He was not in the least concerned with Zaichnevsky's "social and democratic Republic." He was concerned only with imposing a kind of scientific order on the art of destroying an existing society. There are about ten words in Russian which mean "destruction," and he rings the changes on all of them. Everything must be destroyed! No stone must be left standing! In the guise of revolutionaries, the angels of fury and destruction and denunciation have returned to the world, and suddenly it occurs to us that we have heard this voice before—in *Isaiah,* in *Jeremiah,* and in the chapters of *Genesis* describing how the Deluge visited the earth. Behind the stark theses of the *Catechism* lie a fierce religious vindictiveness and a prophet's fervor.

Nechayev portrays the revolutionary in considerable detail. Austere, determined and tyrannical, he wages a cold and unremitting war on the world and on himself. He is the fanatic who dares not let his eyes gleam, for fear of being observed. He is the most dangerous of mortals: the hero dedicated to unheroic ends. His austerity leads to a kind of asceticism. Nicolas Berdyaev, the modern Russian philosopher, has observed that the *Catechism* is unique in its asceticism:

It is a sort of instruction in the spiritual life of a revolutionary, and the demands which it makes are harsher than the requirements of Syrian asceticism. The revolutionary must have no interests, no business, no personal feelings and connections; he must have nothing of his own, not even a name. Everything is to be swallowed up in a single exclusive interest, by the one idea, the one passion—revolution. Everything which serves the cause of revolution is moral. Revolution is the one criterion of good and evil. The many must be sacrificed for the one. But this is also the principle of asceticism. In such a case the living person is crushed; it is deprived of all the richness of the content of life for the sake of the Revolution–God.*

But while Nechayev describes an ascetic rule, the last of the long series of rules which began with St. Basil's extraordinary compilation of regulations for the monks of Annesi, the new catechism describes an austerity which is founded on no morality and the monkish revolutionary receives no solace of heaven. The Christian rule is turned upside-down. All the revolutionary can ever expect to see is the fire of an apocalyptic vengeance. It is the starkest, the bitterest, and the least rewarding of all rules. But it was precisely because the rule portrayed a total self-abnegation that it had a wide appeal. A generation brought up among starving peasants and under a fiercely autocratic government was prepared to live rigorously and to die without reward in the hope that the following generations would fare better. "Destroy everything," wrote Pisarev. "All the good things will escape destruction, otherwise the sooner they are destroyed the better. Hit hard in all directions. It can't possibly do any harm." Pisarev seems to be whispering the words, half afraid of them and on the lookout for reservations. It was the singular achievement of Nechayev that he showed how destruction could be brought about by a group of devotees determined to obey the rules.

Such was the blueprint of the revolution which Nechayev

* Nicolas Berdyaev, *The Russian Idea*, (New York: The Macmillan Company, 1948) p. 117.

hoped to bring about on his return to Russia. With the *Catechism* which he kept in code, the mandate signed by Bakunin, Ogaryov's poem, and a substantial sum of money he was now ready to return. He planned to spend the winter organizing his forces. On February 19, 1870, the ninth anniversary of the emancipation of the serfs, he planned to unleash the civil war which would topple the Czar from the throne. Following the injunctions of the *Catechism,* he had prepared already the list of those condemned to death. At the head of it were General Trepov, the Chief of Police in St. Petersburg, and General Mezentsev, the Chief of the Political Police of the Empire. The life of the Czar was to be temporarily spared, so that "the free peasantry, having broken the chains of slavery, on the day of vengeance will be allowed to break his head and at the same time pull down the tattered garments of the obsolete imperial system." At that moment not only the Czar but the whole imperial family was to be destroyed, leaving no trace behind them. And following the example which Bakunin had attempted many times in the past, Nechayev was determined to capture one of the imperial arsenals. His revolutionaries would be armed to the teeth. This was to be war to the death.

Though the Russian secret police had opened his mail and kept sporadic watch on him in Geneva, they showed a curious lack of vigilance at the border. With the help of some Bulgarian and Serbian revolutionaries, Nechayev made his way to Bucharest, then an outpost of the Turkish empire. Then he slipped over the border, and reached Moscow by the middle of September. Altogether he spent less than a hundred days in Russia and failed to achieve any of his objectives, but in those three months he carried out one by one all the commands of *The Revolutionary Catechism.*

In the years of the peasant revolts of Stenka Razin and Pugachov, the steppes of southern Russia had resounded with a strange, high-pitched Cossack battle-cry: *"Nechayi! Nechayi!"* (Cut! Cut!) Now a silent Nechayev was returning to Russia, hoping to succeed where his Cossack ancestors had failed.

On the Eve

When Nechayev returned to Russia, his first task was to gather together the remnants of the revolutionary organization. He soon found his friend Vladimir Orlov, who had sent him money abroad, and Nikolayev, with whose passport he had left the country. They had preserved their faith in him and were willing to obey his orders. In a short time nine cells, each composed of five members, came into being, together with a special group of trusted advisers known as the "Great Russian Section, Moscow." These alone were granted the privilege of knowing Nechayev's real name: to the others he remained Ivan Petrovich. The central organization seems to have consisted of the young nobleman, Peter Uspensky, who managed the well-known Cherkessov Bookshop; Alexey Kuznetsov, a student of the Petrovsky Agricultural Academy; Nikolay Nikolayev, who had once lived in Ivanovo and was now a student of the same Agricultural Academy; Ivan Prizhov, a forty-two-year-old secretary attached to the college and the author of two books, *The Poor in Holy Russia* and *A History of Russian Taverns;* and Prince Varlaam John Aslanovich Cherkessov, a railway engineer born in Tiflis a year after Nechayev. Two others, a student of the Medical Academy called Alexey Deteils, and the twenty-five-year-old Varvara Alexandrovskaya, the wife of a college professor, seem also to have taken part in the high councils of the secret organization. To these—and to these alone—Nechayev outlined the grand strategy.

The strategy was simple. First, it was necessary to increase the number of cells until all European Russia was covered with a vast network of cells owing allegiance to Nechayev. Secondly, the Imperial Armament Factory at Tula must be honeycombed with agents of the secret organization. Thirdly, on a day yet to be determined by Nechayev all the cells would come out in open revolt, every man armed and disciplined. Inevitably there would be war through the summer, followed by a general congress in October; and Nechayev explained the advantages of an outbreak in the spring by saying that if the insurrection failed in the cities, they would be able to fight along the Volga and the Dnieper with all the advantages of summer weather, and the peasants would be able to find shelter in the forests. As he spoke, his mind moving with delighted incomprehension among the serious problems of revolt, it seems never to have occurred to him that he possessed no military training; and if it had occurred to him, it would not have disturbed him any more than it disturbed Trotsky. He had appointed himself commander-in-chief, and he already claimed to have agents in the Imperial Armament Factory. The number of cells in St. Petersburg was increasing daily. Money was beginning to flow into the revolutionary coffers. Tula was being "cased." Soon Nechayev was able to report to Kuznetsov and Uspensky that "our main strength is not in Moscow but in Tula where we have fifty men in the arsenal on our side" and some time later he reported to Prince Cherkessov: "The men at the arsenal are all ready and we can take over Tula any time we like." Our knowledge of these statements comes from reports which appeared in the *Records of the Moscow High Court*, which began an inquiry into the mysterious affair at Tula at the end of the year. The report entitled *The Affair of the Conspirators Sergey Nechayev, Nikolai Nikola-*

yev, Ivan Prizhov, and Others offers a strange jumble of over-
heard conversations, excerpts from the reports of police
spies, and references to a secret notebook, otherwise uniden-
tified, which contained an account of the comings and goings
of the revolutionaries. From this report we learn that the police were well aware of Nechayev's *alias:* Ivan Petrovich.
They knew that Nikolayev went under at least three *aliases:*
Alexander Vassilievich Belkov, Belkin, and Yegor Anisimov.
But on the whole the report tells us very little about Nechayev's activities and the travails of the conspirators that early
autumn. We know that Nechayev claimed 150 members in
Moscow and some of his most loyal adherents belonged to
the Petrovsky Agricultural College, where Ivanov, Dolgov,
Ripman, and Kuznetsov were students. Among these students Nechayev was always known as Ivan Petrovich. To
other students in Moscow he was Pavlov, which seems to
have been the name he maintained in all his dealings with
Moscow University. We know there were endless intellectual
discussions which were often stormy. We hear of occasional
attempts to blackmail members in order to swell the coffers
of the revolutionary organization. A young army officer in St.
Petersburg was ordered to arrest a former member of the
group and blackmail him into signing a promissory note for
6,000 rubles. It was an unpleasant incident, and though the
promissory note was signed, the 6,000 rubles were never collected. There seem to have been continual financial difficulties, but everyone spoke of Nechayev's amazing optimism.
While the revolutionaries copied out verses, and Nechayev
himself continued to tell disarming lies about Nechayev,
sometimes saying that he had died in Siberia, at other times
referring to "the famous and melancholy occasion when our
Nechayev was shot by the police on the road from Tambov
to Perm," Nechayev himself was never at a loss. He held authority by reason of the mystery surrounding him. Who was
he? No one seemed to know. Was he really the Nechayev

whose name was spoken with bated breath? Meanwhile, Nechayev was certain the revolution would break out in the spring. He sent messengers to Bakunin, announcing that all was well and he hoped shortly to be able to summon the old anarchist back to Russia. To the messengers he explained that if Bakunin asked questions, they must be answered evasively. If Bakunin asked about Nechayev, they must say: "Nothing is known." Nechayev exclaimed: "The old man is the most inquisitive devil in the world. Don't trust him!"

One of the reasons why we know so little about those days in spite of the voluminous evidence brought forth at the trials is that Nechayev trusted no one, continually wore disguise and lived in a world of pseudonyms. He would summon meetings, usually arriving late, explaining that he had just come from a town five hundred miles away. There would be a short discussion, Nechayev would present the orders of the mysterious Society of which he was at once the chief executive and the legislature, and then he would be off again to Tula or St. Petersburg. Dostoyevsky has described such meetings in *The Possessed*, giving them a curiously hysterical air, but in fact Nechayev's meetings with his fellow-conspirators seem to have been strangely quiet. We hear of meetings in which Nechayev said: "Prepare yourselves. In the spring everything will be different. Don't disturb yourselves. Wait for the signal." He was waiting with buoyant optimism for the moment when the Imperial Armament Factory at Tula would fall into his hands.

Everything was going well for the revolutionaries when an incident occurred which was to destroy all Nechayev's carefully laid plans. It was a small incident at first, no more than a clash of temperaments. Once or twice before he had given way to bouts of senseless anger. He slept badly. He was continually rushing from one place to another. Now he gave an order of no importance whatsoever, and when it was disobeyed he flared up, murdered the culprit who disobeyed him and then ran for his life. In a sense he was running from this murder until the day he died.

It began so quietly that afterwards the conspirators had difficulty remembering exactly how it happened. Kuznetsov said later that he thought it began on November 4th. Nechayev, Kuznetsov and Ivanov were having a secret meeting. Nechayev had brought along some leaflets he had written recently. These leaflets were inflammatory incitements to rebellion, written under the title *From Those Who Are United To Those Who Are Scattered*. In brusque tones Nechayev ordered Ivanov to post them on the walls of the students' dining-hall and of the library of the Agricultural College. Ivanov demurred. He explained that it would only lead to the closing of the dining-halls, police raids, the arrest of innocent students. This may have been exactly what Nechayev intended. There was a long pause. Ivanov said nothing at all. He could see Nechayev's anger, the lips pursed, the eyes glaring.

"I tell you," said Nechayev, "the Society has ordered it. Are you disobeying the Society?"

"I refuse to listen to the Society when it tells me to do completely senseless things."

"Then you refuse to submit to the Society?"

"Yes, when it behaves stupidly."

Nechayev turned on his heels. His face was white. He wanted certainties, absolute obedience to commands, the knowledge that everyone was submitting to his will. Ivanov had been a trusted member of the group. It flashed through Nechayev's mind that the police seemed to know far more about the mysterious Society of the Ax than they should ever have been allowed to know. Ivanov was always smiling. He was handsome, well-built, an excellent student. Nechayev had taken to him, but seems to have doubted his loyalty for some time. And then, too, no one had ever dared to accuse Nechayev of stupidity before. The brief conversation ran-

kled, and Nechayev came to the conclusion that Ivanov's refusal must be regarded as an act of rebellion. It was as
though Ivanov was saying: "What is all this about the Society of the Ax? Who gives you the right to issue orders?
Every time you go away and consult the Society, you come
back and tell us that the Society has endorsed your views. I
don't believe the Society exists."

After the meeting with Kuznetsov and Ivanov, Nechayev
disappeared. Presumably he was in Tula, where there was
constant coming and going of revolutionaries. He returned
two weeks later with the announcement that he had obtained a new printing press. There were more discussions
with Nikolayev and Kuznetsov about Ivanov's "act of treason." Nikolayev was startled. He had not regarded Ivanov as
a man capable of committing treason. Nechayev asked what
should be the punishment of a stool pigeon. There followed
long theoretical discussions, but according to Kuznetsov,
who was present at many of them, they came to no agreement. On November 19 there was a meeting between
Ivanov and Prizhov. At the trial Prizhov said they discussed
nothing of any particular importance, but this is unlikely: it
would seem that Prizhov was sounding out Ivanov, and he
later reported on the meeting to Nechayev, who now concluded that Ivanov must be punished. Accordingly he asked
Nikolayev for a revolver and a knife, and ordered Nikolayev
to summon Ivanov to a meeting in a grotto of the Petrovsky
Park. Ivanov was to be told that the new printing press was
hidden there, and Ivanov himself would be placed in charge
of it. By this time Nikolayev was fully aware that Nechayev
planned to murder Ivanov in the grotto.

The Petrovsky Park lay on the northwest of Moscow, on
the outskirts of the city. Some fifty years before it had been
a haunt of the aristocracy. Here the nobility had built little
painted Swiss chalets, danced beside the lake and admired
the flowers. Prince Razumovsky had built an enormous palace

overlooking the gardens, but in 1861 the palace was bought
by the government, pulled down, and the site offered to the
University. The aristocracy had deserted the park, and
wealthy merchants built their suburban houses where there
had once been painted chalets. The gardens were going to
waste. It occurred to the officials of the University that the
site of Prince Razumovsky's palace was admirably located for
an agricultural school with botanical gardens and model
farms. Accordingly, in place of the palace, there arose in
1865 the Petrovsky Razumovsky Agricultural College, of
which Ivanov was one of the few, carefully-selected students.
There were only 150 students. Ivanov knew the gardens
well, and he would have no difficulty finding the grotto. It
was a winding grotto, the kind often frequented by lovers,
and it overlooked a small pond.

It was a dark night with low scudding clouds and thick
snow on the ground. The lakes and ponds in the gardens
were covered with a thin sheeting of ice. Ivanov, accompanied by Nikolayev, made his way to the grotto. It was dark
inside, with no light anywhere. Nechayev was waiting outside. So, too, were Kuznetsov and Uspensky. Prizhov was
standing beside Nechayev. He said later that he did not enter the grotto, but others remembered that he followed
Nikolayev. It was going to be a very simple murder. The
only weapon Nechayev had on him was the knife, given to
him by Nikolayev, which he slipped inside his heavy boots.
Suddenly Kuznetsov, standing outside, heard shuffling sounds
followed by a scream, but it was not the scream of Ivanov.
Nechayev, blundering in the dark, had put his hands round
Nikolayev's neck, and would have strangled him if he had
not recognized the voice in time. All Kuznetsov knew for
certain was that there was a nightmare within the grotto,
whispers, scuffling sounds, sudden pleadings. Then there was
another scream; this time it came from Ivanov.

"So the murder is about to take place," Kuznetsov whispered to himself. "In the dark grotto—"

But the murder did not take place within the dark grotto. Ivanov hurled himself out of the grotto, screaming at the top of his voice, followed by Nechayev, who was wildly waving his arms. Nechayev pushed Ivanov down to the ground, grappled with him and finally sat on him. Prizhov, standing some twenty paces away, said it was so dark that all he could see was a black shuddering mass, and out of the shuddering mass there came Nechayev's clear voice shouting: "Give me the revolver." Both Prizhov and Nikolayev claimed they remained in the grotto. It was probably Kuznetsov who provided the revolver. Ivanov was still fighting for his life. In the death-struggle he succeeded in biting Nechayev's thumb. Suddenly there was a shot, and soon Nechayev was turning the body over to search in the pockets, and then there came Nechayev's voice again, shouting for stones. No one understood what he wanted the stones for until he explained they would all have to help carry the body to the pond. It was all confusion, people running about in the dark, whispering, and then came Nechayev's authoritative voice, telling everyone exactly what to do. He fired another shot into Ivanov's head, presumably because Ivanov was still alive, and then he shot wild, and Prizhov, who felt the bullet whistling past his face, screamed. He had an odd idea that Nechayev was going to kill them all. He kept shouting his name, saying: "I am here! Don't shoot!" He was a simple-minded man, and seems never to have understood what was happening. But when Nechayev ordered him to help carry the body to the pond, with heavy stones tied at the neck and feet, Prizhov went running along with them. "I didn't feel strong enough to help carry the body," Prizhov said later. They dropped the body in the pond. Even then Nechayev bungled, for he suddenly pushed Nikolayev into the pond, and Nikolayev

came out cursing, wet through, wondering whether Nechayev had pushed him in deliberately and not daring to ask.
Then, the murder accomplished, they all went to Kuznetsov's apartment. Nikolayev dried his clothes, Nechayev bandaged his bleeding thumb, and they all sat up half the night
discussing their success in putting an end to the life of an
obvious informer.

In *The Possessed* Dostoyevsky based his account of the
murder of Shatov on the published reports of the murder of
Ivanov, with significant variations. Oddly enough, though
Dostoyevsky mentions the grotto, he makes no use of it;
three conspirators jump on Shatov in the light of three lanterns and almost at once Peter Verkhovensky shoots at Shatov's forehead. A moment later he is going through Shatov's
pockets, and giving instructions for getting the stones and
tying them to Shatov's neck and legs; and then the conspirators, awed, argumentative, and giving way to sudden senseless screams, carried the body to a pond. But Dostoyevsky's
account of the murder is at considerable variance with what
actually happened. Characteristically, he makes his conspirators far more hysterical than they were. They scream; they
indulge in fights among themselves; the swinging lanterns
light up a scene of madmen dancing wildly in circles, some
with handkerchiefs stuffed in their mouths to prevent them
from shouting, others crowding round the dead body and
still others running around in a wild panic. In fact, when
Ivanov was killed, the conspirators appear to have been remarkably quiet and undemonstrative, and though there was
some purposeless running about, most of them stood quite
still, regarding it with considerable detachment like figures
on a darkened frieze. It was Nechayev's responsibility, and
they felt little responsibility of their own.

We know nothing about the further incidents of that
night, but Nechayev's speech to the conspirators in Kuznetsov's apartment may very well have corresponded to the

speech which Dostoyevsky puts into the mouth of Verkhovensky:

Gentlemen, we can now disperse in the knowledge that we
have all fulfilled our duty, a duty which we have each of us
undertaken without feeling any sense of compulsion. And if
you feel unhappy about the matter, may I remind you that you
you will feel still unhappier tomorrow, and there is nothing
shameful in such feelings . . . As for danger, I cannot foresee
any. It would never occur to anyone to suspect any of you,
particularly if you behave reasonably and make no foolish mistakes . . . You understand, you have been called upon to
bring new life into an organization which is dying of stagna-
tion. Remember this, and may it bring you courage. From
now on we have only one aim. We must bring everything
down with a crash. The State will fall, and all its moral
standards will fall with it. We alone are left, we who have
prepared ourselves to take over the government: we shall
bring the intellectuals over to our side, and as for the fools, we
shall let them carry us on their shoulders. . . . Tomorrow we
shall not meet, gentlemen. I shall go into the country for a
while. You will hear from me the day after tomorrow. Meanwhile I think it would be better if you spent tomorrow at
home, and if you made your way to your own houses tonight
going by different routes, two at a time.

In some such way Nechayev must have spoken to the conspirators who were now beginning to regard him with hatred, though they took pains to conceal it. He was at the
height of his power. He was determined to show that he was
impervious to moral principles. Covered with blood, his
hand bitten by Ivanov's teeth, he had led his party of revolutionaries away from the first engagement with the enemy,
and accounted himself victorious. It seems never to have occurred to him that Ivanov was innocent of the crime of being
a police spy, and in later years he would talk proudly of having committed "a political murder."

Nechayev had previously arranged to go to St. Petersburg immediately after the murder. He left by train the next day. The cells he had established were behaving in a way which gave him no pleasure. The students were making no effort to suborn the military or to take over power. Instead they were engaged in endless theoretical discussions. "Remember Karakozov! Go out and murder the government!" He contemptuously dismissed the theoretical discussions as the ravings of incompetent children, and drew up new plans for taking over the state. He told them there was good news from Tula: they would soon have arms. But in fact there was little news from Tula, and Nikolayev, who went to Tula about this time, had nothing to report. Five days later the newspapers announced the discovery of the body of the young student Ivan Ivanovich Ivanov. The body had risen to the surface of a pond not far from the Agricultural College. It was a small item in the newspapers, and the revolutionaries in St. Petersburg paid little attention to it. Nechayev himself thought he had covered his traces, for he returned to Moscow a few days later. He did not know that Uspensky had already been arrested, and that the police were on his trail. Worse still, Ivanov had left a number of documents in his room which clearly pointed to a revolutionary conspiracy, headed by a certain Pavlov. The police were already familiar with Pavlov. Telegrams were exchanged with St. Petersburg. Uspensky, the most intelligent of the conspirators, was beginning to talk. Nechayev went into hiding. It was rumored that he slipped out of a police net by wearing women's clothes. On December 3 Kuznetsov and Prizhov were arrested. From that moment the traces of Nechayev disappear until about the middle of the month when Prince Cherkessov paid a visit to Tula to see the twenty-six-year-old Varvara Alexandrovskaya, then busily occupied in the conspiracy to take over the armament factory. He told her that Nechayev was in extreme danger, and needed her help. He must go abroad again. In Switzerland, or elsewhere, he would obtain money to advance the revolution and help those of the conspirators who were in danger of arrest. Varvara Alexandrovskaya agreed. Early in January, with a false passport, disguised as a woman, with Varvara Alexandrovskaya at his side, and pretending to be her sister, Nechayev slipped out of Russia and made his way to Bakunin in Switzerland.

When he returned to Russia, he came as a prisoner of the Czar.

The Restless Years

Baffled by disease, the perfidy of his friends, his wife's infidelity, and above all by the constant pressures of the secret police, Bakunin had grown weary of Geneva. He complained of the smells in the street and the curiously pervasive *bourgeois* character of the town. It was a place where nothing happened. People played cards, the taverns were crowded with amateur chess players, there were the endless Sunday morning promenades: altogether it was enough to drive you mad. Bakunin thought of going to Italy, but he had already taken part in two attempts to seize power in Italy, and he had no longer any strong attachment for Garibaldi. Accordingly he decided to live in Locarno, on the Italian frontier, where living was cheap and where he hoped to dream away the last years of his life. The fight had gone out of him. He wrote to Ogaryov that he was not in the slightest interested in the possibility of a revolution in France, though he was to change his mind later. "I have absolutely no desire to see a great display of fireworks," he wrote shortly after he had set up his establishment in Locarno, in a letter to Herzen. But Herzen was dying, and the old order was passing. An exhausted Bakunin gazed over Lago Maggiore, dreaming about what might have been, spending odd moments during the day racking his brains over a translation into Russian of an obscure work of "economic metaphysics" by Karl Marx. At intervals he read Proudhon and Comte and continued to work on a leaflet on the subject of suppressing the State.

When Nechayev reached Geneva, he learned to his dismay that Bakunin had fled. He stayed with Ogaryov and disinterred some of the pamphlets they had written the previous year. He gave them to Varvara Alexandrovskaya and bade her return with them to Russia immediately, explaining that the fire of the revolution must be fed. The truth was that he was getting tired of Varvara, who immediately made her way back to Russia and was arrested by the police on the frontier, with the pamphlets intact. Nechayev still had considerable sums of money. In addition to the money he found in Ivanov's pockets there were the dues paid by the members of the secret society. And when Ogaryov pointed to the swollen thumb, Nechayev answered proudly that he had once more been arrested by the police as he slipped over the frontier, he had clubbed the policeman over the head, but there had been a terrible fight. Ogaryov was impressed, and to impress him still further Nechayev explained that wealth was pouring into the coffers of the secret society and all of Russia was on the verge of revolution. He proposed to spend only a few days in Switzerland: soon he would return and "light the faggots under the Czar's throne."

Early in February Nechayev made his way to Locarno. Herzen had just died and Bakunin, still suffering from the shock, greeted his young friend with open arms. "Boy" had not changed. If anything, Nechayev was more dauntless than ever. He repeated the stories of the great wealth which would soon be flowing into his hands, about the mysterious Russian nobleman who was on the point of selling his estate and handing it over to the Society, about the vast prospects of revolution. When Bakunin pointed to the wounded hand, Nechayev told how he had fought off a whole battalion of police officers single-handed. He had returned, Nechayev said, for one last consultation with Bakunin before ordering the revolution.

The long idyll with Bakunin continued as before, but there were problems to be solved. Nechayev's money was running out; there was delay in obtaining the large sums which were due to arrive from Russia; Bakunin was complaining against the drudgery of translating *Das Kapital* for which he had received an advance of 300 rubles against a total fee of 1,200 rubles to be paid on completion of the work. The 300 rubles was already spent, and Bakunin had translated only the introductory chapters. Nechayev offered to relieve Bakunin of the responsibility of finishing the translation. On "official" notepaper, bearing the name of the Society of the Ax in red ink, with an ax, a dagger, and a revolver drawn roughly on the paper, he sent off a letter to a certain Liubavin, a Russian student then studying at a university in Germany who had acted as intermediary and persuaded a Russian publisher to make the advance. Liubavin was told he had committed a monstrous crime. Bakunin was a revolutionary whose life was devoted to the revolution; to demand that he should exploit his talents by hackwork showed an amazing ignorance of affairs. The student was peremptorily commanded to telegraph to Bakunin a release from his obligations. If he refused, the Society of the Ax would take appropriate measures. The letter was unsigned, and Liubavin concluded that it had been written by Bakunin and immediately wrote an insulting letter to Bakunin, recapitulating the contents of the letter received from the Society of the Ax. Bakunin was alarmed. At bottom, he had the *bourgeois* instincts: he always paid his debts. He immediately wrote to Liubavin, announcing that he accepted his obligation and would repay the 300 rubles as soon as circumstances permitted. He regretted however that he saw no likelihood of ever being able to complete the translation of *Das Kapital*. Then he turned on Nechayev and asked for an explanation. Nechayev laughed. He had simply taken the most obvious course, and he was sorry the old man took it amiss. Soon the matter was forgotten, for new problems were arising every day. The fate of the 300 rubles owed to the Russian publisher Polyakov could be relegated to the future. The Russian revolution, too, could wait. The most pressing problem was that the Swiss government had received an extradition order for Nechayev's arrest, and for the first time in his life Nechayev was alarmed. As Nechayev explained with admirable simplicity: "Money is never a problem. If we want money, all we have to do is to hold up the Simplon post. But when the Swiss police are on our track, we have to work much harder."

What happened then could easily have been predicted: Nechayev set Bakunin to work. Writing to Ogaryov on February 8, Bakunin complained bitterly about the amount of work Nechayev had made him do:

> I am late in replying to your letter because Boy is making my head whirl with all the work he sets before me. This morning I had to write an article on the subject of the courtesy of the police who place themselves at the service of foreign powers and go running after thieves, forgers, and brigands so-called . . . The situation of the Russian refugees in Europe imposes upon us the necessity to do everything we can, without losing a moment, to win the public over to our side. Unless we do this, every single one of us may be extradited as though we were the worst kind of thieves and assassins.

Already there were rumors that Nechayev had murdered Ivanov. Nechayev denied them glibly. A little later he was admitting the rumors and explaining that the murder was purely political, and unavoidable: Ivanov had been found guilty of a crime against the revolution. Bakunin was aware there was nothing to prevent the Swiss police from arresting Nechayev on an extradition order. Fearing for his own life and also for Nechayev's, he set to work on a pamphlet which later became the celebrated plea entitled *The Bear of Berne and the Bear of St. Petersburg*, which purported to have been written by a Swiss citizen. It was a heady document, accusing both governments of tyrannical practices, and it did nothing to make Nechayev's position less vulnerable. By this time Bakunin was beginning to lose that perfect faith with which he had accepted Nechayev's least utterances in the past. Nechayev stayed with Bakunin less than ten days and returned to Geneva. There at least he could be sure of complete acceptance of his views. Ogaryov, far more than Bakunin, had fallen under Nechayev's spell.

The idyll between Nechayev and Ogaryov was interrupted by a further idyll between Nechayev and the elder daughter of the "poor, dear, feckless" Herzen, who had died in Paris on January 21. Natalie Herzen, who was known as Tata, was present at her father's death. Shortly afterward she hurried to Geneva to comfort Ogaryov, once her father's *alter ego*. She had inherited a small fortune. She painted well. She had the fine, strong features of her father. She could speak four languages, and she was filled with revolutionary fervor. Ogaryov began to think of a match between Nechayev and Tata Herzen, which would link the foremost of practicing revolutionaries with the family of the great apologist for a Russian revolution. And when, after a visit to Paris in February, Tata Herzen returned to Geneva, Bakunin was thinking in the same terms.

There is no reason to believe that Tata Herzen ever fell in love with Nechayev. But Nechayev lived under Ogaryov's roof, Tata was always by his side, and he set her to work addressing envelopes. Bakunin had been complaining that Nechayev had grown lazy, but the fit of laziness soon passed. Since no money was coming in, the letters to Russia consisted largely of appeals for funds to aid the revolution. Most of these letters fell into the hands of the police, and almost no money came out of Russia. Remembering Tata's skill in drawing, Nechayev suggested that she draw designs for making banknotes. Tata groaned: she had no experience in drawing banknotes and no intention of trying. The problem of money was growing urgent. In March Bakunin arrived in Geneva with the bland suggestion that Tata should help the cause by marrying into a rich family. She was pretty; she was gifted; in what better way could she serve the revolution than by selling herself to a rich admirer? It was not one of Bakunin's more brilliant suggestions and sounds suspiciously like the kind of idea which would occur to Nechayev. For Nechayev was not totally devoid of ideas. He suggested a literary alliance between Tata Herzen and himself; together they would edit the revolutionary magazine *Kolokol* [*The Bell*], which had been founded by her father. Tata threw herself enthusiastically into the plan. Between April 2 and May 9, six issues of *Kolokol* appeared with the names of Natalie Herzen and Sergey Nechayev on the masthead. Neither of the editors had any experience of producing a revolutionary magazine. It was excessively tame, full of praise for Herzen and subdued attacks on Bakunin. There were unsigned open letters written in Nechayev's worst style, and there was none of the fire which characterized the brief pamphlets which Nechayev had begun writing from the moment he first stepped on Swiss soil. Only two assumptions are possible: either Nechayev was deliberately bowing to Tata's more liberal revolutionary ideas, or he was simply using the magazine as an instrument to advance his claim on Tata's fortune. She seems to have admired and feared him by turns, and to have resisted his attempts to seduce her, and she was fond of him to the very end. But she never submitted herself to the orders of the mysterious Society which Nechayev claimed to control and seems to have realized very early in their relationship that it had no existence outside Nechayev's brain.

There remained the Bakhmatiev fund. Since the death of Herzen the fund came under the control of Ogaryov, who could dispose of it as he pleased. Under Nechayev's promptings he decided to give the greater part of it to Nechayev's Society of the People's Vengeance. To give an appearance of legality to the transfer, Ogaryov summoned a meeting of revolutionaries; and in the presence of Tata Herzen, her young brother Alexander, Natalie Ogaryov, and a few other Russian exiles, the money was handed by Ogaryov to Bakunin, who handed it to Nechayev. Both Ogaryov and Bakunin retained small sums for themselves. As usual Bakunin showed his notorious respect for contracts and demanded that all those who witnessed the transfer of the money should sign an affidavit. He had not counted upon Nechayev, who refused on the grounds that such an affidavit involved his honor as a revolutionary. There the matter rested until later in the year when Karl Marx announced that all the money had fallen into Bakunin's hands. Bakunin was so aroused on a point of honor that he drew up a manifesto to be signed by Ogaryov. The manifesto, a wonderful tissue of truth and incomparable falsehood, read:

I, the undersigned, do hereby declare that all the moneys contained in the Bakhmatiev fund were placed in the hands of Nechayev, to be given over to the Russian Committee of which the aforesaid Nechayev is the foreign representative, according to the documents and statements in his possession.

Bakunin had no right whatsoever to dispose of the funds, and did not in fact do so. The right to dispose of the fund belonged exclusively to Herzen and me; and after Herzen's death I alone possessed the right to dispose of it. Bakunin himself took no part in the transfer of the capital sum to Nechayev, which took place in the presence of only two people: Natalie Alexandrovna Herzen and myself.

Unfortunately, on this occasion, I made an unpardonable omission. Having absolute confidence in the revolutionary faith of Nechayev, I did not ask for a receipt. It was only later, when my opinion of Nechayev changed for the worse, that I decided to ask him for a receipt . . . Nechayev refused, offering the pretext that the Russian Committee never acted in this manner. This dishonest attitude on the part of Nechayev only confirmed my suspicion that ideas of morality were completely foreign to him.

The part which Bakunin played in this affair was as follows. After the death of Herzen he persuaded me to give the money to Nechayev as the representative of the Russian Committee, as the single designated revolutionary who could be said to represent the Russian revolution abroad. To this man the total sum contained within the Bakhmatiev fund was given. It was not difficult to convince me that this was the best course to adopt, for I shared with Bakunin an absolute faith in the existence of the Russian Committee, and both of us regarded Nechayev as its chief representative abroad.

Such was Bakunin's contorted apologia with its truths, half truths and lies so inextricably mingled that even now we can hardly disentangle them. The only thing that is certain is that the greater part of the Bakhmatiev fund, amounting to 10,000 francs, disappeared in Nechayev's pockets. Some of the money may have been expended on the cost of publishing *Kolokol*. A good deal of it must have been kept by Nechayev. Bakunin in the affidavit takes care to repeat twice that he received none of the money, so arousing the suspicion that he received a considerable share of it. But the mystery of the Bakhmatiev fund remains.

There are other mysteries concerning Nechayev's brief stay in Switzerland. There is, for example, the mysterious figure of Vladimir Serebrennikov, of whom nothing is known except that he was always to be seen by Nechayev's side. Bakunin regarded him as a rogue, but never enlarged on his crimes. He seems to have attached himself to Nechayev and to have been his constant messenger and confidant. We

know more about a young revolutionary called Semeon
Serebrennikov, a friend of Ogaryov who was one of the witnesses who attended the transfer of the money to Nechayev.

On May 9 Semeon Serebrennikov was standing outside
Ogaryov's house when three plain-clothes men hurled themselves upon him. There was a short struggle, Serebrennikov
heard the words, "Camperio . . . Nechayev . . ." and then
his arms were twisted behind his back and tied with cord.
Protesting, he was removed to the police station, threatened
with a revolver and kept waiting until the superintendent
arrived. His papers were taken from him: passport, letters,
money, banknotes. When the superintendent arrived, Serebrennikov was formally accused of being Nechayev. He was
shown a photograph of Nechayev with the usual police
description underneath. He pointed out that Nechayev's hair
was dark, his own blond, and kept asking to see Ogaryov.
He had difficulty in making himself understood. He knew no
French and could not speak German with ease. He was
thrown into a cell and given ten francs to buy food.

The next day there was a formal interrogation. Once
again he attempted to explain that he was not Nechayev.
He said he was a poor student, the son of a peasant, born in
the village of Znamienka in Ilguinsk district in the government of Irkutsk. Asked to account for his movements during
the previous five years he said he had spent the greater part
of his time studying in St. Petersburg. In April, 1869, he
left Odessa for America by way of Vienna, Berlin, and Ham-
burg. In America he had gone under the name of Guy Ore.
He had stayed there only a few months. He was back again
in Europe in December, studying at the Polytechnic College
in Zurich. Asked whether he knew Nechayev, Serebrennikov
answered that he had encountered a student of the same
name in St. Petersburg, but at the time of the murder he
was safely in New York living with a Russian called George
Leger, 148 Lawrence Street, in the house of a certain Mr.

Rietzel, a teacher of music. This could be checked by the
authorities of New York. Asked to account for his more recent movements Serebrennikov shrugged his shoulders and
said he arrived in Geneva five days ago.

Serebrennikov was kept in prison for a further ten days.
The fourth interrogation occurred on May 20. After the
interrogation he was led into a courtyard. A mysterious visitor was watching him from a window above, evidently someone who knew Nechayev well and who could recognise him.
But the recognition evidently failed, for on the next day, a
Saturday, Serebrennikov was suddenly released. He had been
accused of no crime. There was not enough evidence to link
him with Nechayev. Serebrennikov was furious. He complained that while he was in prison the only reading matter
allowed consisted of two or three twenty-year-old newspapers, a novel published in 1781, and a French grammar
printed about the same time. Serebrennikov was of the
opinion that they were deliberately conspiring to reduce him
to a state of insanity with these old books and newspapers.
The novel particularly annoyed him. "It would have been
useful to a peasant," he said, "but I am a student and
deserve better."

With this, Serebrennikov disappears from the scene, as an
authentic "figure of mystery." He was not quite as innocent
as he made out in the pamphlet which he printed at the end
of the month. The pamphlet was entitled *L'Arrestation de
S. Sérébrénnikov par la Police de Genève,* and purported to
show that the Swiss police were completely out of their
minds and should pay him a large sum as damages for un-
lawful arrest. In fact, Nechayev knew him well and he had
played a small role in Nechayev's revolutionary activity. In
St. Petersburg Serebrennikov had possessed a small printing
press, and, as we have seen, it was on this press that Alexandra Dementieva printed the copies of Tkachev's inflammatory pamphlet summoning the students to revolt. The

printing press was to be mentioned at great length during the trial of the *Nechayevtsi* the following year. For the Russian government the arrest of Serebrennikov was an expensive mistake. On the day of the arrest the Swiss police forwarded a telegram to St. Petersburg, announcing the capture of the dreaded Nechayev, with a full description. The Russians were wary and immediately sent two men to Switzerland to identify the prisoner. One was a watchman attached to St. Petersburg University, the other a watchman attached to the Andreyevsky College, the day-school where Nechayev had once taught theology. When they failed to identify Nechayev, Serebrennikov was released. The Russian police caught up with Serebrennikov four years later when he was working in Prussia. He was extradited, put on trial and sent to Siberia.

Meanwhile Nechayev was still hiding in Geneva and the surrounding villages. He was always on the move, always a little ahead of the police. Ogaryov in his mysterious way continued to keep in touch with him. Once when Nechayev was staying in the little mountain village of Le Locle in the Jura, Tata Herzen was sent on a secret mission to him. A little while later she hid him in her house for a week. It was now known that the Russian government had supplied the Swiss with an extradition order, accusing Nechayev of being a common criminal. Bakunin sent an endless stream of letters and telegrams to Nechayev warning him that he was in danger of imminent arrest. There were letters on May 2, 4, 6, and 9 and two telegrams were sent on the fifth and the seventh. "Why are you silent?" Bakunin complained in one of the letters written from Locarno. "If you have received my letters, why don't you reply? I know nothing of what is happening and understand less." Probably Nechayev could not have replied to the letters even if he had received them. He was on the run. Bakunin rushed to Berne, hoping to head off any action by the Swiss police. He consulted

lawyers and buttonholed judges. The lawyers Adolf and
Gustav Vogt offered to work on behalf of Nechayev. The
Bundesrath Knusebeck explained that although the Federal
Council would probably refuse extradition if the case was
brought to their attention, there was nothing to prevent the
Cantonal Council of Geneva from obeying the order of the
Russian police. At least ten Russian agents were searching
for Nechayev, and they were well supplied with funds. In
panic Bakunin drew up an open letter to his friends in
Geneva, begging them to act quickly. He urged all Russian
émigrés to sign a memorial in defense of Nechayev. Many
signed, though some afterward regretted their signatures
and explained that they signed against the evidence and
without conviction. "Beware of falling asleep on the task,"
Bakunin wrote. "Apply yourselves! Give the largest possible
publicity to this act of cowardice on the part of the Swiss!
Use every weapon open to you—pamphlets, articles in the
newspapers, private correspondence! Keep up an unrelenting
pressure!" In the midst of Bakunin's furious efforts to save
Nechayev there arrived from Moscow a young revolutionary
called Lopatin who asked casually why anyone should trouble to defend a common murderer. Lopatin had an un-
impeachable revolutionary background. He had seen Nechayev at work in Switzerland and in Russia. He poured scorn
on Nechayev as the valiant revolutionary. The story about
the escape from the Peter and Paul Fortress was untrue.
There was no vast revolutionary society in Russia waiting
to obey Nechayev's orders. The scars on Nechayev's thumb
were death-marks left by Ivanov's teeth. "There is absolutely nothing that can be said in his favor," Lopatin explained; and though Bakunin refused to believe Lopatin's
report as it was recounted to him by Tata Herzen, it is clear
that his faith in Nechayev was shaken.

While Bakunin was attempting to move heaven and earth
to save Nechayev from the Russian police, an obscure

quarrel broke out between the two revolutionaries. All we know is that the quarrel involved Ogaryov and related to some conditions which Bakunin laid down. Writing to Ogaryov on June 14, Bakunin refers haltingly and in veiled tones to the causes of the rupture which now seemed inevitable:

> . . . I now feel it is my duty to state clearly and categorically for the benefit of Neville [Nechayev] the conditions I have already mentioned to you. My mind is made up, I shall not and cannot take back my words, I refuse to make a single backward step. Whether he accepts my conditions depends very much on your attitude toward me. He will accept them if you tell him to, as you will if you come to the conclusion that it is just, useful, and necessary to lend me your support. I have done my best to convince you, and I have given you all the information I have. All I can do now is to wait for your reply and for his . . . Of course "Boy" is obstinate, and I too, once I have made up my mind, have not the habit of changing it. *Ergo,* a rupture with him, at least from my side, now seems inevitable. If we all agreed, acting with complete unanimity, we might be able to make some impression on his pigheadedness; on the other hand we might fail completely. In any event we must put an end to the affair once and for all.

Neither Nechayev nor Bakunin has left any clues about this sudden alteration in their relations. Already in February Bakunin had written to Ogaryov about "the conditions on which he could give himself up to the cause." He told Ogaryov that he had overcome all false shame. "Up to this moment we have acted as pure idealists: we have served the cause only with our aspirations, our desire to perform great deeds, occasional pieces of propaganda. But if anyone wishes to perform on a large scale, he must know a great deal and dare splendidly." Bakunin added that it was also necessary to have control over considerable resources. But it is unlikely that the estrangement arose as the result of Nechayev's failure to support Bakunin financially. Their differences lay much deeper. Both were impoverished, bitter, remorseless in their desire for power. In their different ways they had outlived the need for one another. Generosity was a quality which Bakunin retained to the end: it was not a quality we can associate with Nechayev, who felt no gratitude for Bakunin and no generous impulses towards any man. There came a blunt letter from Nechayev announcing he would arrange a rendezvous at a time and place to be determined later. Then there was silence.

A week later Bakunin heard that Nechayev had slipped out of Switzerland. He had taken with him a box containing Bakunin's entire international correspondence, hundreds of private letters and letters of introduction written many months before. There could be only one reason for the theft. Horror-stricken, Bakunin wrote to his friend Talandier in London:

Neuchâtel, July 24, 1870

My dear friend,

I have just heard that N. has visited you, and you have given him the address of our mutual friends (M. and his wife). I am forced to the conclusion that the two letters which O. and I sent to you, warning you to keep him away from your doors, failed to arrive in time. Without the least exaggeration I believe this delay to have been an absolute disaster. And if it seems strange to you that we are warning you against a man to whom we have given letters of introduction, letters written in the warmest terms, then remember that these letters were written in May, and since then we have been confronted with some grave incidents—incidents which have made us break off all relations with N. At the risk of appearing to be out of our minds, we believe we have the sacred duty to warn you against him. And now I shall try to tell you very briefly the reasons why we have changed our opinion of him.

It is perfectly true that N. is the one man most persecuted

by the Russian government, which has covered the whole continent of Europe with a cloud of spies determined to find him in whatever country he can be found. It is true too that the Russian government has demanded his extradition from Germany as well as Switzerland. It is also true that N. is one of the most active and energetic men I have ever known. When he serves what he calls the cause, he never hesitates, stops at nothing, and is as merciless toward himself as toward others. This is the chief quality which attracted me to him, and it was this which made me over a long period of time seek out an alliance with him. There are some who say he is simply a fraud. This is a lie! He is a dedicated fanatic, and a very dangerous fanatic: with him an alliance can only be disastrous. And this is why: there was a time when he did actually belong to a secret organization in Russia. This organization however no longer exists. All its members were arrested. N. is alone now: alone he represents what he is pleased to call the Committee. With the Russian organization decimated, he is busy preparing a new one abroad. All this would be natural, legitimate, and extremely useful, but his methods are reprehensible. Deeply impressed by the disaster which destroyed the secret organization in Russia, he came to the conclusion that if he was to form a true and indestructible society, he would have to base it on the political principles of Machiavelli and adopt the motto of the Jesuits: "Violence for the body, lies for the Soul."

Truth, mutual confidence, fast friendships—these can only exist among a dozen individuals who form the inner sanctum of the Society. All the rest must be no more than blind instruments of the Society's will, expendable according to the whim of the twelve, who are bound together by the sternest oaths. It is perfectly permissible to deceive, compromise and steal from the underlings: it is even permissible to lose them. He is wholly the conspirator. And so, now that you have received N. because we sent our own letter of recommendation, and you have given him your confidence and recommended him to your friends—to M. and Mme M. in particular—what will happen when he has entered your world? Let me tell you.

First, he will tell a host of lies in order to increase your sympathy and confidence in him, but this is not all. The sympathies of lukewarm men, by which I mean men who are not wholly dedicated to the revolution, men who have other interests, men with family ties and love affairs and friendships and social relations—such men he regards as unworthy, and he will do everything he can to submit them wholly to the cause, and quite without your knowing it, he will try to take over your whole life. To do this, he will spy on you and attempt to get possession of all your secrets, and if left alone in a room in your absence, he will open all your drawers, read all your correspondence, and if he finds a letter which in some way compromises you or your friends, he will steal it and guard it carefully for his own purposes of intimidation. He has done this with O., with Tata and other friends, and when we faced him with the charge, he dared to say: "So I did it? Well, that's our system. That is how we treat enemies—we have to compromise *everyone* who is not completely with us." By this he means all those who are not completely convinced of the complete validity of his system and have not promised to apply it themselves.

Then, too, if you introduce him to a friend, his first aim will be to sow dissension, scandal, and intrigue between you. If your friend has a wife or a daughter, he will attempt to seduce her and get her with child, forcing her beyond the limits of conventional morality and so place her that she is compelled to make a revolutionary protest against society.

Every personal tie, every friendship, everything . . . all these he will regard as evil, and he will do his best to destroy them, and he will do this because these things weaken the effectiveness of his secret organization. Do not, I beg of you, cry out that this is an exaggeration! All this has happened and can be proved. When he is unmasked, this poor N. is so childlike, so simple in spite of his systematic perversity—he even thought he could convert me and begged me to develop this theory in a Russian journal which he wanted me to publish. He has betrayed the confidence of us all, stolen our letters, horribly compromised us—in a word, he has behaved like a vil-

lain. His only excuse lies in his fanaticism! Without knowing it,
he is terribly ambitious, because he has come finally to the
conclusion that the revolutionary cause can be identified with
his own person, and so leads the life of a martyr, full of privations and unbelievable hard work: therefore you cannot call
him an egoist in the worst sense of the word. He is a fanatic,
and fanaticism has led him into becoming an accomplished
Jesuit—there are moments when he is no more than a beast.
Most of his lies are white lies. He plays the Jesuit game as
others play the game of revolution. But in spite of his naïveté,
he is extremely dangerous, because *every day* he commits
crimes, abuses confidences, acts treacherously; and it is all the
more difficult to prevent these things from happening because
one hardly suspects their possibility. In spite of all this he is a
force to be reckoned with, because he has immense energy.
And so it was with immense sorrow that I broke with him. I
thought of how service to our cause demands immense re-
serves of energy, and how rarely we come upon anyone so
richly endowed with pure energy. But after thinking the matter out, I came to the conclusion that no other course was
open to me, and now that we are apart, I must keep fighting
him to the bitter end. Believe it or not, his last project was to
form a group of thieves and bandits on Swiss territory, evidently with the intention of bringing about a revolution. I
have prevented that by making him leave Switzerland, and it
is quite certain that if he had continued with his project, this
group of bandits would have been captured within the space
of a few weeks—he would have been lost, and everyone else
would have been lost with him. His friend and companion S.
is an outright scoundrel, a brazen liar, without the excuse or
the saving grace of fanaticism. He committed innumerable
thefts of papers and letters from me. And these are the fellows whom M., even though warned by J., has thought of introducing to Dupont and Bradlaugh. The evil has been done,
and we must do what we can to put it right, making as little
noise as possible and without scandal.

(1) In the name of your peace of mind, the peace of your
family and your own dignity, I beg you to shut your door to

them. Do this without any explanations: simply cut off all connection with them. For many reasons we do not want them to think we are waging war on them all along the line. They must think these warnings against them are coming from our enemies—and this statement might very well be true, since there have been some very energetic accusations against them stemming from the general council in London. Please do not unmask us too prematurely. They have stolen our papers, and we must get them back somehow.

(2) Persuade M. that the safety of his whole family depends upon breaking with them. Warn them about how he will systematically try to corrupt and seduce young women, and in this way wield power over the whole family. I am distressed beyond words at the thought that they have got M.'s address: they will publicly denounce M. They told me quite openly, and in the presence of witnesses, that they are perfectly prepared to denounce their enemies to the secret police; and by enemies they mean those who are only lukewarm to the revolutionary faith; and they regard denunciation as a perfectly legitimate means to an end. To take over a person's family secrets and thus hold a whip over them—this is one of their most important weapons. I am so terrified at the thought that they have M.'s address that I beg him to move to another lodging, and so avoid discovery. And if M. continues to be infatuated by his own judgment and continues his relations with these gentlemen, then I am sure that there will be terrible consequences, and these will arise as a consequence of his own blind vanity.

(3) You and M. must warn all our friends to be on their guard against these gentlemen. N., the most obstinate of players, will lose the game—the other is lost already. None of our friends must be allowed to fall into the general pattern of ruin. It is all very sad and humiliating, especially since I recommended them, but truth is the better part and the greatest remedy against all evils.

Bakunin was quite capable of writing fifty-page letters, and this letter to Talandier is by no means the longest he wrote. Yet it is one of the most illuminating and certainly the most despairing of all his letters. Written in bile, in the extreme assurance that he had at last seen evil face to face, he paused long enough to offer Nechayev a tribute of baffled admiration. He was bemused, as he had never been bemused before; it was beyond all comprehension, he said, and yet there was nothing performed by Nechayev which he had not himself encouraged and performed a hundred times. Even the name of his friend terrified him; he dared not write it down in full; and he went bitterly complaining against the injustice of "Boy" to anyone who cared to listen to him.

Meanwhile Bakunin had performed a useful service to humanity. The letter to Talandier provides the perfect summary to the nihilist character, and belongs to the great series of "Characters" written during the seventeenth and eighteenth centuries. Bakunin saw the danger and recoiled in horror. The huge terrifying insolence of Nechayev frightened him, as later it pleased Lenin; and what is apparent throughout this long letter is a kind of envy of Nechayev, a deep love, and even an understanding; it is as though Bakunin is saying, "He is terrible beyond words; he has compromised me; but he is singularly great in his terrible way." Bakunin had only been playing with destruction; this was the real thing. He had written once: "The desire for destruction is at the same time a desire for creation." He had only half believed it. Now for the first time he saw this belief parading in the flesh.

Stung into fury by his loss, Bakunin writes with quite extraordinary penetration of the nihilist character. Himself a nihilist or nearly a nihilist, he is able to relate the construction of the nihilist mind when projected to its ultimate extension. So Dostoyevsky describes Kirillov with immense understanding, and Hitler (though he was pretending to be doing something else) described his own nihilism in a speech he delivered after the blood bath of 1934. Mostly, it is only the nihilists who write convincingly about the nihilist character. Bakunin was so frightened of Nechayev that he remained in hiding for six weeks. He knew he was not innocent. He expected the vengeance of Nechayev. Strangest of all is the underlying quietness and composure of the letter. It is as though Bakunin was setting about the task of stripping Nechayev of his adornments quietly, tenaciously, knowing that the task was necessary, and not only because it was necessary to warn Talandier: it was also necessary that he should himself be warned.

The letter to Talandier was only one of many. He wrote to his friend Mroczkowski in London, begging for every scrap of available information about Nechayev. What had Nechayev told him? Where is he? Who is he staying with? Had Bradlaugh and Dupont been warned against him in time? To another correspondent he wrote urging that every effort should be made to steal back from Nechayev the papers which Nechayev had stolen from him. "I beg you to break off all relations with Nechayev and his little friend Woldemar S.,* and afterward do everything you can to destroy your traces." From Locarno he wrote to Ogaryov on July 28, admitting that the worst had happened. His letters of warning had been received too late. Mroczkowski had introduced Nechayev to "that iconoclast Bradlaugh" and to Dupont, an influential member of the International Workingmen's Association. Nechayev was planning to publish *The Bell* in London. Everything was going badly, but thank heaven, Ogaryov had sent him a packet of tea. We can leave Bakunin as he brews the tea and commiserates with himself on the loss of his secret journals.

In London Nechayev fared badly. Within a few weeks Bakunin's letters caught up with him. He seems to have

* Vladimir Serebrennikov, who accompanied Nechayev to London. He used the name Woldemar Sallier.

quarreled with Vladimir Serebrennikov, and with immense difficulty he produced two numbers of a new Russian periodical called *The Commune* (*Obshchina*) which purported to be the organ of the Russian Socialists. The first number appeared under the date-line September 1, 1870, but probably came out some weeks later. It contained a veiled attack on Herzen, "the grand old man of the revolution who only knows how to play at liberalism." It also contained an open letter to Bakunin and Ogaryov, accusing them of being reactionaries, revolutionaries "of the most incompetent kind" and men who had mismanaged the funds entrusted to them. In the open letter Nechayev demanded the balance of the Bakhmatiev fund, but unknown to Nechayev, Bakunin had signed on July 21 a statement to the effect that he was borrowing 450 francs from the fund and proposed to return the money within three weeks or at the latest on the 15th of August. It can be assumed that Ogaryov and Bakunin now regarded the fund as their own private repository, to be used as they thought fit, and there was not the least likelihood that they would entrust the balance to Nechayev.

There was little Nechayev could do in London. In January, 1871, he was in Paris. In March he was once again in Zurich, working with a Serbian passport as a house-painter. There were rumors that he visited Lyons during the few days when Bakunin placed himself at the head of the Committee of Public Safety during the Commune, but Bakunin found no trace of him and it is unlikely that Nechayev, whose French was always poor, could have made headway in France. He returned to Zurich because he was known there, and still had a handful of friends. It was the time when the International Workingmen's Association was at the height of its power, and the First International had no sympathy for Nechayev's methods. He lived secretly, and was often penniless. Serebrennikov remained in London, and it sometimes pleased Nechayev to send messages to Serebrennikov who would then transmit them to Switzerland, giving the impression that Nechayev was still in England. Penniless, desperate, going under half a dozen different names, living with obscure Rumanian and Serbian revolutionaries, Nechayev still planned a revolution and he was still surrounded by a loyal but improvident band of followers, but the original impetus was wearing thin.

At the beginning of July, 1871, there opened in St. Petersburg the trial known as "the trial of the *Nechayevtsi*." Some eighty-four of the followers of Nechayev had been rounded up. The courthouse was open to the public; the newspapers were encouraged to publish full reports of the proceedings. Nearly everyone who had come in contact with Nechayev in Russia was under arrest. Nechayev's chief lieutenants, Orlov, Nikolayev, Prizhov, Uspensky, Kuznetsov and Mme. Dementieva were brought to the witness stand, and gave full accounts of their dealings with Nechayev. From diaries, documents, and telegrams the police were able to fill in a complete history of the hundred days Nechayev had spent in Russia. The public was appalled by the extent of the revolutionary society and by the extreme youth of the conspirators: their average age was just over twenty-two. Many had been kept in prison for nearly two years. One had committed suicide; another had gone mad. They included the sons of peasants and members of the nobility, the widow of a general, the cousin of a famous composer, the son of a Finnish landowner, a number of students from Turkestan with names like Djavad Ishkhanov, and an obscure Frenchman with the extraordinary name of Pajou de Moncey. At the trial *The Revolutionary Catechism* was read out at length together with Ogaryov's poem and most of the documents which Nechayev produced with Bakunin's assistance in the early days of their friendship. The *bourgeois* were fascinated and terrified by the emergence of "the Nechayev monster." An alarmed public prosecutor described the conspiracy as "a dagger thrust at the heart of the monarchy." It was more than a dagger. It was a threat which was to hang over the dynasty to the very end, and the witnesses for the prosecution took pains to point out how close Nechayev had been to raising the standard of revolt. But not all the evidence pointed towards a strong revolutionary movement. Asked by the President of the Court how many cells of conspirators there had been, the prisoner Dolgov could remember only four: there were, he said, cells around Kuznetsov, Ivanov, Nechayev, and himself. When he was further asked whether the organization was a strong one, he answered: "No, it was very, very weak."

Weak or strong, Nechayev's influence was dreaded by the Czar, who asked for daily reports and held special meetings at which the implications of *Nechayevshchina,* all that could be understood by the portent of Nechayev, were discussed at length; and at some time during the trial he ordered the arrest of Nechayev even if it meant taking "extraordinary measures."

Some of the witnesses at the trial pretended to an ignorance they clearly did not possess. Some like Semeon Kuznetsov pleaded not guilty. Others like Ripman pleaded "guilty to belonging to a secret society whose aim, known and accepted by him, was a social uprising among the people." Those who had taken part in the murder of Ivanov related the incident at length to a hushed court, holding nothing back; and in the fading pages of the journals of that time, we can read the details of the murder as seen by the four participants—only Nechayev's own account is lacking. But the death of Ivanov was neither the main nor even the most important subject to be aired at the trial. The main subject was Nechayev, whose absence only made him all the more present, a ghostly mocking criminal who defied the might of the Czarist police to arrest him. Who was he? Where did he obtain his strength? This man who called himself Pavlov and

Ivan Petrov, Dmitri Feodorovich and Captain Panin, who
wore his disguises well and sometimes appeared in women's
clothes, the chief of the *Narodnaya Rasprava*, the People's Vengeance, or those other societies which proliferated
around him, the Society of the Ax, the Society of the Five,
who was he? And if you arrested him and tortured him to
death, how could you be certain that he would not arise
again?

The mystery of Nechayev was not solved at the trial; it is
still unsolved. The witnesses confessed that they had never
understood him, but they feared the powers he wielded,
those mysterious threats which he called down in the name
of vengeance. But there were strange omissions at the trial.
Very little was said about Nechayev's attempt to capture the
arsenal at Tula, and the President did not press too hard in
his inquiries about how Nechayev had hoped to take over
supreme power. Dolgov was asked by the President whether
the aim of the Society was to prepare an uprising among the
people. Dolgov answered evasively: "Nechayev said the people were ripe for an uprising and we must help them in
every possible way." The President reminded Dolgov that
they had been talking about an uprising. What kind of
uprising? "Well," said Dolgov, "I thought deputies would
come together from various places and introduce new laws."
But everyone else knew that the uprising would not consist
of an assembly of lawyers.

Later the government regretted that it had held the trial
in public. Three hundred had originally been arrested:
these had been winnowed down to eighty-four. The jury
decided to acquit all but those who had been close to Nechayev and those who participated in the Ivanov murder.
Alexey Kuznetsov, who had spent a year and a half in jail,
was sentenced to ten years hard labor, while his brother
Semeon was acquitted. Prince Cherkessov was sentenced to
deprivation of all rights and permanent exile in Tomsk.

(As a member of the nobility he could not safely be sentenced to prison.) Shortly afterward he escaped abroad, dying in London in 1925. Uspensky received the sternest punishment, fifteen years' imprisonment. Nikolayev, who had taken part in the expedition to Tula and given Nechayev the knife with which Ivanov was stabbed, received only seven years and four months' imprisonment. Prizhov received a sentence of twelve years imprisonment to be followed by permanent exile in Siberia. He survived his years of imprisonment and died in Siberia in 1885. Of the others who received short terms, Peter Tkachev escaped abroad in 1873 shortly after completing his sixteen months' sentence. Later he married Alexandra Dementieva, who was released from jail in January, 1872, and ordered to live in Novgorod under police surveillance. A short while afterward she received permission to leave Russia "without the right to return," and she was present at Tkachev's bedside at the Hospital of St. Anne in Paris when he died in 1882. Alexandra survived him by forty years. Deteils received four months' imprisonment and five years' police surveillance. The President, addressing those who had been found not guilty, reminded them that they were in the same position as all other honest citizens. Nothing had been proved against them, and therefore they could hold their heads high.

The trial was over, but the mystery of "the Nechayev monster" remained. Frightened by the possibility that the monster would emerge again, the Czar repeated his explicit instructions for Nechayev's arrest, and incensed by the conduct of the President at the trial, he discussed with Count Pahlen, the Minister of Justice, how such trials should be conducted in future. In the following year there appeared over Count Pahlen's signature a new law withdrawing political cases from the ordinary tribunals. Henceforth political trials would be judged by special tribunals composed of senators appointed by the Emperor alone.

The trial had left the public with mixed feelings. There was the pleasant shiver of apprehension at the mysterious spectacle of "the Nechayev monster," the spider in the midst of an endless web. There was the pleasant knowledge that the police had once more been defeated: as the result of a trial lasting from July 1 to September 11 the police, far from proving their capacity to nip revolts in the bud, had only shown an amazing incapacity to understand what was happening beneath their eyes, and they had failed to arrest Nechayev, whose audacity delighted many, even though the details of the murder of Ivanov were singularly depressing. Vera Figner, who was in Switzerland at the time of the trial, recalled reading about it in the newspapers. "I read about them every day," she wrote later, "but I must say that it was only the murder of Ivanov, described in all its tragic detail, which made any impression on me—all the rest was inexplicable and passed me by." But Dostoyevsky read the published reports avidly. He knew one of the defendants, a relative of his wife. He had begun to work on *The Possessed* in 1867, but he could make no headway with it. By January, 1871, he had written only two chapters. When the trial opened in July, he hurried to St. Petersburg and he was one of the spectators in the public gallery. The figure of Nechayev intrigued him, and under various disguises Nechayev appears in the novel, now as Shatov, now as Kirillov, now as Peter Verkhovensky. From the Nechayev trial he borrowed names, incidents, complete situations, though later he went to some pains to deny that the influence of Nechayev is present in the novel. In *The Diary of a Writer* he wrote: "I myself am an old Nechayev, or else— perhaps—might have been a follower of Nechayev, I am not sure. In the days of my youth it might certainly have happened." And in the notes which he wrote while planning the novel he would sometimes write the name of Nechayev where he had intended to put the name of Verkhovensky.

Nechayev's presence in the novel is profoundly evident in the scenes where Verkhovensky summons the millennium for the benefit of Stavrogin. Speaking in the authentic accents of Nechayev, Verkhovensky announces the destruction of the civilized world:

> Culture is unnecessary! We have had enough of science! Without science we have material enough for a thousand years, but one must maintain discipline. The only thing that is lacking in the world is discipline. The thirst for culture is an aristocratic thirst. The moment you have a family or fall in love you get the desire for property. We will destroy that desire: we will make use of drunkenness, slander, spying. We will make use of incredible corruption. We'll stifle every genius in its infancy. Everything must be brought to one common denominator: complete equality.

Dostoyevsky, in spite of his abhorrence of socialism, took care to present Verkhovensky as an adventurer, not as a socialist revolutionary. He draws the figure of a Verkhovensky drunk with power and thoughts of power, engaged in an intrigue of vast dimensions, but the intrigue is an end in itself, deriving its strength from Verkhovensky's determination to play the game of destruction for its own sake, without remorse and without enjoyment, simply because the world does not deserve its boasted civilization; and when Stavrogin accuses Verkhovensky of being an "ambitious politician," Verkhovensky laughs in his face:

> So you mean I'm a rogue? Well, and why should you be worried about what kind of man I am? I'll tell you what I am. This is what I have been leading up to. It wasn't for nothing that I kissed your hand. Well, it is necessary that the common people should know what we are up to—all the rest are "waving cudgels and hitting out at their own men." Oh, if only we had more time! That's the trouble—we haven't enough time! We shall proclaim destruction—why? why?—well, because the

idea is fascinating! And then too we must get a little exercise! We'll have a few fires, we'll spread a few legends. Every mangy little group will be useful. I'll find you some splendid fellows in these groups, and they'll be glad to do a little shooting, glad of the honor. We'll make such a mess as the world has never seen. Russia will be plunged in darkness, and the whole earth will weep for its old gods.

But to the very end Dostoyevsky remained confused, and the pen often falters when he comes to describe Verkhovensky's actions. He wrote once: "Nechayev partly Petrashevsky." It was as though Dostoyevsky, who had himself taken part in the Petrashevsky conspiracy of 1852, was determined to hug Nechayev to his breast. He repeats too often that there is nothing of Nechayev in *The Possessed,* but the novel is bathed in the light which came from Nechayev, and his own admissions mingled with denials only prove the extraordinary hold which Nechayev had upon his imagination.

While Dostoyevsky was busy writing *The Possessed* and the brooding image of Nechayev still hung over St. Petersburg, the physical Nechayev was wandering restlessly over Switzerland, searching desperately for a hiding place. He lived from hand to mouth. He made occasional sums of money by sign-painting. Very few people knew where he was staying. Vera Figner, who was in Zurich at the time, said that hardly anyone suspected his existence among them. A few who met him begged him to leave the country for his own sake. Nechayev replied that he chose to remain, and in any event those who wanted to get rid of him were clearly doing so for selfish reasons: in a country brimming over with small clandestine revolutionary organizations, they were afraid Nechayev would take over. Lonely, embittered, still dreaming of future conquests, still talking about a revolutionary society which would overthrow the Czar, Nechayev lived in one garret after another.

One day in the spring of 1872 Nechayev appeared in Zemphyr Arbore-Ralli's house in Zurich. Arbore-Ralli had been one of Nechayev's first associates at St. Petersburg in 1869. He had been arrested in March, 1870, after the failure of the first student uprising. Released a few days later, he was arrested again in Kishinev and thrown into the Peter and Paul Fortress, but no evidence of any consequence was brought against him and in October, 1871, he was released and sent into exile. By the end of the year he had escaped abroad, and now he was studying quietly, with no particular passion for revolutionary activity. Nechayev's visit surprised him. It was the first time he had seen Nechayev outside Russia. Nechayev asked for shelter, and stayed at the house for a few days. As Arbore-Ralli describes him:

> He had changed a good deal. There he was—thin, of medium height, nervous, biting his nails to the quick, and his eyes were burning and he kept making sharp gestures with his hands. He was not a good talker and he spoke Russian with a broad Vladimir accent. He had still learned no French conversation, though he could somehow explain himself in the language and he read the language with only a little use of the dictionary. All he had when he came was a small handbag and two books—the *Confessions* of Rousseau and the *Mémoires Authentiques* of Robespierre. During his stay with me neither of us spoke about Ivanov. He knew why I said nothing, for it was I who had introduced Ivanov to Uspensky during my stay in Moscow.

Arbore-Ralli had been a friend of Karakozov and an intimate of Nechayev's. He had listened approvingly in the days when Nechayev spoke of "the destruction of those monsters in gleaming uniforms sprinkled with the blood of the people." He had introduced Nechayev to all his friends, but he had learned to regret his admiration for the revolutionary, and after a few days he reminded Nechayev that the police were on his trail. Nechayev made his way to La Chaux-de-Fonds, high up on a plateau in the Jura Mountains, where some anarchists had established cooperative workshops. It was a small town, and according to Prince Peter Kropotkin the least attractive of all Swiss towns, for "there is no vegetation there, and it is open to bitterly cold winds in winter, when the snow lies as deep as in Moscow, and melts and falls again as often as in St. Petersburg." Here Nechayev settled under the name of Linders, working at odd jobs, still resolutely dreaming of revolution. Vladimir Serebrennikov was in London, and some days later Arbore-Ralli received through the mail a mysterious letter from London written on notepaper decorated with the sign of the Ax and *The People's Vengeance* in red ink across the top. Together with the letter were a number of pages in cypher, which Arbore-Ralli was ordered to send to Nechayev. Amused, Arbore-Ralli wrote to Nechayev at La Chaux-de-Fonds and suggested it would be much simpler if Nechayev wrote directly to Serebrennikov: there was no purpose in playing this conspiratorial game of ciphers, and in any event Arbore-Ralli had no desire to act as intermediary. Nechayev had previously begged Arbore-Ralli to come to La Chaux-de-Fonds. The invitation was refused. Unknown to Nechayev, Arbore-Ralli was in touch with Bakunin. Soon an alarmed Bakunin was sending Nechayev urgent warnings to leave the country. Remembering the pamphlet which Bakunin had once composed in defense of Nechayev's right to stay on Swiss soil, Nechayev replied with his accustomed pride: "I too have friends in Berne, and they would have warned me if I was in danger."

The danger was drawing closer. From time to time Nechayev slipped into Zurich. More and more he was coming to see a great hope in the young Polish revolutionaries. He met one of them called Turski, also a refugee, and a member of the Polish Socialist Party, at that time containing no more than twenty members. At the head of the Party was a certain Adolf Stempkowski, who was the secretary of Greulich, the leader of the Swiss Socialists. He had escaped from Russia after the Polish uprising in 1863. He spoke Russian with a Polish accent, and was well-known among the Russian *émigrés* in Switzerland. Like Nechayev, Stempkowski worked as a sign-painter. Once long ago he had the reputation of being a stool-pigeon, but he worked so hard on behalf of so many revolutionary organizations that he was now in everyone's good graces. Turski arranged a meeting between Stempkowski and Nechayev. For three weeks Nechayev had been receiving urgent warnings from Bakunin to leave Switzerland. "This is no longer 1870," Nechayev answered. "It's only the Bakuninists who want to get me out of the country." In this he was wrong: the Russian police also wanted him, and Stempkowski was their paid agent.

As usual Nechayev had laid his plans deeply. He had discussed at length the possibility of infiltrating into Bakunin's organization. It was Turski's opinion that Stempkowski would be able to provide any information about Bakunin that Nechayev wanted. "He detests Bakunin," Turski said, "but superficially they are on the best possible terms. See him. He will give you all the information you want." Nechayev hurried to the rendezvous in a Zurich restaurant. Stempkowski was all affability. Suddenly he raised his hand, making a beckoning sign. Nechayev thought he was summoning a waiter. Immediately two plain-clothes detectives pounced on Nechayev, removed his revolver and dragged him screaming out of the restaurant. Some Russian and Serbian students were outside the restaurant. Nechayev called to them. There was a brief struggle, and for a few minutes Nechayev was free. The police however were determined to arrest him, and the students were not particularly concerned about Nechayev's fate. "It would have been very easy to have saved Nechayev," a witness said later, "but no one really wanted

to. We remembered the murder of Ivanov, and we thought
he deserved punishment. We even helped the police to arrest some of Nechayev's would-be rescuers."

A few hours later Nechayev was removed from the Zurich
prison and handed over to Russian police officers on the
Bavarian frontier. It was August 14, 1872.

The Swiss police officers had acted in good faith. From
St. Petersburg there had come an extradition order drawn
up with all the proper codicils and an outline of the evidence against "one Sergey Nechayev, student, charged with
the murder of Ivan Ivanov, student, on November 24,
1870." The date was wrong, but that was of small consequence to Nechayev as he made his way back to Russia.

A few days after Nechayev's arrest Vladimir Serebrennikov, Nechayev's strange *alter ego,* appeared at Arbore-
Ralli's house. The documents stolen from Bakunin had been
preserved intact. Serebrennikov offered to sell them for 400
francs. Hiding his eagerness, Arbore-Ralli bought them and
a few days later, with the help of Armand Ross, the sea-
soned revolutionary who had been Bakunin's secretary for
many years, he set about examining the documents. Among
them was found the letter in which Bakunin promised to
submit himself entirely to Nechayev's will, even if Nechayev
should order him to forge banknotes. There was a copy of
The Revolutionary Catechism, faithfully copied out in Bakunin's handwriting. There were diaries, letters, manifestoes,
cuttings from newspapers with Bakunin's annotations, complete lists of Bakunin's visitors, and a copy of the numerical
cypher which Bakunin employed in his correspondence. It
was all there, down to the last telegram. Presumably the
documents were handed to Bakunin. From this moment they
disappear from sight.

With Nechayev under arrest, Bakunin showed himself astonishingly free from bitterness. He had good reason to hate
Nechayev. It was not only that Nechayev had repeatedly

maligned him, stolen his documents and laughed in his face. There was also the matter of the celebrated letter which Nechayev had written to Karl Marx's publisher. Marx was vengeful, and at the height of his power. He had watched Bakunin's growing popularity within the International with alarm. At the Congress of the International in Basle in 1869 Bakunin had been the figure who stood out among the revolutionaries as the one most likely to capture the International for his own purposes, but in the Congress which took place in London in September, 1871, Bakunin was absent and Marx was in full control. He ordered a full inquiry into Bakunin's relations with Nechayev. *The Revolutionary Catechism* was now well-known and Marx believed or pretended to believe that it was the work of Bakunin. A certain Utin, who later became a contractor to the Czarist Army during the Turkish war of 1877, was asked to prepare a full record of the Nechayev trial and of Nechayev's relations with Bakunin, and this document was formally presented to the Congress of the International at The Hague the following year. On the insistence of Marx Bakunin was drummed out of the International. Bakunin was deeply perturbed, stung to the quick by "this germano-judaic *complot* against me." But he refused to express any horror at Nechayev's perfidy, and could think only of the days when Nechayev came to him and he welcomed the boy with open arms. He wrote to Ogaryov in November:

> Some secret voice tells me that Nechayev who is utterly lost and certainly knows it—this Nechayev who is so confused and vitiated—is far from being banal. This time his heart will reveal all his old courage and primitive energy. He will perish like a hero, and this time he will betray no one and nothing.
> So I believe, and soon we shall know whether I am right. I do not know what you feel, but for my part I am deeply sorry for him. In all my life no one has done so much harm to me—so much premeditated harm—but I am sorry for him nevertheless.

He is a man of rare energy, and when I met him for the first time, his heart was burning with love and compassion for the poor oppressed people of Russia: his soul was stamped with the true suffering of the sickness of our age. Only his outward aspect was unclean; inside he was pure . . .

From the day when Nechayev was handed over to the Russian police, he behaved as Bakunin had prophesied.

The Tiger Caged

Captured, Nechayev was still a force to be reckoned with. Legends hung about his name. The police officers who guarded him and kept him shackled in specially-reserved compartments of the train which brought them by a round-about route through Smolensk to St. Petersburg, and so to the Troubetskoy Bastion of the Fortress of Peter and Paul, wondered at the power of the legend. There was the young revolutionary with the straggly beard and the deep-set eyes, looking no more dangerous than any young Russian student, but at every station it was necessary to send off telegrams to Count Levachov indicating the exact time of arrival and the probable time of departure, and the condition of the prisoner. It was assumed that he would attempt to escape. At every station armed guards were sent to watch over the train. He was not only heavily shackled and fettered, but two policemen were chained to him. At moments amused and tolerant, at other moments wildly facetious and brutally angry, Nechayev watched the policemen with the supercilious air with which he regarded all authority. It was as though he was saying throughout the journey: "All these shackles are quite useless. I shall escape. I possess an idea which is far stronger than your chains." The telegrams sent to Count Levachov are still preserved. We know the exact time to the minute when Nechayev's train passed through the towns on the railway. Finally—and we can almost hear the sigh of relief which went up in government circles in Moscow and St. Petersburg—we know that he was received in the Peter and Paul Fortress at exactly nine o'clock on the morning of October 19, 1872, and that shortly afterward he was interviewed by Count Levachov.

The interview appears to have been brief. The Count was affable. He explained that there might be "a certain mitigation of your fate" if Nechayev gave the Russian government a complete outline of his organization. Nechayev parried, and suggested that he was in a position to make conditions. Among these conditions was a sweeping change in the nature of government authority, with Nechayev himself as "a special advisor." Nechayev talked for some time about the inevitability of the revolution and hinted at his own commanding position among the revolutionaries. Levachov said afterward that Nechayev's conditions were "brilliant and profitable for him, and very bad for us." After a while Levachov called his bluff and reminded Nechayev that he had been captured in secret, no one knew what had happened to him and he was at the complete mercy of the government. Nechayev answered: "You can take my life away, but not my honor." He was still playing the game of the powerful revolutionary, though he possessed hardly a single disciple. Levachov seems to have been convinced that Nechayev, though not so powerful as he pretended, was still a formidable adversary.

The meeting with Count Levachov took place in a cell in the Troubetskoy Bastion, where some of the most dangerous prisoners had been kept in solitary confinement. There was only one row of cells in the Peter and Paul Fortress more carefully guarded. This was the Alexis Ravelin, where Alexis, the son of Peter the Great, had been kept through the greater part of his life. Count Levachov had hinted that Nechayev would be thrown into the Ravelin unless he cooperated with the government. Nechayev knew the consequences. In the Alexis Ravelin prisoners were kept until they rotted away and went mad and died in the squalor of their small and miserable cells. He knew, too, that he was being treated with the implacable vengeance reserved for an arch-enemy of the state.

In his damp cell, lapped by the waters of the Neva, Nechayev waited. He shouted abuse at his guards and ordered them to bring the prison superintendent into his presence, and when the superintendent arrived, Nechayev pointed out that he had been captured illegally; he had abjured his Russian nationality; he was an *émigré* like all the other *émigrés;* and he should be freed unconditionally. He asked for pen and paper, to write a letter to the Czar. Neither paper nor pen were given to him, and though the prison superintendent took note of all Nechayev's remarks, and a full report on Nechayev's behavior was sent to the Czar, he was left to the silence and loneliness of the dark dungeon and the ministrations of the guards who wore soft felt boots and moved noiselessly about. He wore the prison dress which consisted of a green flannel dressing-gown, immense woolen stockings of an incredible thickness and boat-shaped yellow slippers which he could hardly keep on his feet when he walked. The silence deepened. In the end silence alone could kill a man. Within a few months it could reduce him to imbecility. In her memoirs Vera Figner observed how after several months of silence in the fort her vocal chords weakened and her sense of time became strangely distorted. When she was released, if anyone dropped a silver teaspoon, she had to exert all her will to prevent herself from crying out, so great was the strain on her nervous system. Silence bred silence, and there came a time when she had no desire to speak.

The silence of the Peter and Paul Fortress was broken at regular intervals by the chimes of the bells in the spire of the fortress cathedral, which chimed the liturgical response "Have mercy, O Lord" every quarter of an hour and the canticle "How glorious is our Lord in Zion" at every hour. At midnight they chimed "God save the Czar." The bells, though they broke the silence, also reinforced it.

The fortress was a city of the dead. Within the Cathedral lay the dead Emperors and their marble monuments. Monks and holy men lived there, performing perpetual masses for the dead kings. The dying prisoners in their tomb-like cells were evidently taking the place of those sacrificial offerings which were once offered at a king's burial. Perpetually expiating their crimes, they represented the permanent offerings to the dead. But the fortress was also a city of the living: there were streets with shops, and visitors were occasionally escorted through the place, to admire the Cathedral and marvel at the high walls and place candles at the feet of the stone saints who stood in niches along the prison walls.

October passed, and then November, and Nechayev was still alone in his cell, fed three meals a day—the allowance for food was 50 kopecks—and every afternoon he was allowed out of his cell for a short walk while a guard cleaned it. The walls were damp and thick, very dark, and there was a small heavily-grilled window eight feet from the floor. An iron bed, an iron table, a commode, a paper-thin woolen coverlet, a Bible, a kerosene lamp which was kept burning all night: nothing else. The food was slops. The damp air brought on asthma. Iron rings, rusted but still immensely strong, were fixed to the walls: to these the prisoners were chained. But more terrible than the privations of the prison was the ghostly autumn mist which penetrated the cells and hung over the high walls, a mist which blocked out the light. And through the mist came the silent warders in their black uniforms, always walking in pairs and under orders never to talk with the prisoners.

In this silent world anything might happen. A man might freeze to death, or be bludgeoned by a warder in the corner of his cell, and no one would know or care. At various times in the past it had been rumored that prisoners had been quietly hanged or poisoned at the whim of the prison governor. But under Alexander II, who desired to know everything that happened in the vast domains of his empire and spent his days brooding over interminable reports, the Peter and Paul Fortress had become a hive of bureaucratic efficiency. Daily reports were sent about each prisoner to the head of the Third Division; many of these were placed on the Czar's table. Nechayev did not know for certain, though he may have guessed, that an endless stream of reports on his behavior was being sent out from the prison offices. Officials in the highest circles of the land were busily poring over reports and debating over his fate.

But what should be done with the prisoner? Should he be killed quietly, without anyone being the wiser? Should he be left to rot inside the fortress? In an audience with the Czar, Count Levachov pointed out the advantages of a well-staged public trial: it would help to destroy the legend Nechayev had created around himself and it would intimidate the revolutionaries by showing them they were powerless in the face of the Russian secret police. Accordingly the Czar agreed to a trial early in the New Year, and at 5:30 on the afternoon of December 22 Nechayev found himself under a police escort, with Major Remer in command, outside the walls of the Peter and Paul Fortress. He had been told only that he would be put on trial in Moscow.

The usual fantastic precautions were taken. Once again he was chained to two police officers, and once again telegraph messages were sent to Count Levachov whenever the train passed through a station. Near Moscow the train was shunted onto a siding, and a heavy guard surrounded him as he descended from the train.

The trial opened on January 8 at twelve o'clock, with President Dreyer as the presiding official, a jury, and a court

of assessors. It was brief and explosive. Nechayev's attitude
to the court was calculated to offend. He hammered away
at the greatest weakness in the prosecutor's case—he had
been arrested illegally, in a foreign land. He saw himself
as the heroic defender of freedom, refused to answer questions, hurled abuse at the prosecutor and defended the killing of Ivanov as "a purely political matter." He played
deliberately to the gallery. With his hands thrust in his
pockets he glared at the President and shouted: "I do not
recognize this court! I am an *émigré!* I do not recognize your
Emperor or your laws!" Shortly afterward the President
ordered him to be removed. As Nechayev marched out,
there was sympathetic applause from the gallery, and Dreyer
firmly reminded the audience that if there was another outbreak he would order the police to remove them from their
seats.

When Dreyer considered that Nechayev had had time to
cool his heels, a message was sent to him saying that if
promised to behave he would be allowed to enter the chamber. Nechayev marched back. He had promised nothing.
The prosecutor began to ask leading questions. To all these
questions Nechayev shouted: "Hurrah for the Zemski
Sobor!" This reference to the States-General established by
Peter the Great and then abandoned was calculated to in-
flame the audience, and once more there were sympathetic
murmurs from the audience. Dreyer decided to take the matter in his own hands. He asked Nechayev point-blank
whether he regarded himself as guilty of the murder of
the student Ivanov. Nechayev answered that he was being
tried according to the laws for common criminals, whereas
the murder of Ivanov was clearly of a political character.
The medical reports read at the trial of the *Nechayevtsi,*
with details of how Ivanov had died by bullet wounds, stran-
gulation, and drowning, were now read out again as important parts of the evidence against Nechayev. Nechayev

assumed an air of profound indifference. He leaned forward on his elbows, pouted, rolled his eyes at the gallery, pushed out his lips and pulled at his beard. At times he sat with arms akimbo. An observer during the trial described him: "He is about twenty-five, not tall. He wore a black silk jacket, breeches and a dirty waistcoat. Nothing extraordinary about his face—you will see such faces commonly among young dandies. Thick, but not long chestnut-colored hair. Rather narrow, deep-sunken eyes. A thin prickle of hair on his upper lip. His profile is sharply outlined, but when you see him full face the broad forehead makes the face look square and rather vulgar." Evidently he was not a prepossessing person at his trial, but he had no intention of being prepossessing. His aim was to show derision of his judges, and in this he succeeded.

All through the indictment, the reading of the evidence and the cross-examination, Nechayev clowned. He beat time with his left hand, looked vaguely at the public gallery as though he was searching for someone, in the middle of the President's questioning, and then for long periods he would sit quietly, twisting his beard and his thin mustache, forming the hairs into braids, or else smoothing his hair or silently playing an invisible piano on the ledge in front of him with his right hand. When the prosecutor had completed a long speech of denunciation, Nechayev remarked quietly: "It is humiliating to defend myself against such obvious calumnies. All Russia knows that I am a political criminal. I repeat what I have already said to Count Levachov—the government can take my life away, but not my honor!" Then he smote himself on the breast.

For this behavior he was once more dismissed from the court. What happened then is not clear. According to Nechayev he was taken to an empty room and set upon by police officers. The police officers denied beating him, but they may have been so angered by his contempt and impertinence that they could hardly prevent themselves from beating him. Police officers, then as now, regarded the beating of prisoners as a conventional exercise. When Nechayev was again allowed to enter the court he was in a fiery temper and began to denounce the officers. He was silenced by the reading of the verdict. He was sentenced to twenty years in Siberia, and he was dragged from the court, shouting: "Long live the Zemski Sobor! Down with despotism!"

On the next day in his Moscow prison Nechayev called for paper and ink and wrote a letter to Count Levachov:

Count!

When I was sitting in my cell in the Peter and Paul Fortress, you came to me and asked me to explain the real purposes of my activities. You said that if I told the truth there would be some "mitigation of my fate." At that time I refused to furnish you with any explanations. But now my fate is decided, and the time has come when I think I can partly satisfy your wishes and place the facts in proper perspective. The words of a man condemned to twenty years imprisonment in Siberia should convey only the desire for the truth—no one should doubt the truth concealed in them. In this letter I propose to give you the information I promised long ago.

In the following, I shall base myself only on facts, but the facts I have in mind have scarcely anything in common with the administrative system as practiced in this uncivilized country. While talking of facts, let me tell you of one fact of considerable importance. Yesterday, in the Hall of Justice, applause broke out. As a result the President decided to throw me out of the chamber. I was dragged into a corridor and then into an empty room, where a police officer began to beat me over the back and legs. The atrocious behavior of the officer was all the more shocking because I never showed any enmity towards him and was always coldly polite and well-mannered. For myself, I do not believe that any government can take pride in the fact that it has these knights of "club law" among its officers. I know that the reforms of three or four years ago were meant to make "club law" impossible . . .

But you asked me about my activities. Count, my fate is decided or almost decided. I shall go to Siberia, and this is why I must speak the truth, and it seems to me that you in your high position deserve only the truth, and nothing else will have any meaning for you. The high government post which you hold gives you the opportunity to see things as they are. And so, putting aside all dreams of utopia, I urge you to consider that Russia is on the eve of a political revolution. Everywhere the desires straining within society are assuming more radical and more destructive channels: everywhere there are small conspiracies and plots against the overpowering strength of the government, but these small conspiracies can coalesce into large conspiracies, and these in turn to furious revolutions. But I do not want these things to happen. Freedom from above is better than freedom from below. Above all, I believe it is the task of our time to work for constitutional revolutions rather than the bloody revolution which tears down a whole people.

Myself, I am a son of the people! My first and only aim is the happiness and well-being of the people. Here we see Stenka Razin and Pugachov once more ascending the scaffold, as in France they would be ascending the guillotine, and on the other side we see the people being fired on and put to inconceivable suffering. But I know that in the end the people have the power to put the people in power. The task of all men of good will in this stormy age is to avoid that inevitable terror which will come about if the people decide to tear down the thrones of the mighty.

You asked me to describe the purposes of my activities. These are the purposes.

Nechayev signed the letter "*Emigré* Sergey Nechayev, transformed by Mezentsev from a political into a common criminal." Underneath the signature he wrote a postscript: "I shall go to Siberia with the deep assurance that millions of voices will soon be shouting: 'Long live the Zemski Sobor!' "

The letter is a complex document: many purposes were inextricably woven into it. Nechayev seems to have had considerable regard for Count Levachov and some hope that he might be able to bring about constitutional reforms. Levachov was close to the Emperor. He possessed a singularly brilliant mind, and had treated Nechayev fairly, if distantly. The letter formed an apologia for his own actions and at the same time, since the Count was bound to be informed of Nechayev's behavior at the trial, it demonstrated that Nechayev was in full command of his faculties. By implication Nechayev was saying: "I clowned during the trial, and did so deliberately, to show my contempt for your jurists. But I have a mind that can see clearly, and you should use me as a consultant." As always he was playing for high stakes.

It was the custom when prisoners were sentenced to long years of imprisonment in Siberia to hold a ceremony of public degradation. The authorities doubted whether the ceremony would serve any useful purpose in the case of Nechayev. There was the danger that he might be rescued by the mysterious friends he was always hinting at. There was the very real possibility that a few determined revolutionaries might, if they succeeded in capturing Nechayev, use him as a symbol of resistance against the government. If anything, he had by his contempt of authority during the trial increased his own legendary stature. But by January 20 it had been decided that the government would risk the ceremony of public degradation. On that day Count Shuvalov wrote a memorandum to Prince Dolgoruki, the Governor-General of Moscow:

Although existing laws and regulations must be carried out to the letter, I have the honor to inform you that the daring behavior of the prisoner at his trial demands that the complete observance of the law shall be accompanied by extraordinary measures of security to prevent anyone from recognizing him or helping him to escape.

Nechayev was in prison in the Sustcherskaya district north of the river. Count Shuvalov's memorandum referred to the difficulties of transporting Nechayev from the prison to the Horse Parade south of the river. The Horse Parade was the usual place for the public degradation of prisoners.

It was decided that the ceremony should take place at night, with as few witnesses as possible. Major Remer, Lieutenant Popov, and a sergeant accompanied Nechayev in a closed carriage at eleven o'clock at night for the journey south of the river. The idea of taking Nechayev in a carriage was not a very good one. He made several efforts to escape. At the Horse Parade the carriage was met by a military escort. Alone and fettered, standing under a symbolical gallows, surrounded by a hollow square of soldiers and policemen, Nechayev faced his accusers. His sentence was once more read out to him. Drums rolled. A solemn prayer was read by a priest, for the ceremony involved a kind of symbolical execution and at the end of the ceremony the prisoner was supposed in some mysterious way to have passed out of life altogether, his long exile in Siberia to be accounted no more than a passage to limbo. Usually the prisoners are too awed by the ceremony to make speeches. Nechayev was not awed. While the drums rolled, he shouted at the top of his voice: "The guillotine will soon be standing where I am! It will lop off all your heads! Don't fear, in two or three years your turn will come!" A little later he shouted: "Down with the Czar! Hurrah for freedom! Long live the Russian people!" When he was being lifted into the carriage he was still shouting: "I am on my way to Siberia! I know millions of people are on my side! Down with despotism! Hurrah for freedom! I am a political prisoner, but I am being treated like a common murderer! I have received no trial—only a mockery of a trial!" Soon afterward his voice was drowned by drums.

Nechayev had every reason to believe he was about to make the long journey to Siberia. From Siberia, however, too many prisoners had escaped. The Czar ordered him imprisoned in the Alexis Ravelin of the Peter and Paul Fortress.

The journey from Moscow to St. Petersburg was made in secret and by a roundabout route. He left Moscow by train at 8:05 in the morning of January 26. It is possible that an attempt to rescue him was made at the Nikolayevsky Railway Station, but the reports are confused. At Smolensk the following night Major Remer telegraphed the usual report to Count Levachov. A lawyer, passing along the platform, was told by some railwaymen that "the famous conspirator Nechayev" was on the train. The secret therefore was not so well kept as Count Levachov hoped. The train swung west to Vilna and then to Tsarskoe Selo. At 9:45 on the night of January 28 Nechayev passed through the gates of the Peter and Paul Fortress for the last time. The clothes he wore during the trial were removed from him and he was put into prison garb. The prison records of the fortress, remarkable for detail, list the clothes taken from him: a hat of lambs' wool, a black cloth coat, a jacket, half boots, thick cloth trousers, waistcoat, shirt, drawers, and a pair of copper shirt studs.

From now on his life was to be a ceaseless fight with the prison. The Czar, who regarded him as a mortal enemy, had decided to discredit him by annihilating him. For years no word would ever be heard from him. For years no one knew whether he was alive or dead. The Czar himself sent a message to the military governor of the fortress: "Put Nechayev discreetly and forever in the fortress." Many years

later, after the Bolsheviks had come to power, there was
found the original order written by the governor of the
prison, Bogorodetsky. The order is dated January 29th,
1873, the day after Nechayev had been admitted into the
fortress. It reads: "I command that Sergey Nechayev, deprived of all rights and imprisoned yesterday under the
orders of His Majesty in the Alexis Ravelin, shall be placed
in cell number 5 in the greatest secrecy and guarded with
the greatest vigilance. His name is never to be pronounced,
and he is to be known only by the number of his cell."

The achievement of Nechayev had only just begun. He
fought a long war against authority even when he was
chained in a cell so small that if he stretched out his arms he
could touch both sides. From the first he was a nuisance. He
asked for books, demanded a retrial, hinted at the powerful
forces who were even then determined to rescue him. When
Count Levachov asked him again to join the Third Division,
he refused abruptly and turned his back on the Count, just
as he had turned his back on President Dreyer at the trial.

By order of the Czar a weekly bulletin on Nechayev's
health, and how he spent his time, was prepared by the
prison officials on the basis of daily reports. In these reports
the prisoner's name is never mentioned.

On February 9, 1873, the first report was issued:

The prisoner in cell number 5 of the Alexis Ravelin has
from February 2 to February 9 behaved quietly and courte-
ously. He wakes each morning at 7, and has gone to sleep
at 9:30 except on February 2 when he woke at 7:45 and
went to bed at 11:30. He sleeps well.

During the day he reads the *War Gazette* of 1869, and often
walks about the cell, rarely lying on the pallet. Recently he
has been behaving more affably than usual, his expression is
happier and he is beginning to look people in the eyes where
previously he avoided a direct gaze. Previously he answered
everyone roughly in a cutting voice, dropping his eyes.

These strange bulletins were prepared until the day Nechayev died. The first two bulletins are known to have been
read by the Czar, and it is probable that Alexander II continued to read them until he was killed by terrorists when
returning to the Winter Palace after a review. The first
bulletin hints at explosions of temper during the first week
of Nechayev's imprisonment. These explosions were rare.
From early in February he decided to fight the government
with a cool brain and all the weapons at his command. He
decided to keep his body and brain active. Though chained,
he practiced gymnastics in his cell. He asked for books—the
list was endless, and included John Stuart Mill's *Political
Economy*, Gervinus' *History of the XIX Century*, Louis
Blanc's *History of the French Revolution*, Jules Clarétie's
History of the Revolution of 1870-71. For some weeks nothing was done. The library of the Alexis Ravelin was not so
well served with books as the library of the Troubetskoy
Bastion, and there was some doubt whether inter-library
loans were permissible. In the end permission was obtained
from Count Shuvalov to let Nechayev read all the books he
listed except Louis Blanc's *History of the French Revolution*. Nechayev was not too downcast. He had already read
the book in Switzerland.

On the twenty-third of February a second bulletin was
sent to the Czar:

> The prisoner in cell number 5 of the Alexis Ravelin has
> from February 16 to February 23 behaved quietly. He is now
> reading the *War Gazette* for the year 1871 and is generally
> cheerful. Exception is made under the date of February 19,
> the first day of Lent. Given Lenten food, he remarked: "I
> have no belief in God and none in Lent. So give me a plateful
> of soup and some meat, and I'll be satisfied." On February
> 21 he walked about continually, often lifted his hands to his
> head, was thoughtful and went to sleep only at 1:30 in the
> morning.

This bulletin was written by Major Remer, who seems to have been permanently attached to Nechayev.

Nechayev suffered no ill consequences following his refusal to eat a Lenten supper. He announced that he intended to compose a history of the Czardom, and asked for pen, ink and paper. These were given to him. He began a long war against the stupidity of librarians and asked to be allowed to have a complete library in his cell, saying that it was impossible to compile a worthy history of the Czardom without a vast number of books. He asked for Robert von Mohl's *Geschichte und Literatur des Staatswissenschaften,* a surprising demand since he knew almost no German. The continual demand for books served a double purpose: it occupied his time, and the reading of the books sharpened his brain: also, he was patiently devising a code formed by making small pencil marks under letters, and in this way hoping to communicate with other prisoners. Many years later, when Olga Natanson was imprisoned in the fortress, she came upon the penciled code-marks. "I knew Nechayev was in the fortress and not in Siberia by the marks he left in the library books." But during the early years of Nechayev's imprisonment no one except the prison officials and the Czar knew he was there.

Nechayev's plan was simple. He would insert a small wedge, and then see whether he could push it deeper. Already, even in those early months, he was beginning to exert an extraordinary influence over his guards. He would ask them simple questions. They would refuse to reply. But all the time Nechayev was watching them closely. He observed their eyes. He devised questions which they could hardly fail to answer. Once they had spoken to him they were at his mercy. Little by little he was driving the wedge deeper. He used the same tactics with the prison officials in charge of the library. When he saw they were sympathizing with his desire for books, he sprung the trap by asking them to communicate with his sister and fetch "the small library, now in my sister's house, which belonged to me when I was an *émigré*." He never received these books, but the attempt showed his audacity.

Life in the fortress continued silently and without change. The prison records say that May 16, 1873, he was transferred to cell number 7 for a few days. The official reason was the removal of the double winter windows and their replacement by summer windows. Presumably someone in authority had demanded a thorough search of the prisoner's cell. On October 2 the river rose and the Alexis Ravelin was threatened with flood-water. The officials held their breaths. No orders had been received about what should be done to Nechayev if his cell were threatened with flood-water. But the waters subsided, and Nechayev spent the winter alone with his books in his clammy cell.

At some time during the second year of his imprisonment Nechayev shared his cell with a certain Shevich, a former guard's officer who had been involved in a scandal at Court. The reasons for making Nechayev share his cell are obscure, and nothing is known about Shevich except that he was white-haired, had long been considered insane and had been a prisoner of the Alexis Ravelin for more than twenty years.

Reports on Nechayev's behavior were still being sent to the Czar and to the head of the Third Division. The report for April 19, 1874, read: "No change has been observed in the prisoner in cell number 5 of the Alexis Ravelin. He behaves very quietly, and spends his time reading and writing." But Nechayev was not quiet. In his own way he was stirring up trouble. By this time he was on good terms with the guards, who were already calling him admiringly "our eagle." By whispers and subtle hints he had conveyed to them that he was an important personage, of royal blood. The guards, remembering the fate of Alexis, half believed him. They slipped food into his cell. Some years later they were to give him a plan of the fortress and send messages out for him, but in these early years he was still the young tiger calculating how to force a passage through the bars and he had not yet learned that the simplest way was to force the keeper to unbolt the gate.

The years passed slowly. The ferocious revolutionary ferment which was to arise in Russia in the late seventies had already begun. The movement known as "To the people" was spreading like an epidemic, and in 1873 was in full progress. All over Russia young college students were working in villages and factories, disguised as laborers and farmers. They forged passports, scattered revolutionary pamphlets and spoke in quiet, educated voices of putting the Court and the government into the hands of the executioners. They modeled themselves on the young Rakhmetov, the hero of Chernyshevsky's *What Should Be Done?* who lived the pure ascetic life and subjected himself to intense privations as a preparation for revolutionary activity. Young doctors appeared mysteriously in obscure villages, saying they had come to serve the people. They demanded no payment. They modelled themselves on the portrait of Bazarov in Turgenev's *Fathers and Children,* which had appeared in 1862, though they disputed many of Turgenev's judgments. They disputed in particular Turgenev's statement that the nihilist "refuses to bow down to authority, and will never accept any principle of faith, however much that principle may be revered," claiming that they had faith in the people, and that was enough. Soon the small group of convinced terrorists known as the *Narodnaya Volya* (the People's Will) would hurl itself in single combat against the powers of the government. Meanwhile there were daily arrests and the prisons were filling with young students. Throughout Russia the revolutionary ferment was increasing. Ironically, Nechayev knew nothing about it.

In the third year of Nechayev's imprisonment a strange

incident occurred. As usual, he was behaving quietly, immersed in his books. Suddenly the door of his cell was flung open and he was confronted with General Potapov, chief of the Corps of the Gendarmerie. The general had come with a renewed offer to Nechayev: if he would outline all the ramifications of his conspiratorial activity and serve the Third Division as a spy, he would be given his freedom. Nechayev was incensed. He struck the general fiercely across the face, drawing blood. The guards hurled themselves on Nechayev in time to prevent a second blow. Bleeding from the mouth and nose, Potapov left the cell. Nechayev himself recorded later that he received no punishment for his attack on the general.

This incident occurred in January, 1875. Six months later, in July, the prison governor, alarmed by the increasing revolutionary activity in Russia, had a long interview with Nechayev. In the course of the interview Nechayev offered to write a detailed letter to the Czar outlining the measures he thought necessary to bring the revolutionary activity to an end. A letter to the Czar, supposed to have been written by Nechayev at this time, has come down to us, but it is written in a style so unlike his usual style that it appears to be a forgery. But on January 30, 1876, Nechayev did write a letter, which he addressed to "His Imperial Majesty Alexander Nikolayevich, Lord and Emperor of the Russian People," and there is not the slightest doubt of its authenticity. It is a long letter, written in the familiar hard, unrelenting style. He begins with the assertion that he has been arrested illegally and imprisoned without trial, and goes on to accuse the Czar of deliberate duplicity. He asks why he has never been told "the conditions agreed upon with the Swiss government, by which I, the *émigré* Sergey Nechayev, was handed over to the judgment of the Russian court." He goes over the familiar ground. He remembers that he was removed from a prison in Zurich at night, unexpectedly and without warning, and was not aware he was to be handed over to the Russian police until he had crossed the frontier and was greeted by Police-Inspector Sevastyan-sky. All the old griefs are set out. Once again he refers to the murder of Ivanov as a purely political crime. Why should he be sentenced to perpetual imprisonment? He has done nothing worthy of the punishment. He has offered repeatedly to help His Imperial Majesty to put an end to the revolutionary ferment in the country. The Czar must realize the unforgivable nature of his crime. Nechayev demanded an immediate trial as a political prisoner and hinted that if this was not brought about he would shake the throne of the Czar of All the Russias to its foundations.

With this letter Nechayev sealed his own fate. The long honeymoon was over. The Czar read the letter. On February 7 he summoned the head of the Third Division to his presence, and gave orders for condign punishment. Two days later there was a meeting of the prison officials to inquire how the orders should be carried out. On February 14, while Nechayev was making his usual daily walk in the prison garden, guards rushed into his cell, searched it thoroughly and removed all the writing material and all the books. When he returned to the empty cell, he was told that the books and paper had been removed as a punishment. He stared hard at the bare walls and said in a clear voice: "Very well." The bulletin issued at the end of the week goes on to say: "He was strangely quiet during the rest of the afternoon, but at four o'clock he began to scream." Four o'clock is the time when darkness falls over St. Petersburg in February.

As a further punishment he was made to wear the fetters on his wrists which he had been allowed to discard when writing.

For nearly two years he felt the full force of the Emperor's vengeance. Though he was eventually allowed to read again, all writing materials were refused him. Now more than ever he came to resemble the old, shaggy ferryman in Tolstoy's *Resurrection* who lived on the bank of a Siberian river and who was so angry at all things and all men that he refused to bear a name, to recognize any authority, or to bow to any man.

The long fight for books and paper and a modicum of freedom had been lost. The years had aged him. His face was lined, and he suffered from prison pallor. His name was still dreaded, and there were still prison officials who trembled in his presence. But the young tiger suffered from fits of shivering, and at night he could be heard singing, in a cracked voice, strange melancholy songs. He slept badly. Some thought his mind was already unhinged. But he had the courage of despair, and gradually he began to exert authority over the guards. He was not defeated yet. He had still seven years to live, and in the course of those seven years he was to exert a strange, invisible power over the prison and over the revolutionaries of Russia.

The Shaking of the Bars

"If it were desired to reduce a man to nothingness," wrote Dostoyevsky in *The House of the Dead*, "it would be necessary only to give his work a character of uselessness." In the gray twilight of his cell Nechayev was slowly dying of the disease of uselessness. Once a day a guard entered and silently removed the drawer of the commode; three times a day he was handed food through the bars; the bells of the cathedral chimed every day with terrible regularity; every day there was the dull boom of the noon gun and every midnight the bells in the cathedral spire chimed "God save the Czar." And so it would go on until the day when the guards would find him lying dead in a corner of his cell.

From the beginning Nechayev had decided to fight back, but there was little strength left in him. The skin at his wrists and ankles was suppurating. His face had the pale blue color of prisoners who have been long buried in their cells. His lips quivered uncontrollably. Everything in the cell, the narrow iron bed, the brick stove, the commode, even his own body, was chained or bolted to the walls; he had become no more than an extension of the cell. Yet he was determined to fight on. At the first sign of government weakness, he would pit all his remaining strength against his enemies. He was waiting for a momentary accident, a moment of inattention when the warders were occupied elsewhere, but this moment was long in coming.

It was the misfortune of Nechayev that he represented in the eyes of the autocracy all the mysterious forces which were known by the name of terrorism. Alone, with only his cunning to guide him, he had inaugurated a secret society with ramifications through all strata of society. That the secret society had no further existence after Nechayev's arrest seems never to have occurred to the Czar's ministers: they suspected its influence everywhere, and every new outbreak of terrorism was attributed indirectly to Nechayev.

But his greatest misfortune was that the years of his imprisonment coincided with a remarkable resurgence of revolutionary activity in Russia, and while the revolutionary activity was at its height, he could neither hope for redress nor exert his power over the movement. The years 1876-1879 marked the culmination of vast and carefully contrived outbreaks of terrorism. Bakunin died in July, 1876. He had never enjoyed a very great influence in Russia. He belonged to an age when revolutionists thought the battle could be waged by inflammatory manifestoes alone. Now the time of the scientists and the engineers of revolution had come: the key-word was organization, and among the revolutionaries were the most knowledgeable experts on high explosives. Instead of Nechayev with his *Revolutionary Catechism* and his strange power over young students were men like Zhelyabov and Kibalchich, both experts in the use of explosives, the one a superb organizer, the other the possessor of one of the finest scientific brains then known in Russia. Now for the first time it began to seem possible that the Czar might be overthrown. His whole palace might be blown up, his train hurled off the railway lines, his lines of communication and his very existence at the mercy of the revolutionaries who planned his destruction coldly, poring over maps and time-tables and books of analytic chemistry. The romantic period was over, or nearly over, for there were still a few revolutionaries prepared to employ Nechayev's methods: conspiracy, bluff, intimidation, the threat of vast peasant uprisings. Such a threat was employed in 1875 by Jakob Stepanovich, who took the name of Dmitri Naida and secretly showed the peasants a Golden Charter printed in gold letters on satin, and ostensibly signed by the Czar. The charter purported to be an appeal by the Czar to his faithful peasantry, urging them to kill their landlords and live in an anarchist paradise. For some months peasants in the Chirigin and Cherkassi districts swore to follow the Czar's precepts, but the movement came to an end when a drunken peasant revealed the whole story to a soldier.

For a government on the defensive the behavior of young students who went about educating the peasants was more worrying. In 1876 and 1877 the police arrested more than a thousand of these students, keeping them in jail over long periods. Finally in September, 1877, a public trial of 193 students was held, all that were left after the winnowing process had been carried out. Eighty prisoners had died in jail, while others had committed suicide. All the 193 were regarded by the police as dangerous revolutionaries.

The trial, which lasted until January, 1878, was conducted with intense bitterness on both sides. The defense pointed to the sickly faces of the accused, who had been starved in prison. They recalled the names of the prisoners who had died under arrest. They listed the crimes of the autocracy and went over to the offensive. In the eyes of the revolutionaries the hero of the trial was Ippolit Myshkin, the son of a non-commissioned officer, arrested for a bold attempt to rescue the philosopher Chernyshevsky from his prison in Siberia. "This court," Myshkin shouted, "is worse than a brothel where girls sell their bodies to earn a living! Here are Senators who out of cowardice and servility, and the hope of promotion and decorations, sell other people's lives, sell truth and justice to the highest bidder—" In the crowded courtroom the President's bell was continually ringing for silence. When the trial ended the autocracy had lost again. Only ninety-four of the prisoners were sentenced, mostly to short terms of imprisonment. The Czar was infuriated by the obstinacy of the jury in bringing in such verdicts. In his memorials and in the annotations he wrote on the margins of police reports he described the revolutionaries as "ridiculous," "headstrong," "men without character or principles." He seems never to have understood that they were intelligent, ruthless, and determined people, and he continued to place in positions of authority men who were completely incapable of dealing with the problem.

Among these was a certain General Trepov, the Chief of Gendarmerie in St. Petersburg. The singer Chaliapin, who came to know him well, has described him as a dandy who scented himself, wore immaculate gold-braided uniforms, continually twirled a small blond mustache and behaved with studied brutality at all times. He was handsome, widely interested in the arts, and seemed unaware that his face was pitted with smallpox. He had a habit of inspecting prisons and houses of detention. At these places he allowed his brutality free play. Encountering a political prisoner called Bogolubov, Trepov ordered him to remove his hat. Bogolubov refused. Trepov was incensed, rushed at the prisoner, gave him a blow across the face and demanded an apology, and when the prisoner refused, ordered him to be beaten with birch-rods.

Such incidents had happened frequently, and the revolutionaries were powerless to prevent them. This time it was agreed that General Trepov must be punished. Various groups of revolutionaries discussed methods of punishing him, but it was the young revolutionary Vera Zasulich, then living under police surveillance in a village near Moscow, who decided to take the matter in her own hands. She hurried to the Gendarmerie. On the excuse that she wanted to present a petition, she was allowed into the general's office.

There she whipped out a revolver and shot him. He was severely wounded, but recovered in time for the trial. The Emperor had suggested that it would be dangerous to hold the trial in public. Count Pahlen replied that her guilt was undeniable, and in any event she had confessed to the crime and the jury could hardly contravert her evidence. The Emperor seems to have been satisfied with the reply and made no further attempt to interfere in the trial.

Vera Zasulich was defended by one of the best advocates of the time. Once again the defense went over to the offensive. Not Vera Zasulich but General Trepov was being tried. The defense listed the general's crimes, spoke of the young girl's idealism and defended the revolutionaries against the police. Against all the evidence, the jury brought in a verdict of Not Guilty. There was wild applause, and the judge had no alternative but to order her release. While Vera Zasulich was being mobbed in the corridors of the court, General Trepov signed an order for her immediate rearrest. He was too late. The crowd surged round her. She was lifted into a carriage driven by a young artillery officer, Sidoratsky. Suddenly a shot rang out. Sidoratsky fell dead. In the confusion Vera Zasulich slipped out of the carriage and was carried through the crowd to safety. A week later she was on her way to Switzerland.

The Czar was incensed, but there was little he could do. Immediately after the attempt on Trepov's life, he summoned General Mezentsev, Chief of the Political Police of the Empire, and discussed methods of dealing with the terrorists. It was Mezentsev who suggested that the sentences imposed on the convicted prisoners in the Trial of the 193 be severely increased. Mezentsev also suggested that crimes against the state be dealt with by summary courts. There was provocation enough. Arrests continued all summer. Mezentsev sent telegrams to all the governors urging the implacable punishment of all revolutionaries. At nine o'clock in the morning of August 4 General Mezentsev, accompanied only by an aide, was walking through one of the main streets of St. Petersburg when a fast carriage pulled up beside him. Out of it leaped a former artillery officer, Sergey Kravchinsky, with a naked sword in his hand. He killed Mezentsev and then jumped back into the carriage, having left the sword firmly embedded in the general's body. The carriage was being driven by the fastest horse in St. Petersburg. Kravchinsky escaped into hiding, and soon afterwards disappeared from the country. On the same day there was printed a pamphlet composed by Kravchinsky under the title *A Death for a Death*. In the pamphlet he explained at great length why he had killed Mezentsev, set out the general's crimes, and detailed the consequences if the government determined upon revenge. "Our aim," said this remarkable pamphlet, "is the destruction of the existing economic structure and the removal of social injustice." Under the name of Stepniak, Kravchinsky continued his revolutionary activity from abroad.

The killing of Mezentsev by Kravchinsky was the turning-point. Henceforth the revolutionary movement in Russia was to become increasingly violent and to move closer to Nechayev's conception of what a revolution ought to be.

Nechayev was still guarded closely. The small empire which he wielded over the guards, the secret meetings with high officials, his studied insolence and his furious determination, all those hidden resources which he guarded as he guarded over his own sanity had led him nowhere. He was so much a prisoner of the Czar that he was unable to smuggle a single letter out of the fortress.

How well the Alexis Ravelin was shut off from the outside world can be seen from the testimony of Tolstoy. In 1878 he applied to the governor for permission to visit the Ravelin where a distant relative, Prince Volkonsky, a prominent Decembrist, had been imprisoned many years before.

The governor offered to show him all over the fortress: all, except the Alexis Ravelin. "You must understand the terribly stringent rules which have been laid down for the Ravelin," explained Baron Maidel. "There are only three people who are allowed to enter the Ravelin and leave it alive: they are the Emperor, the Chief of the Gendarmerie, and myself." Tolstoy was puzzled. He had served under Baron Maidel in the Crimea. He could see no real reason why his innocent request should be refused. "It is the order of the Emperor," said the Baron. "No prisoner shall ever leave it alive."

Later, these rules were apparently changed. A prisoner who went mad was removed to an insane asylum. A few—a very few—prisoners were allowed to leave the Ravelin for Siberia later, when the fortress was jammed with prisoners following the wave of revolutionary unrest in the eighties. But until the spring of 1879 rigorous laws were still applied to the fortress: and when the laws were changed, it was only because the government had no alternative.

That spring, an unprecedented number of new prisoners entered the fortress. They were the prisoners whom General Drenteln, the new Chief of the Third Division, regarded as too dangerous or too important to be sent into ordinary prisons. The fortress officials accepted the new prisoners with ill grace. "We will have to take them, but we do not want to take them," Baron Maidel wrote to the Minister of the Interior. With this new influx, it was no longer possible to put prisoners into isolation cells, for the only way in which men could be isolated in the fortress was by placing them in cells surrounded by two empty cells. Originally, Nechayev had been placed in a cell which had one empty cell beside it, the other being occupied by a madman. Soon it would necessary to put other prisoners close to him. Meanwhile the prison guards, overworked by the presence of increasing numbers of prisoners, silently rebelled. And when in April, 1879, the young revolutionary Solovyov shot at the Czar outside the Winter Palace, sending the Czar running to the shelter of the nearest doorway, running not in a straight line but in zigzags, avoiding death by a singular display of acrobatics, the guards brought the news to Nechayev, who appeared strangely unmoved.

"I've told you a hundred times that it would happen," Nechayev told the guards. "I myself belong to the Party of the Succession. I cannot tell you what position I hold in the society, but it is an extremely high one. Solovyov was one of our recruits. Remember, the Party of the Succession will eventually come to power. Make no mistake, there will be many more attempts against the Czar by the Party, of which I have the honor of being a member."

Nechayev's Party of the Succession was as nebulous as all the other political parties he had fathered, and considerably more aristocratic, for among its members he included many Grand Dukes and some Ministers of the Government. In the name of the Party Nechayev promised high rewards to the guards who helped him. They would learn in time that he had been fighting for them, not for himself. All those wasted years he had been trying to reach out to them, and now at last they were beginning to treat him far more seriously, their new-found trust in him mingled with a sense of guilt because they had not sufficiently helped him in the past. It was only when he claimed partial responsibility for Solovyov's attempt on the Czar that they began to fear "our eagle." "I have been suffering here without ever having committed a crime," he told them. "I have worked only for the peasants, for you and your fathers. I tell you, there will be a revolution, an end to the Czardom. It will happen as it happened in France. We will take the land from the landowners. The factories will belong to the nation." Once more he hinted that he was a prince of the Royal House. Since no one knew his real name and he was always referred to as "the well-known state prisoner," and since many princes and counts had been imprisoned in the Alexis Ravelin, the guards hardly dared to dispute his claim.

Toward the end of the year the revolutionaries attempted to derail the imperial train on the Moscow-Kursk railway. Once again Nechayev took credit for the deed. He prophesied that very shortly the whole of the Czar's family would perish. There was evidence that the revolutionary movement was gaining impetus. For the revolutionaries 1879 was a good year. Early that year Prince Dmitri Kropotkin, Governor-General of Kharkov, a cousin of the anarchist Prince Peter Kropotkin, was shot and killed as he left the theater. On April 25, a month later, an attempt was made on General Drenteln, the Chief of the Gendarmerie. On August 26 the Executive Committee of the *Narodnaya Volya* formally condemned Alexander II to death. Martial law was declared through all European Russia, unlimited discretionary powers were given to the governors-general, and exile by administrative process was for the first time authorized by the Czar. But the vast powers placed in the hands of the police were often misused, and the stupidity of the police was equalled by the cunning of the revolutionaries. One of their most cunning and most adroit plans concerned an attempt to blow up the Winter Palace itself.

In the autumn of 1879 a young peasant, Stepan Nikolayevich Khalturin, was working as a carpenter in the Winter Palace. He was a joiner and polisher, had been employed in several St. Petersburg factories and was an excellent workman; he was also a member of the Executive Committee of the *Narodnaya Volya*. He had founded the Northern Workers' Union. When the union was crushed, Khalturin vowed vengeance upon the Czar, and sought the permission of the Executive Committee to enter the palace as a common workman. Gradually he would accumulate single-handed a sufficient store of dynamite to blow up the palace. All he needed was the dynamite, which he stored under his pillow in his sleeping quarters in the cellar. Though heavy guards were placed at the entrance to the palace, there were no guards at the gate through which the workmen and servants entered. Accordingly, he accumulated a large store of dynamite. The problem was then to discover when the Czar would be in the palace dining-room—it was decided to fire the dynamite when the royal family was sitting down to dinner. Khalturin pretended to be weak in the head. He was always scratching his neck and asking innocent questions and was a great favorite among the other workmen and the guards who occasionally visited the cellar.

In November, 1879, the police arrested a revolutionary, discovering on him a plan of the palace in which the dining-room was marked with an ominous red cross. A detachment of soldiers was thereupon sent to search the palace. Khalturin showed astonishing coolness during the search. His luggage was examined, but none of the soldiers thought to look under his pillow. A post of gendarmerie was established permanently in the cellar. Khalturin went about his work as usual, and was particularly admired by the corporal of gendarmes, a man called Petrotsky. He continued to pick his nose, scratch at his neck and tell droll pointless stories. He played the part so well that Petrotsky one day brought his daughter to the cellar and explained to Khalturin that she would make an admirable match. Khalturin laughed slyly. "I'm just a peasant," he said. "I just don't know what I'd do with her." Everyone laughed. A few days later the Czar himself passed through the cellar on a quick tour of inspection. Khalturin remarked bitterly: "I'd have killed him if I'd had a hammer handy." One day Khalturin had a long discussion on the subject of terrorism with Petrotsky. They were two or three feet away from the hidden store of dynamite. "I'm just a stupid peasant," Khalturin said. "All this talk about terrorists—I don't understand. Tell me, please, what does a terrorist look like?" Petrotsky laughed: "Oh, they're easy to recognize—desperate-looking fellows with wild eyes! You can tell them at once!" Suffering from migraine headaches which came from the fumes of dynamite under his pillow, Khalturin took immense pains with his plan, and until long afterwards no one suspected him; and he failed in his purpose by a hairbreadth. He had every reason to believe that the Czar was in the dining-room when he exploded the dynamite. In fact the Czar had been delayed by an audience with Prince Alexander of Hesse, and he was just about to leave for the dining-room when the dynamite exploded. It was twenty minutes past six o'clock on a dull February evening. All the lights went out. There were screams in the dark. For half an hour it was believed throughout St. Petersburg that the Czar was dead within the ruins. But the royal family had escaped. The explosion killed ten soldiers, wounded thirty-three more, and injured twenty-three civilians. The floor of the dining-room was wrecked and all the windows were broken. The next day there appeared all over St. Petersburg placards announcing that the Executive Committee of the *Narodnaya Volya* regretted the deaths and injuries of the soldiers and civilians but took entire responsibility for the attack. The Executive Committee promised to continue a relentless struggle with the dynasty, until social reforms were carried through. Khalturin himself escaped to Rumania. Two years later, in March, 1882, he returned to Russia, killed General Strelnikov in the streets of Odessa, was arrested on the spot and executed a few days later.

The explosion in the Winter Palace filled Nechayev with renewed hope. He told the guards: "We have failed this time. Watch out! The next time we shall succeed!"

Of all the years which Nechayev spent in prison, the year 1880 was the happiest. Once more his influence was being felt among the guards. An immense hope welled in him. The

explosion in the Winter Palace had led, as the revolutionaries had hoped, to an effort of reconciliation by the Czar.
Exactly a week after the explosion Loris-Melikov, a convinced liberal, was given semi-dictatorial powers, and for a
brief period there was instituted a "dictatorship of the
heart." The revolutionaries took full advantage of the new
government's weakness and pursued their attacks relentlessly.

Meanwhile in prison the battle of the books went on. The
policy of the prison governor changed with each passing
month. There would be weeks in which Nechayev would be
allowed to read only journals, other weeks in which all the
resources of the prison libraries were thrown open to him.
If he was found to have written messages in code, the
books would stop. With innocent eyes, Nechayev would ask
why he received no books, and the prison governor was in
no position to offer explanations to his most insolent prisoner. One day at the end of March, 1880, Nechayev, after
his daily walk in the prison garden, returned to his cell to
discover that once more all his books had been removed,
with the exception of a single issue of the *Official Journal*.
He was outraged, summoned the guards, demanded his
books and wept when they explained that they were helpless in the matter—the order had come direct from the
prison governor. Nechayev waited a few days, then one
night he carved a letter to the Emperor with a broken teaspoon on the walls of his cell. To make the letters stand out
more clearly, he filled them with his own blood. The letter
read:

> To His Imperial Majesty, Lord and Emperor,
> Alexander Nikolayevich.
> YOUR MAJESTY!
> At the end of my eighth year of solitary confinement, the
> Third Division, without any provocation whatsoever on my
> part, has deprived me of my last means of exercising my mind

—the reading of new books and journals. Not even General Mezentsev, who tore me to pieces with a flogging two years ago, dared to deprive me of this occupation. Evidently the Third Division is determined that I should spend my days in a state of debilitating idleness. Evidently they have determined to destroy my mind by inactivity. My strength has declined during many years of suffering in prison. I believe they are firmly of the opinion that they can drive me down the road of madness or suicide.

I have no desire to share the fearful fate of my unhappy neighbor in the prison, whose insane screaming gives me no peace at night.

I have the honor to inform Your Majesty that the Third Division of the Imperial Chancelry may deprive me of my mind only by depriving me of my life: not otherwise.

PALM SUNDAY 1880
S. Nechayev

According to the prison records he was still complaining that he received no journals on July 21, but by the end of July the stream of books opened up again, and until the following year when it was decided to let him rot to death he was allowed to read as he pleased. This was the year when he came to maturity, swiftly extending his influence. His guards presented him with a plan of the prison fortress and smuggled notebooks, paper, maps, and forbidden journals into his cell. Except for the freedom which he desired above all things, he needed only the presence of a revolutionary companion to make him happy; and in November even this gift was given to him.

Stepan Grigorievich Shirayev was originally a peasant from Saratov. He had studied at the Saratov gymnasium, and spent two years studying veterinary science at Kharkov. In 1876 he emigrated, and worked as a smith in Paris and London. Returning to Russia, he joined the *Narodnaya Volya* and became a member of its Executive Committee.

Because of his expert mechanical knowledge he was one of the conspirators chosen for the task of setting mines under the Moscow-Kursk railway over which the imperial train was due to pass. The mines failed to explode. Arrested on December 4, 1879, he was brought to trial only in October of the following year. He was condemned to death, but the Czar commuted the penalty to imprisonment for life. On November 10 Shirayev was thrown into cell number 13 of the Alexis Ravelin.

Nechayev was overjoyed. Letters were passed between their cells. For the first time Nechayev learned the details of the revolutionary organization of the *Narodnaya Volya*. Here at last was a revolutionary party he could respect. He learned that the members of the party had the utmost admiration for him and would listen to any advice he gave them. They exchanged secrets. Nechayev broached the most cherished of all his plans: a plan to take over the Peter and Paul Fortress on the day when the imperial family attended a service at the Cathedral. Then the Czar would be captured and the successor proclaimed. Shirayev was skeptical, but he offered to submit the idea to the Executive Committee if any means could be discovered to send messages outside the fortress. On this subject Nechayev was an expert. There were now enough guards in his power, and he arranged with a certain Andrey Orekhov, one of the prison warders, that a letter written by Nechayev should be smuggled outside the fortress and given to a certain Dubrovin, who lived nearby. Dubrovin, like Shirayev, came from Saratov. He was a revolutionary who belonged to the *Chorny Peredyel* party, worked on the periphery of the revolutionary movement, and was prepared to risk his neck for Nechayev. The message sent to Dubrovin was given to Grigory Isayev, a member of the Executive Committee of the *Narodnaya Volya*. The effect was electric.

Vera Figner has told in her memoirs the extraordinary

impression produced by the letter. One evening in January, 1881, she was sitting in her apartment in the Voznessensky Prospekt, waiting for Isayev. It was a time of terrible strain among the revolutionary organizations, because an attempt on the life of the Czar had been planned, the police were already suspicious, and few of the revolutionaries thought they would survive the attempt. There were two other members of the Executive Committee with Vera Figner. It was ten o'clock. Suddenly Isayev burst into the room, his coat covered with snow. He placed a thin sheaf of papers on the table and said quietly, as though it were a matter of no importance at all: "A message from Nechayev —from the Ravelin."

"Are you sure?" Vera Figner asked.

"Yes, quite sure," Isayev nodded, and then there was a long awkward silence. It was as though the redoubtable Nechayev, the most legendary of revolutionaries, had sprung into the room beside them.

Vera Figner was stunned. At twenty-nine she was an experienced revolutionary. She had grown up with the revolutionary movement, and knew all the active revolutionaries of her time, but she had never set eyes on Nechayev, who belonged to the generation immediately before her own. She had read the interminable accounts of his trial, and bitterly regretted the death of Ivanov. In 1872 she left Russia for Switzerland, and she was in Zurich at the time when Nechayev was arrested by the Swiss police. She knew a good deal about Serebrennikov and many of Nechayev's friends. Serebrennikov, indeed, had been her favorite, and she remembered how he had been arrested and was later released, when a watchman from the Andreyevsky Academy declared that Serebrennikov did not in the least resemble Nechayev. But in Switzerland Nechayev seems to have had almost no connection with the Russian *émigré* students at the University: he belonged to the past and was almost forgotten. And now he had suddenly emerged from the grave. Spirited back to Russia, he had disappeared so completely that no one knew where he was imprisoned or whether he was still alive.

In silence the revolutionaries read Nechayev's long letter. As usual he wrote crisply, in a business-like way. He wrote as "a revolutionary removed from the main stream of the revolution should write to the comrades who are still in freedom." He spoke of his overmastering desire to escape from the fortress, and he talked succinctly about the way the revolution had immeasurably broadened its base since his arrest. Listening to Nechayev's letter, Vera Figner was aware of a sense of guilt. She had hated him in the past. Now it seemed to her that all the dark stains in Nechayev's character could be explained and washed away. The blackmail, the extortions, the murder of an innocent man, all these could now be explained as deliberate inventions by his enemies. Above all, he showed himself resolute, determined to help the members of the *Narodnaya Volya* and the possessor of a fantastically pure revolutionary imagination.

More letters came. In these letters Nechayev revealed what had happened to him during the long years of his imprisonment. He had fought off despair. Hands and feet chained, living in a dark cell alone, he had succeeded at last in exerting his influence over his jailers. He told how he had examined minutely the character of every soldier and warder who was brought into contact with him. "I observe incessantly, notice everything and store my memories." He was full of praise for the work of the *Narodnaya Volya*. He spoke of how the prison authorities had offered him his freedom if he turned informer, and how he was flogged and placed in solitary confinement when he refused. He said he had only one desire: freedom to work for the Executive Committee.

If Nechayev had written the letter a few weeks earlier the

subsequent history of Russia would have been different. At this moment the Executive Committee was immersed in a plan to assassinate the Czar. To attempt to liberate Nechayev from the prison would involve a complete change of plan. There is a story that the Executive Committee wrote to Nechayev and offered to abandon the attempt to assassinate the Czar and instead concentrate on efforts to release him. The story, though sometimes denied, may well be true, for there exists a long letter from Nechayev to the Committee in which he outlines two methods by which he could escape: one method involved a long pipe which would somehow be thrust through the soft earth under the fortress, coming out into the open in the small garden where Nechayev took his daily walks. Down this pipe Nechayev would slide to freedom. It was a wonderful, fantastic and probably impractical idea. The second method involved the large-scale bribing of the officers and guards at the fortress. There survives a letter from Nechayev which says: "Forget about me for a time and go about your own affairs. I shall watch from afar with the deepest interest."

But this was only the last of a long series of letters in which Nechayev exhorted his revolutionary comrades to deeds of daring and resource. Andrey Zhelyabov, a stern, patient, and superbly gifted executive, dealt with the correspondence. Nechayev formed an excellent opinion of Zhelyabov's capacities, and at one time suggested that Zhelyabov should become the revolutionary dictator. His old impudence and joy in life returned. He suggested that the *Narodnaya Volya* should distribute millions of copies of a false proclamation, ostensibly from the Czar:

> We, Alexander II, Emperor and Autocrat of all the Russias, Czar of Poland, Duke of Finland, etc. etc. on the counsel of Our Most Beloved Consort, Her Imperial Majesty the Czarina, and also at the entreaty of the Princes and Grand Dukes, etc. etc. and in consequence of the repeated requests

of the entire Nobility, have thought it fitting to return the peasants to serfdom, to prolong the period of military service, and to overthrow the houses of prayer of the Old Believers etc. etc.

This proclamation was never issued. Undeterred, Nechayev sketched out a secret *ukaz* ostensibly from the Holy Synod, to be issued after the assassination of Alexander II:

Almighty God having seen fit to put Russia to this supreme trial, we have the misfortune, O Brethren, to inform you that the new Czar, Alexander III, suffers from a confusion of the mind and no longer comprehends affairs of State. Therefore the loyal clergy are in duty bound to offer secret prayers at the altar for his miraculous return to health; and let none of you confide this secret to anyone.

These letters were smuggled out through soldiers, prison guards, and servants employed in the fortress. In return the *Narodnaya Volya* sent him long coded letters, money, even food. He was not always pleased with the letters from the Executive Committee and occasionally complained against their tone. "Do not thank me for any compliments I may have written," he wrote. "The success of your organization cannot spring from a bourgeois conscientiousness. Our enemies will grow fat on it. By being scrupulous, you will make your task more difficult. It may even cost you hundreds and thousands of deaths."

In time the messengers from the fortress came in direct contact with the revolutionaries. They did not of course know them by name; but they knew "the dark one," "the red-haired one," "the one who is broad and fat, wears a little black beard and has his lips turned up at the corners." About a hundred letters were exchanged in a period of a little more than two months. Then the blow fell.

On March 1 Grinevitsky hurled the bomb which killed

Alexander II. A few days previously Zhelyabov, who had organized and planned all the complex aspects of the assassination, was himself arrested. On him there was found 25 rubles, five copies of the newspaper of the *Narodnaya Volya,* and a number of letters in code written by Nechayev. On March 10 a further windfall came into the hands of the police—more letters and a list of names, pseudonyms and addresses, found in the possession of the revolutionary Sophie Perovskaya. The code-names were easily translated: Andrey Orekhov became Petukh, a certain Shtiklov became Shtulov. The conspiracy within the Peter and Paul Fortress was soon scotched, and to add to Nechayev's miseries Baron Maidel, the governor of the fortress, died. In his place there was appointed the stern and sharp-featured General Ganetsky, the hero of Plevna.

On the day when the news of the assassination of Alexander II reached the fortress, Nechayev addressed his guards: "Now you see I was speaking the truth. We have killed him. I was the first to warn you. I told you the Czar would be killed if he did nothing for the peasants."

It was almost the last act of the outrageous drama which Nechayev had been playing. From now on he could hope for no mercy, and no mercy was ever shown to him. Slowly, impenitently, fighting tooth and nail almost to the last breath, mocking his accusers and certain of his revolutionary vindication, of the triumph of his desperate desires, he went down to his death.

The Tiger Dies

Throughout the spring and early summer of 1881 the Czarist police worked as they had never worked before. Implacable in their determination to root out the terrorists, they made wholesale arrests and winnowed out their prisoners at their leisure. The "dictatorship of the heart" had been proved a failure. By May 11, Loris-Melikov had resigned. In his place there came the more forceful Count Ignatiev. The power behind the throne was the Procurator of the Holy Synod, Konstantin Pobedonostzev, who hoped "to drown the revolution in Jewish blood." "I will force one third of the Jews to become Christians, another third I shall force to emigrate, and I shall see that the remaining third starves to death." It was as though Hitler and all his legions were alive on Russian earth.

At some time between March 20, when Baron Maidel died, and July 19, when Adjutant-General Ivan Stepanovich Ganetsky sent a strange letter to Count Von Plehve, the recently-appointed Chief of the Gendarmerie, Ganetsky for the first time visited the Alexis Ravelin and addressed his prisoners. He was seventy years old, but his voice was strong and vibrant. He had in his possession the evidence proving that Nechayev had suborned the guards; and he was determined that there should be no repetition of the offense. The speech he made as he stood at the great iron door leading into the casemate was directed mainly at Nechayev.

He threatened dire punishment for any infraction of the regulations. Nechayev, his nerves at breaking point, subsequently wrote a complaining letter to the Czar:

Sovereign!

The new commandant Ganetsky, immediately after his assumption of power over the fortress, made a speech to the prisoners in the Ravelin concerning the events of March 1st. The character of his speech and all the circumstances surrounding it were entirely improper. The speech was not delivered in a room specially prepared, but in the corridor and not far from the casemate door. The speech, which was spoken in a thundering voice, was chiefly destined for my ears—this was quite clear from the contents. It was delivered in such a way that I heard every word clearly. This intimidating speech failed in its aim. The oblique threats made by General Ganetsky did not terrify me; on the contrary they showed me that under the pressure of recent events, the officers of the administration are going out of their minds; and having lost their wits, they are in process of losing their dignity.

The Alexis Ravelin is a secret prison—no inspectors ever penetrate here. Formerly there were abuses, such as one might expect in a prison remote from the world. The late commandant, the respected Baron Maidel tolerated the swinewarder Philimonov, but while fulfilling his austere duty, the Baron set his face against allowing the prisoners to be tortured. Now, after hearing Ganetsky's speech, this swine of a Philimonov shamelessly snatches away our last morsels of hope and declares that he is doing this in accordance with instructions received from the commandant. I have therefore begged the commandant that I should be fed from the guards' canteen with coarse tea and porridge—in spite of the inadequacy of such meals, they would be altogether preferable to the meals from the precious store supplied by Philimonov!

All those who are in any way employed in the Ravelin are now of the opinion that they can oppress the political prisoners to their hearts' content. Since the arrival of the new com-

mandant the guards have become impertinent and provoca-
tive. The time allowed me for exercise has been reduced from
two hours to twenty minutes. Worse still, for a whole month I
have not been allowed out of this stifling casemate. Ganetsky
has even ordered the ventilation passages to be closed. Apparently his purpose is to prevent me from making ink out of the
soot. The glass in my high window was clean in the old days:
through this glass I could see a little space of sky. What terrors
assail the heart of a prisoner alone in his cell, condemned to
perpetual imprisonment, deprived of the consolation of watching the clouds in their progress and the gleaming of the
stars at night.

Two commandants: General Korsakov and Baron Maidel,
six chiefs of gendarmes beginning with Count Shuvalov and
ending with General Cherevin, and President of the Supreme
Council of Ministers Loris-Melikov—all these have visited me,
and all these have seen the clean window-pane, and not one of
them was of the opinion that a clean window-pane threatened
the safety of the state, and it is a fact that I . . .* under investigation over many weeks and months. But I was not a prisoner
"under investigation," and it is now ten years since I was first
deprived of my liberty: the burden of watching over me apparently involves no high political principles, but being completely arbitrary and impersonal has been entrusted to the
prison authorities.

I had one personal enemy—General Mezentsev. He kept me
in chains for two years, but he did not shut out my view of the
sky. I had another enemy—General Potapov, whose face I
once struck. He had the right to hate me, but he took no revenge on me. He knew well enough that to take revenge on a
man deprived of his freedom is to have the soul of a beast.
General Potapov behaved like a man. I do not know whether
General Ganetsky possesses any of those feelings which are
properly called human, but I do know—judging by his visit
to the Ravelin and how he stood for an hour by the casemate
door and gazed approvingly upon the misery of the prisoners
through a crack—that he finds a good deal of satisfaction in

* Some words are omitted in the manuscript.

contemplating the suffering of others, and this is a satisfaction which can hardly be called human. Of course he has no desire to hurl me into an abyss of despair. He sees the tears and torments and the baffled rage of the prisoners, and no doubt he listens to the wild screams of frenzy which come from my poor companion in misery imprisoned in the casemate beside mine, a poor devil sentenced to solitary confinement to the point of madness. Oh no! I gave Ganetsky no satisfaction—he did not see me in tears. I want him to live on, and when the time comes for him to be dragged to the scaffold, we shall see whether he shows a hundredth part of my own peace of mind, my own self-control.

In the year 1875 I wrote a detailed letter to the highest authority in the land, in which I demonstrated to your august father that Absolutism had had its day. I said that the foundations of an absolute monarchy were shattered beyond recall. Only by granting a Constitution can our ruler save Russia from the horrors of revolution. I said it was necessary to introduce without delay a liberal representative system, and unless this was done, there would be no way of avoiding internal unrest, and there would continue to be insolent attempts on his life by men prepared to suffer nothing to come in their way. I said that in a few years it may be too late. The turn of recent events has only confirmed my prophecy. The reaction after the catastrophe of March 1st was inevitable. It was in the order of things . . . but the scale of the reaction and the way it has been prolonged will inevitably result in oppressions, and these oppressions in turn will further endanger the rule of the people who think they can govern the country.

I am a victim of a gross injustice. I was placed on trial in Moscow, deprived of all my fundamental juridical rights. They not only did not allow me to choose defending counsel, but they refused to furnish me with copies of the evidence taken in open court. I was not informed of the charges. Sentenced to twenty years imprisonment on the basis of unproven accusations hurled at me by the prosecutor—accusations which are clearly against all the evidence, as everyone in Russia knows— I was denied the right of appeal. Further, I was deprived of every possibility of exercising my rights, for they gave me no copy of the judgment and refused to give me ink and paper so that I could complain to the proper quarters. I was taken in the depths of the night from the scaffold and then by roundabout ways, traveling half-way across Russia, to the Peter and Paul Fortress. There I was buried alive, placed in solitary confinement, deprived of everything. I do not expect the new governor to lighten my woes, and I would not be surprised if this letter made everything worse.

Louis XVI only understood the terrible sufferings of prisoners when he was himself given over to the mercy of the Bastille.

Nowhere in the world are administrative officials so strict as they are in Russia; nowhere else are those who govern more shamelessly determined upon vengeance.

Without shame, I have accounted it my duty to acquaint Your Majesty with the conditions of my life in prison. The utmost punishment has been inflicted on me in the name of Your Majesty. But is this Your Majesty's true desire? I shall suffer all these privations willingly, if I could know that this was the intent of Your Majesty's imperial purpose. But to be a victim of Your Majesty's will and to be deprived of humanity and to be silent . . .

I am at the end of my tether. Written in blood, with a nail.

This was the last letter Nechayev wrote to the Czar, and probably the last that he ever wrote. With its hesitations and ambiguities, its desperate pleadings, the fierce hammering on single themes, it shows Nechayev at his best—and his worst. As he recalls the injuries inflicted on him, the hurts are magnified, and there are swift changes of perspective, sudden alterations of mood, immense gaps. His mind, slowly eaten away by the corrosive poisons of loneliness and the bafflement of a man who once had power within his grasp, pleads insistently: so does his body: but the pleadings turn in different directions and recoil upon themselves. At the very end he demonstrates his most secret desire: some recognition by Majesty. But it was the peculiar privilege of the Czar that he could be more powerful when he was silent than when he spoke, and in the long-drawn history of Nechayev's imprisonment nothing is so remarkable as the prisoner's determination to be heard in a void of silence, and the Czar's determination to use silence as his most formidable weapon.

A copy of Nechayev's letter, written in lampblack, reached Ganetsky, who was a soldier and therefore was not likely to have any sympathy for Nechayev's diatribes against the Czar. Only two things in the letter concerned him, as prison governor—the fact that Nechayev was able to write at all, and Nechayev's accusations against the quality of the food. On July 19, 1881, Ganetsky sent a copy of the letter with a covering note to Von Plehve. Presumably no one had warned him not to mention the prisoner's name: for the first time in years a communication from the prison boldly avoided the familiar words: 'the prisoner in cell number 5.' Ganetsky wrote:

> Prisoner Sergey Nechayev, who has been deprived of all rights and is kept in the Alexis Ravelin, has been found writing a complaint to His Majesty. The writing is in lampblack which would appear to be mixed with kerosene.
>
> I am enclosing a copy of the document for Your Excellency's attention, and I have the honor to inform you that Nechayev is in the highest degree unstable, rude, and insolent to all those who have official dealings with him. His pretense at finding the food unsatisfactory merits no attention whatsoever. I can testify personally to the great care which is taken in the Alexis Ravelin for keeping the food fresh, and that it is of the highest quality . . .

It is unlikely that Ganetsky wrote with his tongue in his cheek. Well-intentioned, an excellent officer who had earned the affection of his men in the battles against the Turks, he occasionally visited the prison kitchens, tasted the food and was always remarking on its high quality. If the Czar ever read the letter, he would have smiled contentedly. It had taken a good many years, but at last they had Nechayev where they wanted him: squirming, begging for mercy, insolent as always, but with the knowledge of eventual defeat written in every line of the monstrous and wonderful letter. There was no abject surrender, but then no one had ever hoped to see Nechayev surrendering abjectly. The long processes of expiation were beginning to bear fruit; and those who were watching Nechayev carefully from the shadows could reflect that a *mea culpa* would soon be heard from the remote cell in the Alexis Ravelin. They could have killed him. Instead they demanded an interminable act of expiation; and for them the importance of Nechayev's letter must have resided in the knowledge that Nechayev was perfectly aware what was demanded of him.

Suffering from scurvy and dropsy, his lungs choked by the foul air of the Ravelin, his mind the prey of doubts and sudden paralyzing dreams of grandeur, Nechayev was slowly losing the one thing he valued more than his physical body—his will-power. At the beginning of the year he had the guards at his mercy and was corresponding freely with friends outside the prison. By midsummer he was saying: "I am at the end of my tether." He was closer to the end than he could ever have suspected.

In the heat of the St. Petersburg summer the obscure madman Beidemann, who had kept Nechayev awake on so many nights, was removed from his cell. Beidemann had been regarded as a harmless eccentric who suffered from nothing more serious than prison fever, but at last he was seen to be quite mad, and on July 3 Ganetsky gave orders for him to be removed to an asylum.

The relief which followed Beidemann's removal was followed immediately by the shock of Shirayev's death. Shirayev was in cell number 13, and Nechayev had maintained contact with him through the prison guards. Dr. Gavril Wilms, the prison doctor, announced Shirayev's death in his usual dry and unilluminating manner. He wrote in his report of August 18, 1881:

> The prisoner suffered during the spring from a light catarrh complicated by occasional hemorrhages. In spite of the medical assistance given to him, there appeared signs of tuberculosis in the left lung at the beginning of July. He died at six o'clock this morning.

Dr. Wilms had no particular incentive for keeping the prisoner alive, and seems to have botched his work. He was sixty years old, stoop-shouldered, "gray as the moon and dry as a stick." Polivanov said of him that "there was something in his manner and his voice so repulsive and impertinent that he was entirely unlike anything you expected to see in a doctor." The death of Shirayev was a blow to Nechayev, for it cut at the roots of his communications with the outside world, and it was some time before he was able to announce to the *Narodnaya Volya* the passing of one of their chief lieutenants. Later, the *Narodnaya Volya* announced that Shirayev died in September, and it is possible that Nechayev himself did not know the exact date of Shirayev's death.

Into Shirayev's cell came the prisoner Leon Philipovich Mirsky, and with his coming Nechayev's fate was sealed.

Mirsky was the pure amateur of revolution, where Nechayev was the ardent professional. On March 13, 1879, Chief of Gendarmerie Drenteln was driving through the streets of St. Petersburg. He was Mezentsev's successor as chief of the Third Division. Mikhailov, the revolutionary leader of the *Narodnaya Volya*, had selected him as a proper target for the revolutionaries, and was arranging for his execution when Mirsky, the twenty-year-old son of a Polish nobleman, riding a beautiful white racehorse, suddenly took it into his head to kill the chief of gendarmerie himself. He followed the general's carriage, fired several shots through the window and then made off. The general was wounded, but gave orders for the driver to give chase. When his white horse stumbled and fell, Mirsky with superb presence of mind simply beckoned to a policeman and said: "My good man, this horse is hurt; just look after it while I go and get the groom." Then he took a droshky, went straight to Mikhailov's hiding-place and announced with an air of bravura: "I have just killed Drenteln, and now, my dear fellow, have the kindness to inform my mistress where I am hiding."

Mikhailov was shocked, but there was little he could do. Drenteln had not been killed. The attack had been bungled. Worse still, Mirsky, an aristocrat to the finger-tips, had attacked the general out of bravado. Mirsky's mistress, Elena Kestelmann, who went by the name of Lilia de Chateaubriand, was informed, brought to Mikhailov's hiding-place and immediately went into hysterics. Mirsky was still wearing the impeccable riding clothes which he always wore on horseback, and seemed not in the least perturbed by the trouble he had caused. He was perfectly prepared to ask Mikhailov to produce another horse from Tattershall's, and then he would ride back to his own home and perhaps kill another policeman on the way. With great difficulty Mikhailov succeeded in convincing him that he must go into hiding. He slipped out of the city, and made his way to Taganrog.

Meanwhile, Elena, who was bearing his child, was being closely watched, and Mikhailov had to change his hiding-place. A good number of St. Petersburg women, who regarded the morning ill-spent if they had not been able to observe through their lorgnettes the familiar young nobleman riding past, wept into lace handkerchiefs. The revolutionaries cursed in silence. They tried to make him go abroad, but he refused; and some months later he was arrested. The house where he was staying was surrounded; he tried to fight his way out, was wounded, arrested, and placed on trial.

In the courtroom he wore a black morning coat and white tie. He was contemptuous of legal assistance, smiled impassively and was courteous to everyone. He admitted the crime. The newspapers reported that "he presented a very gentlemanly appearance," and there was a gasp of horror in the court when he was sentenced to death.

But Mirsky was not hanged. Instead he was taken to the Peter and Paul Fortress. The trial at the military court had lasted two days. Within three days Drenteln was being asked whether he thought the prisoner could be used in a manner "suitable to the advantage of the government," and within a month it was decided to remove Mirsky from the Troubetskoy Bastion where he was originally placed to the Alexis Ravelin. It was explained to him that as an officer and as a loyal subject of the Czar he could serve his country by reporting on the prisoners. Mirsky agreed, and at half past two in the morning of November 28 he was taken to cell number 1. On the same day General Schmidt who was temporarily in charge of the Third Division, wrote two reports: one to the Czar saying that Mirsky had been taken to the Ravelin, the other for the files saying that he was being sent that night to Siberia.

As a stool-pigeon Mirsky was incompetent. No information of value was received from him until the early autumn of 1881 when the police, having checked through the mysterious documents in cipher found in the possession of Sophie Perovskaya at the time of her arrest, came to the conclusion that they represented the code-names of the guards in the Peter and Paul Fortress. They realized at last that Nechayev had been communicating with the outside world. Mirsky was informed. He was ordered to report any conversations between Nechayev and his guards, and he was also asked his opinion about the meaning of the code-words. Nechayev, who had previously taken a sharp dislike to Mirsky, now began to talk with him openly. By December the police were in complete possession of all the information they wanted. The guards were put on trial. Nechayev himself was removed to cell number 1, and fed on bread, water, and a little soup. Except for one last appeal to the prison governor, nothing more was ever heard from him.

The prolonged trial of the guards revealed Nechayev's secret power in the prison. An astonished governor learned that half the warders in the fortress were in some way implicated in efforts to free Nechayev, or to carry messages for him, or to bring him recruits. Four officers and thirty-five warders were involved. All were summarily punished, and sent to Siberia.

Of the last year of Nechayev's life almost nothing is known. Chained to the wall, never allowed out of the cell, his tongue turning black, suffering from scurvy, he was left to rot. The scurvy may have been the worst. The fortress was full of prisoners who had been arrested in the round-ups following the attack on the Czar in March: these prisoners clamored for sugar, lemons, and milk in the hope of warding off the scurvy. Ganetsky inspected the prisoners and came to the conclusion that something had to be done, and we have full records of the number of lemons and the number of bottles of milk bought for the prisoners in the Alexis Ravelin during this time. In July, 1882, thirty-one lemons were bought, and sixteen bottles of milk. In August there were thirty lemons and thirty-eight bottles of milk. In September the bottles of milk shot up to 108, but in November only fifteen lemons were bought. Nechayev's scurvy was so bad that Dr. Wilms ordered for him a half-bottle of milk and half a lemon every day.

On June 1, 1882, Ganetsky wrote to Von Plehve:

The prisoner in cell number 1 in the Alexis Ravelin, formerly held in cell number 5, has requested a Bible and the presence of a spiritual counselor. I regard this as a strange development,

for the prisoner has never previously shown the slightest desire
for instruction in the true faith.

Von Plehve replied that neither the Bible nor a spiritual
adviser should be given to Nechayev. He knew the risks.
Somehow, by means that Von Plehve could only suspect,
Nechayev would use the paper of the Bible for writing
messages and the priest for distributing them. From this
time nothing more was ever heard of Nechayev. His
punishment was now absolute: no books, no light, no air. He
was to be left severely alone; no one must talk to him, while
his body slowly decayed, with festering sores at the ankles
and wrists.

On November 21, 1881, Dr. Wilms stepped into the quiet
cell, having been summoned by an astonished warder. Nechayev was lying dead in a corner. Dr. Wilms made a brief
examination, and wrote on official notepaper his usual brief
report:

> I have the honor to inform you that the prisoner in cell num-
> ber 1 in the Alexis Ravelin died in the morning of November
> 21 around 2 o'clock. His death was caused by dropsy compli-
> cated by scurvy.

In such simple terms did Dr. Wilms sign the death certificate of the man who had put terror into the heart of the
Czar. Ganetsky, who could hardly believe the news, came
to examine the body. It was certainly Nechayev, but no one
who had known him during his revolutionary days would
have recognized him. He was swollen monstrously, as people
swell when they are starving, and his skin was a strange
blue color. Ganetsky gave orders for the chains to be
knocked off and then dispatched a message to Von Plehve,
informing him of the death and asking for orders. Von
Plehve decreed that the body of "the well-known prisoner"
(he did not mention the name) should be buried secretly at

the dead of night, and that all his clothes and possessions should be burned.

That night, at one o'clock, Nechayev's body was taken from the fortress to the Preobrazhensky railway station and removed to an unknown burial ground. On the same night there was a bonfire of Nechayev's effects. These consisted of a pair of trousers, a fur cap, a short fur coat, a summer coat and a summer jacket, a warm flannel shirt, a pair of drawers, a cravat, a bowler hat, chamois gloves, mittens, a pair of woolen stockings, one pair of half-boots, and two handkerchiefs.

It was exactly twelve years to the day since the murder of Ivanov.

The secret of Nechayev's death was well-kept. For some months already the revolutionaries thought he was dead. When in March, 1882, Alexander Mikhailov and Morozov were thrown into the fortress, they made inquiries about Nechayev, but though he was then only a few yards away from them, they could learn nothing. They assumed that he was dead already. It was rumored that he had been taken to Schlusselburg and murdered on the way, and for years afterward it was believed that he had been hanged in the corner of his cell. There were circumstantial stories about how Ganetsky had given him poison, and other stories about how Nechayev had beaten his brains out against the walls of his cell. The secret was kept until 1917, when the Social Revolutionaries who had inherited many of the qualities of the revolutionaries of the *Narodnaya Volya,* opened the records of the secret police. Then for the first time it became known that Nechayev had died in a way no one had suspected—of starvation.

Nechayev was the most obstinate, the most astute in attracting legends to his name, and the most potentially dangerous of the revolutionaries who fell into the net of the Czarist police. Others were to follow—Zhelyabov, Sazonov,

Kaliayev, a hundred thousand more. Slowly, patiently, often with immense courage and resource, they sapped away at the foundations of the Czarist state. None of them ever guessed that the followers of Karl Marx and Engels would inherit the state they were attempting to overthrow. In the year of Nechayev's death, the members of the Executive Committee imprisoned in the Peter and Paul Fortress smuggled out a message to the people of Russia. Called *From the Dead to the Living* the letter repudiated the violence of the early revolutionaries:

> Brothers and sisters, we are sending you from our graves what may be our last greeting, our testament. On the day of our triumph do not soil the glory of the revolution with any acts of cruelty or brutality against the vanquished foe. May our unhappy fate not only be the price of Russian freedom, but may it also serve to bring about a more peaceful and more humane society. We salute our country, we salute all mankind.

This letter, written in the same month that Nechayev was calling for a Bible and a spiritual counselor, was signed by Morozov, Isayev, Alexander Mikhailov, Kolotkevich, Kletochnikov, Aronchik, and Trigoni. They are names now, and few people are concerned with them. They were survivors of a small revolutionary group which changed the course of Russian history, for they brought about the death of the Czar Alexander II and were indirectly responsible for the tormented years of reaction which followed. The acknowledged leader of this group was Andrey Zhelyabov, who once said of Nechayev: "He was the greatest of them all." It was Lenin who said of Zhelyabov that "he was the most resolute of the mechanics of revolution." The line of succession passes through Nechayev and Zhelyabov, and comes at last to Lenin.

ZHEYABOV   a drawing made at his trial

ZHELYABOV

History moves too slowly. It needs a push.

The Rebels

"Everything in Russia will one day end in a dreadful uprising, and the Autocracy will fall in ruins because so many people are crying out against the Czar."

The words were written by the Hanoverian Ambassador shortly after Peter the Great tortured the Czarevich Alexis to death in the Peter and Paul Fortress, but they might have been written at almost any epoch in Russian history. The fear of a dreadful peasant uprising was deeply rooted in the autocracy; so too was the fear of assassination, though the Czars usually died in their beds. Alexander II was the first Czar to fall at the hands of an assassin coming out of the people, his murder planned and directed by Andrey Zhelyabov, the son of a peasant.

No one ever looked less like a peasant than Zhelyabov. The long face with the wide arching brow resembled the intellectual. Tall, well-built, with rosy cheeks and lively blue-green eyes, he could be taken for a doctor or a lawyer, or even for a professor. When he had money, he dressed well. He was proud of his long dark curly beard, his fine hands, his ability to mix well and inspire devotion. He was riddled with ambition, and was rarely humble for long. Women adored him, and the blue-blooded Sophie Perovskaya, the daughter of a Governor-General of St. Petersburg, became his mistress and seemed to recognize in him something of her own aristocratic sensibility. Magnificently virile, contemptuous of weakness, strangely impersonal so that often we have the impression of a man watching himself in the hope of detecting his own flaws, he was, as Lenin said, "the true mechanic of revolution and one who never lost his nerve." Vera Figner spoke of him as "our leader and tribune," and it is clear that he dominated the Executive Committee which pronounced sentence of death on the Emperor and on high officials. Others detected an aristocratic note of casualness in him. The young terrorist Rysakov said he was "completely fascinated" by Zhelyabov's presence, the quick mind, the sense that Zhelyabov was standing at the hub of history. The blue-green eyes, the richness of his voice, the way he would sometimes in the middle of a long discussion start roaring like a schoolboy, reminding everyone not to be too serious while remaining himself deadly serious, his habit of stroking his long beard or passing his hands over his hair, his extraordinary composure at moments of crisis—all these things were remembered afterward with affection and gratitude. Nechayev was called "the eagle": always remote, always strangely condescending, so that even when he was drawing up plans for destroying half of Russia he seemed to be conferring a favor. Zhelyabov was called "Tarass" after the swashbuckling hero of Gogol's *Tarass Bulba*. The name fitted him, though he had little talent for swashbuckling. He was heroic and larger than life; a rich sap flowed in his veins; he knew what he was doing. In all this he was singularly different from Nechayev who seemed so often to be at the mercy of his obsessions.

Zhelyabov was born in 1850, the son of serfs, at Sultanovka in the Crimea. At the age of four he was sent to live with his grandparents. His grandmother, who was born a free Cossack, taught him Cossack songs. He never forgot the songs and would sing them in a clear, deep baritone, even when the police were on his track and he had to be asked to keep silent for fear that the police would recognize his voice.

He was proud of his Cossack blood; and the memory of the great revolts of Stenka Razin and Pugachov burned in him. He learned to read at an unusually early age, and fell in love with Pushkin's poetry, especially the rich, gilded poem called "Golden Fish." From his grandfather, a sectarian, he learned to read Church script. Then for a while his father's master took an interest in him, taught him and then sent him as a boarder to a school in Kerch in the Crimea. Tall and thin, quick-tempered—he was always getting into scrapes—he developed a passion for reading, and was counted an unusually good scholar: he was good enough to receive the school's Silver Medal, and with this he was entitled to entry into the Civil Service. If he wanted to, he could go on to the University with a small bursary—the first wave of reform under Alexander II had produced a sudden need for educated men, and it was beginning to be considered both by rich merchants and by the landed aristocracy that the endowment of scholarships was a proper tax on income. Zhelyabov received a bursary amounting to 30 rubles a month from the estate of a certain Lududaki. He had been born a serf; he had spent part of his childhood as a groom on the estate of his father's master; and he was now well on his way to becoming an educated man.

All accounts of those early days speak of his gaiety. His friend Chudkovsky described him as "above medium height, with rosy cheeks, large smiling eyes which are extraordinarily expressive, and with black wavy hair." The veteran revolutionary Breshkovskaya remembered him as "tall and rosy-cheeked, with large lively ever-gay eyes," the possessor of "a vigorous figure and beautiful face, radiant with happiness." His eyes, which were described as being the color of the Black Sea, meaning that they were a luminous blue-green, seemed sometimes to be lit by interior fires. He danced well, but a little too vehemently. He had a passion for rid-

ing the swings in the public park and liked to make the complete circle, forcing the swing up until he was sailing high
above the crossbar. And even his poverty—for the small bursary was hardly more than the wage of an unskilled laborer—
was something to be dismissed with a smile. Wherever he
went he was perfectly at ease, and he gave the impression of
a man who took a dancing delight in life.

Zhelyabov left the Kerch gymnasium in June, 1869, and
entered the law school of the Novorossisk University at
Odessa with the fall semester. It was a brand-new university
founded only four years before, while the city itself was new
and gleaming: it had been founded by Catherine II in 1794.
With its port and naval base and great gardens, it was growing faster than any other city in the empire, overflowing with
the Greeks, Jews, and Armenians who came to make their
fortunes.

We know very little about his life at the university.
Though he had only one suit, he never complained of poverty. Poverty was something that an ex-serf could expect according to the nature of things. He seems to have been free
with his money, and occasionally gave lessons. He took his
meals at the *Kuhmisterka,* the canteen provided for young
students at the university where meals could be bought at
cost price or less. We know that he spent the long vacation
of 1870 as a tutor to a rich family near Simbirsk on the
Volga. If he received any salary, he must have spent it
shortly after returning to the university, for the university
records note that in October, 1870, he was excused from paying attendance fees on the grounds of poverty, and a little
while later he received from the university authorities a
special grant of 350 rubles from a fund founded by the same
Lududaki who had originally granted him a bursary. He
was well-behaved in classes, and he was constantly being
praised for his diligence in his studies.

The year 1871 was unusually exciting for Russian students

in Odessa. It was the year of the Paris Commune, the trial of the *Nechayevtsi,* and of Count Dmitri Tolstoy's educational reforms. It was also the year when American grain competition was felt for the first time, resulting in a decrease of grain exports and a general lowering of the standard of living in Odessa, which had become by this time the fourth largest city in Russia. The effect of the grain competition was a disastrous pogrom, in which the shops of Jewish merchants were looted and burned. Zhelyabov, as a Cossack, seems to have had no sympathy for the Jews, though he took no part in the pogroms.

Count Tolstoy's educational reforms were based upon an attempt to eradicate all revolutionary tendencies in the schools and colleges. Discipline was to be stricter. New curricula were announced, with an emphasis on the classics, Latin and Greek. Such dangerous subjects as history, Russian literature, geography, and the natural sciences were severely curtailed. The inevitable result of the new laws imposed by the Minister of Public Instruction was to send floods of students to the universities abroad, where learning was encouraged and Latin and Greek were not prescribed as a kind of mental hygiene. And throughout Russia young revolutionaries now began to hold secret classes in the courses which Count Tolstoy regarded with such horror.

With the help of three friends, Zaslavsky, Zhelyesnak, and Goldstein, Zhelyabov decided to ignore the new law and opened a secret college for girls. The girls adored him and flocked to his lectures on Russian literature; other students lectured on physics, geometry, and arithmetic. Zhelyabov was acquiring a talent for oratory and a passion for reciting poetry. He would recite Pushkin's poem "Winter" or a translation of Hood's "Song of the Shirt," and afterward explain the social implications of the poems—the desperate winters faced by Russian peasants, the miseries of factory life, though he knew nothing about factory life and there are no desperate winters in Odessa. It was the time when the movement to the people was at its height, and there was nothing particularly outstanding in Zhelyabov's determination to educate a number of middle-class girls. Later he was to acquire some experience of the real "to the people" movement. Dressed as a peasant, he worked sixteen hours a day on a farm, while attempting to instil revolutionary principles in the peasants' minds. It was an unsatisfactory experience. "From the moment they wake up to the moment they go to sleep not a single thought ever enters their heads," he complained. "All they have is their zoological instincts. You can't do anything with the peasants: we shall have to rely on the industrial proletariat."

With the illegal school thriving and his own legal studies progressing normally, Zhelyabov could look forward to a pleasant career as a lawyer known for his slight radical tendencies. He might have remained a lawyer all his life if it had not been for a professor with the unlikely name of Valtazar Vlassievich Bogishich.

Professor Bogishich was a Czech who spoke Russian badly and suffered from an unruly temper. He was nervous. He had only recently come to the University. He disliked the informality of Russians and preferred the staid formality of the Austrian universities. Professor Bogishich saw the student Avram Baer lounging on his bench and shouted: "Do you think you are in a tavern? If you can't behave better, get out!" The student attempted an explanation and a muttered apology. Bogishich thought he was being impudent or misunderstood what the student was saying, and suddenly screamed: "Get out! Silence! Get out!" Then Bogishich came down from the podium and pushed the student out of the lecture-hall. Some students thought they saw the professor kick the student, but there is some doubt about this. After a brief delay the professor returned to the podium and continued the lecture.

The matter might quite easily have ended there. Bogishich was not disliked. Professors have been known to flare into sudden tempers, only to apologize at the end of the lecture. But when the students came to talk about the matter afterwards they decided they had good cause to punish Bogishich. He had used too much force and he had used the word *kabak*, which implied a low-class tavern, rather than the less vulgar word *traktir*. Also, he had failed to offer any apology. The appropriate punishment followed. Four days later, on October 20, when Bogishich was due to deliver his next lecture, there were no students in the classroom, but the corridors were crowded. Students hissed, whistled, and whispered comments on his behavior, as he passed by them. Bogishich was outraged and sought the advice of the Vice-Rector, who offered to meet with the students the following day. Expecting to find only the students who had attended the professor's class, the Vice-Rector was surprised to find a mass meeting. He called for representatives from among the students to discuss the matter. Zhelyabov, who had never attended any of Bogishich's lectures, was one of the delegates. There was a conference with the Rector, which Bogishich was invited to attend. The professor bore no grudge; the representatives of the students were conciliatory; it was believed that with a simple apology the whole matter would pass over.

On Saturday, October 23, Bogishich's classroom was well attended, but there was no sign of the professor. Thinking it over, he had come to the conclusion that he would lose too much face by making an apology. The students were in an uproar. Someone began singing a bawdy song. Bogishich had made two mistakes: he had failed to keep his promise given to the student representatives; he had also failed to understand the student temper. There were shouts: "Bogishich, resign!" The matter was getting out of hand. The students refused to return to classes unless an apology by Bogishich was forthcoming. The Rector ordered the immediate convocation of the University Council. The derisive shouts and songs of the students could be heard during the conference. Nervous professors began to imagine there would soon be riots. It was agreed that the ringleaders must be put on trial before the University court and an expression of profound regret should be sent by the faculty to the injured professor. The faculty members wrote a memorandum to Count Dmitri Tolstoy, who deliberately misread their liberal protestations and telegraphed:

> Am in entire agreement with University Council. Request Governor General take strictest measures to put swift end to disorders. Expelled students to be banished immediately from Odessa.
>
> *Count Tolstoy*

With the blessing of the Governor General and the Minister of Public Instruction, the Rector decided upon a full investigation. The examination of witnesses lasted a week. The evidence of Zhelyabov and more than fifty others was heard, and soon the punishments were handed down—one student was expelled for a year, though allowed to continue his education elsewhere, and two others including Zhelyabov were expelled without the possibility of continuing their education. Colonel Knoop, the head of the Third Division in Odessa, thought the punishments too severe. He regarded the students as innocent and blamed the professor, saying that Bogishich was deliberately making a mountain out of a mole-hill. A certain Professor Sechenev announced boldly: "Professor Bogishich is the single cause of all our present disturbances." But the verdict of the Rector was final, and on November 11 Zhelyabov was arrested and placed on a ship sailing for Kerch. A crowd of admirers came down to the docks, waving flags, singing songs, loudly protesting Zhelyabov's innocence. About this time, feeling that the whole affair had gone beyond the bounds of reason, Bogishich himself tendered his resignation, and it is possible that the matter might have ended there if it were not from the very beginning evident that Count Tolstoy wanted an excuse to put the students in their place. Floods of telegrams were exchanged between Odessa and Moscow. Bureaucrats sitting nearly a thousand miles away were passing judgment on matters about which they knew nothing. Against his will Colonel Knoop was ordered to see that the decisions taken in Moscow were rigorously carried out; and when the police learned on November 15 that Bogishich had accepted a post at Warsaw University, they ordered him to remain at Odessa. A weary Bogishich resumed his lectures on November 17, and the incident was closed.

Zhelyabov had learned his lesson: anyone who stands up against established authority must be prepared to pay for the crime. He was not particularly bitter. At the last moment the Vice-Rector had summoned him into his office and offered to let him resume his studies in the following year. The Vice-Rector had not however taken account of the authorities in Moscow, and when Zhelyabov applied for reentry on the following September, Moscow played a Jesuitical trick. Zhelyabov had been banished for a year. He could therefore not return to the University until November, and it was clearly impossible for a student to enter the University so late in the scholastic year. Thereupon Zhelyabov gave up the struggle, and made no more effort to enter a university.

At the age of twenty-two he had few qualifications for earning a living. He had studied Latin, French, and German in the Kerch Alexandrovsky Gymnasium; he had read widely in Russian literature; he had a smattering of the law.

At the best he could become a tutor. And when he returned to Odessa at the expiration of a year's banishment, he hoped to settle down as a teacher in some rich family. But he was too famous or notorious in Odessa; no jobs were forthcoming and he made his way to Kiev. There he was employed as tutor in the house of a certain Yahnenko, a business man who had made a small fortune in sugar and lived on the outskirts of the city. Yahnenko had two daughters, Tassi and Olga. Zhelyabov promptly fell in love with Olga, the younger and prettier one.

If Semeon Yahnenko had been a little less good-natured and a little less indulgent to his favorite daughter, the marriage might not have taken place. His sympathies were liberal. He liked Zhelyabov, who was presentable, charming, and altogether the kind of young man he wanted to have in his family. Zhelyabov was not an intellectual, but he would make a good manager of a sugar factory. Olga was hopelessly in love. She was gay, quick, talented, and sang well, though Tassi sang a little better, and at one time the family had thought of making her a concert singer. Olga was the apple of her father's eye, and when she announced in the spring of 1873 that she was going to marry Zhelyabov, her father merely asked whether she had chosen the date of the wedding. She said they would be wed in the summer, and would then return to Odessa, a far more modern and progressive town than Kiev. Olga was just twenty, her husband twenty-three.

The marriage was ill-starred from the beginning. Zhelyabov had married her because she was pretty, affectionate, confiding, and easily swept off her feet by his stories about the need to serve the people. Olga believed him implicitly, and never ceased loving him, though she missed the comforts and luxuries she had enjoyed at home. She missed her grand piano and her singing lessons, and the little house parties on the Kiev estate where the landowners gathered and listened to Olga accompanying herself on the piano. "All you do is to delight the ears of plutocrats and aristocrats," Zhelyabov said bitterly. "Now we must get down to work." Work consisted of lessons in midwifery for Olga and a teacher's job in an orphanage for her husband. With his Yahnenko connections he could have entered an excellent career, but he chose to do otherwise. There seems to have been no bitterness between Yahnenko and Zhelyabov. They understood one another, and if the boy wanted to live in poverty and serve the people, that was his affair. If the young couple needed money, they knew where to find it.

Olga was shocked by poverty. Zhelyabov, who knew poverty well, simply laughed. One of his friends, Semenyuta, has described their living conditions. "It was a shabby dark room on the outskirts of the town. Two or three chairs, a rickety table and an unmade bed with a mattress like a pancake." But they were out most of the day, and they were still too much in love to be unduly perturbed by the appearance of the room. And though Zhelyabov felt an insistent need to serve the people, and had chosen the job at the orphanage largely because it brought him in contact with the poor, neither possessed revolutionary leanings. Zhelyabov had learned his lesson. He was determined to attract as little attention to himself as possible. He would not be a great lawyer. He would spend his days humbly serving the people.

It had not always been like that. Occasionally, when he was living on the Yahnenko estate, he would slip away and meet the young revolutionaries of Kiev, who were forever discussing the social and political theories of Lavrov and Chaikovsky. Groups of students, who called themselves members of the "Chaikovsky Circle" would meet secretly, discuss books, ponder the corruption of the government, and attempt to hammer out a program for the future. It was not

yet a full-blooded revolutionary movement, for no general
program had been agreed upon; and Prince Peter Kropotkin who entered one of the groups of the Chaikovsky Circle
in 1872 speaks of meetings at which nothing more serious
than Stanley's expedition to Africa in search of Livingstone
were discussed. But the innumerable Chaikovsky Circles
were close-knit, foreign books on the labor movement in
western Europe were being studied, and Alexander II was
credited with the belief that these discussion groups might
one day overthrow his throne. He once remarked that he
wished he could corral all the members together in a single
town, where he could keep watch on them. But the idea of
the concentration camp had not yet reached Russia, and he
merely imprisoned any members he could lay his hands on.

In Kiev the discussions of the Chaikovsky Circle were held
in secret, usually in an unfurnished house. Katerina Breshkovskaya paid a visit to one of these meetings where Zhelyabov was present. Axelrod, a young revolutionary who later
became a close friend of Karl Marx, had summoned the
meeting in a house which the builders had not yet finished
building. They had to walk through the dark streets in the
outskirts of the city to find the house. They found a plank
table, oil-lamps, benches, nothing more. Present were Axelrod, a rich landlord called Dalinsky who had returned from
abroad to make inquiries about the possibility of revolution
through the Chaikovsky Circles, a man called Emme who was
the acknowledged leader of the group in Kiev, and another
young revolutionary called Rashevsky. Dalinsky had
brought Zhelyabov with him. They discussed whether they
should open schools in the villages. Emme and Dalinsky felt
schools were a waste of time; they needed their energies for
more exciting endeavors. The speeches were long, slow,
and hesitant. Breshkovskaya maintained that even if they
introduced no program for opening schools in the villages,
at least they should make an effort to educate the older chil-

dren. Histories of various educational experiments were recited. At one point Axelrod pointed to Zhelyabov approvingly, saying he had been born a serf and had done brilliantly as a university student—what more proof was needed to demonstrate that education was necessary? Various resolutions were passed. Zhelyabov was restrained and respectful, and hardly opened his mouth. At last Breshkovskaya and Axelrod fell soundly asleep, and the discussion went on without them. Writing forty-five years later Breshkovskaya was slightly patronizing. It was her opinion that Zhelyabov must have been "astonished by the interest we took in him, and obviously pleased to see the sincere joy with which the *intelligentsia* welcomed and accepted a comrade who had risen from the people." It is much more likely that Zhelyabov was amused by a good deal of talk which led to nothing.

Except for these rare visits with Emme and Dalinsky in Kiev, Zhelyabov had shown no particular interest in the revolutionary ferment of his time. Even in Odessa, when he was living in the slums, he took part in none of the liberal movements. He liked fishing. He associated with his old friends at the University. He developed an interest in chemistry, and asked his friend Semenyuta to give him lessons. Semenyuta refused, saying he was altogether too clumsy with his fingers to play about with test-tubes. The conference in Kiev must have had some effect on him, for he began to spend the evenings giving free classes to workmen. Early in 1874 he seems to have been on the fringe of a Chaikovsky Circle instituted by a certain Makarevich, a student who posed as a shoemaker. When Makarevich was arrested, Zhelyabov sent a letter in cypher to Madame Makarevich, telling her about the arrest and urging her to get from her parents the money to bail her husband out, and gave directions for forwarding the money. The police intercepted the letter. Zhelyabov was arrested, and brought before Colonel Knoop. His ex-

planations were apparently satisfactory, for the colonel wrote
in response to enquiries from St. Petersburg:

> Zhelyabov cannot possibly be accused of belonging to the
> Makarevich circle. He has explained the whole situation to me
> with complete frankness. His part in the affair arose solely
> from his chivalrous acknowledgment of the claims of per-
> sonal friendship. His personal character and social position—
> he recently married the daughter of a highly respected munic-
> ipal councillor—make his guilt extremely unlikely.

Knoop added that he had authorized the release of Zhelyabov on bail of two thousand rubles, but St. Petersburg,
remembering the troubles at the Novorossisk University, had
already placed the finger of suspicion on Zhelyabov. Knoop
received a telegram: "Arrest Zhelyabov immediately." Accordingly Zhelyabov was committed to prison, where he remained for four months, while Yahnenko and Knoop together attempted to pull strings to release a man who was
only too obviously innocent. It was four months later before
Knoop received the authorization to release Zhelyabov from
prison on a bail of three thousand rubles. It was a beautiful
spring day in March. Zhelyabov had entered the prison with
his usual gay demeanor: when he came out his jaws were
set and the sparkle had gone from his eyes. "From that
day," he said afterward, "I became a revolutionary."

Yahnenko, the municipal councillor and owner of innumerable sugar factories, had paid the bail, and did not let his
son-in-law forget it. Olga was still in love, but the marriage
already was breaking up. Zhelyabov gave lessons and went
out on long silent fishing expeditions. This was the time
when the Slavs were rising against the Turks in Bosnia and
Herzegovina. Zhelyabov collected funds for the rebels, and
he would have joined the revolutionary movement against
the Turks if he had been allowed to go abroad, but being

on bail, he was under police surveillance, and not allowed to leave Odessa.

There was nothing in the law to prevent him from going out on the Black Sea in his fishing-boat or talking to the young naval officers of the port. Though moody, he still made friends easily; and at some period during the two and a half years when he was out on bail, the dedicated revolutionary became a close friend of a dedicated officer of the Russian Imperial Navy, a man who was infinitely loyal to the Czar. At that time Lieutenant Rodzhestvensky was a young torpedo-boat commander who liked nothing better than to show Zhelyabov around his gleaming torpedo-boat and take him out on trials. Tall and well-built, with a biting tongue, a quick mind and an abiding interest in social problems, the lieutenant was a model Russian naval officer. Strict with his men, he demanded and received their affection. He was already famous for his physical courage. Thirty years later Rear-Admiral Rodzhestvensky, Chief of the Naval Staff and Commander-in-Chief of the Second Pacific Squadron steamed half-way round the world to meet a shattering defeat at the hands of Admiral Heihachiro Togo in the Straits of Tsushima. By that time Zhelyabov's revolutionary adventures were only a memory, and a whole new school of terrorists had arisen to terrify the Czar.

Zhelyabov admired the torpedo-boats and would sometimes go out for four or five days. From the officers he gained a considerable knowledge of high explosives. Once he nearly blew himself up, and at another time, when a torpedo exploded prematurely, he received a splinter in the arm which prevented him from bending his elbow for some weeks. Through the naval officers he met some of the officers at the Artillery Academy. From them he learned about shells, emplacements, parabolic arcs, and range-finding. He was an apt pupil. Sometimes he would lead the conversation toward social questions. Once an officer offered to devote his whole time to the revolutionary movement. Zhelyabov, already regarding himself as a revolutionary, answered: "Stay where you are! You will be of much more use to us in the Army." Then for long periods he would disappear from Odessa—police surveillance had been relaxed—and would go to Kerch and work on the farms, exhausting himself with physical labor, singing Cossack songs to his baby son who was born in 1876, living quietly, so quietly indeed that the Yahnenkos thought all ambition had been burned away in him. He had been in prison, and the prison had poisoned him. He was only one more of the quiet, bitter students without jobs, rootless and hopeless, who were beginning to see that the country was in desperate need of a revolution. Except for his student speeches against Bogishich he had received no prominence, and he was a little puzzled when in September, 1877, he was ordered to surrender his bail and found himself once more in prison. What had happened was that the government had decided upon a general round-up of revolutionary elements and a mass trial (which came to be known as the Trial of the 193) was about to take place in St. Petersburg. As the least important of the prisoners, Zhelyabov was almost the last to be arrested. The trial ended in January, 1878. Zhelyabov was acquitted, and immediately made his way back to Odessa, where he was faced with the almost hopeless task of earning a living by tutoring. He almost decided to spend the rest of his life working with peasants on a farm. He had a police record; he was regarded as a young firebrand who had escaped a long term of imprisonment only by a miracle; and his future could hardly have looked darker.

In prison he met Sophie Perovskaya. It seems to have been only a brief meeting, but Zhelyabov was deeply impressed by her. Small and graceful, with a delicate nose, full lips, and light blue eyes below a high arching forehead, she be-

longed to the highest aristocracy. Her grandfather had been
Minister of Public Instruction, her father had been Governor General of St. Petersburg at the time when Karakozov
attempted to assassinate the Czar in 1866. For his inexcusable carelessness in allowing the attempt to take place, the
Governor General was summarily dismissed from his post.
He had enjoyed great power. Frustrated, he made the lives
of his family miserable, and Sophie hated him. She hated
his political views, his continual bullying of the servants,
his boasting and his debts; and she possessed a fierce love
for her mother, a woman of great beauty. Sophie was sixteen
at the time of the Karakozov affair. Three years later, when
the General fell ill and went abroad to take the cure, Sophie
remained in Russia, staying with family friends.

Among these friends were members of the Chaikovsky
Circle. She listened to them. She had a deep contempt for
talk, and cried out for action. Living alone, studying for
the diploma which would enable her to earn a living by
teaching, refusing all aid, translating and copying to pay
for her rent, wholly absorbed in the revolution, she was a
thorn in the flesh of the students who were happily content
to spend the rest of their lives discussing the revolution.
Sophie wanted revolution now. She was nineteen when she
was arrested for the first time, for agitating among workmen on the Nevsky Prospekt. She spent a year in prison,
and was then released on bail with orders to remain on the
family estate in the Crimea. Prison only quickened her revolutionary ardor, and in the general round-up which pre-
ceded the Trial of the 193 she was among the first to be
arrested. Acquitted at the trial, she went underground.
Alone among the prisoners at the trial Ippolit Myshkin had
received a heavy punishment. Sophie immediately embarked
on a plan to rescue him while he was being transferred
from one prison to another. Failing in this, she went to
Kharkov, to organize the release of prisoners there. The

attempt failed. The police were now on the watch for an extraordinary slip of a girl who seemed to be wielding vast powers among the revolutionaries, and they trapped her one day when she was secretly visiting her own estate in Crimea. She was exiled to Archangel province, two thousand miles away. She seems to have enjoyed the journey and was on good terms with the guards who treated her politely, so politely that when she had a chance to escape between Simferopol and St. Petersburg she decided to remain with them because she did not want them to be punished if she escaped. Later she changed her mind. When they were nearing Archangel and were spending the night at a small railway station, Sophie slipped out of the room and quietly boarded a train for St. Petersburg. She had no money. When the inspector asked for her ticket, she pretended to be a giggling peasant girl on her way to the capital for the first time. In fact she often resembled a peasant girl, and Vera Figner who knew her well once remarked on the peasant quality of her face. "With her short flaxen braids, her light blue eyes and her childishly rounded cheeks, you would have thought her a peasant until you saw the high sweep of her forehead." Breshkovskaya, who was also one of the prisoners at the Trial of the 193, presents a slightly different picture:

> She was as pure and calm a figure as if she had stepped out of the classic drama of ancient Greece. Her young fresh face expressed peace of mind, calm wisdom, and superiority over her surroundings. Even her smile was as serious as that of a mature man. She was very small and very youthful, and had a round, fair face, rosy cheeks and delicate features.

There was one other prisoner at the Trial of the 193 whose life was to be intimately associated with Zhelyabov. He was the young scientist Nikolai Kibalchich, the son of a parish priest, a man with a smooth rounded forehead, deep-sunken eyes, a fine Greek nose, a short black beard and the look of a dedicated intellectual. His wide-ranging mind was already occupied with problems of flight and jet propulsion. He spent two years at an engineering college and then transferred to a medical school. He knew German, French, and English, and was already immersed in social problems. He took little exercise, often forgot to eat, and studied technical journals all day. One day he was caught giving a prohibited book to a peasant and was thrown into prison for three years. At the trial he was sentenced to a further two months' imprisonment and then released. The damage had been done. He might have lived out his life quietly as a brilliant research professor. Instead he became the revolutionaries' expert on high explosives.

By arresting so many young students and then being compelled to acquit nearly all of them, the government showed itself incompetent to deal with the revolutionary situation. Instead of heading off the revolt, it had only made the revolt more certain. Exasperated students cried out for a rallying point. Their hero was Ippolit Myshkin, but Myshkin was in jail. There was no leadership, only a host of discussion groups and a handful of ineffective revolutionary societies. The Trial of the 193, however, consolidated the opposition, and gradually the secret society which called itself *Zemlya i Volya* (which may be translated Land and Freedom, though *zemlya* implies the physical earth and *volya* has a vast range of meanings including those of "will" and "the pure determination to achieve an object") began to assume the ascendancy. It was not a powerful society. In December, 1876, it held its first demonstration outside the Kazan Cathedral in St. Petersburg. They had planned to organize thousands of workmen in great processions, but no more than two hundred people gathered to listen to the fiery speeches of the nineteen-year-old George Plekhanov. The police did not even trouble to disperse the small crowd;

they sent a few hoodlums to heckle the speaker and beat up the crowd, and then arrested the ring-leaders at their leisure. Plekhanov escaped abroad. Among those who were left was a certain Alexander Mikhailov, a nineteen-year-old student at the Technological Institute whose passion for secret conspiracy entitles him to be regarded as the *éminence grise* of the early revolutionary movement. His hand is visible in many of the attacks on government leaders during the next two years. He was connected with the assassination of Mezentsev in 1878 and with Mirsky's attempt on Drenteln in 1879, and he was close by when Alexander Solovyov fired five shots at the Emperor on the morning of April 2nd, 1879. In the early days of the *Zemlya i Volya* he assumed the role which Savinkov was to play after the turn of the century.

Mikhailov had a passion for order, a clear mind, and a contempt for nervous and excitable revolutionaries. He usually distrusted Jews and Russians from southern Russia. He lived alone, very quietly, attracting no attention to himself and pouring scorn on the young nihilists who wore blue spectacles and long hair. He was the mechanic of revolution. For days on end he wandered through the streets of St. Petersburg, taking careful note of all the dark alleyways, the police stations, the escape routes. He constructed careful maps and sometimes gave the impression of a general about to take over the city. He spoke in a clipped, matter-of-fact voice, and refused to play the Russian game of talking for talking's sake: when visitors came, he opened a bottle, poured out a glass of vodka for each guest, and then replaced the bottle in a cupboard. He would allow a few minutes for drinking, then collect the glasses and insist that the members get down to business. A party member given the task of copying addresses complained that it was bad for his eyes. "Excellent," said Mikhailov. "You can carry on until you go blind." He had Nechayev's brand of obstinacy and Nechayev's wide understanding of political forces, but his words were tempered with gentleness.

Among other things Mikhailov gave himself the task of organizing the finances of *Zemlya i Volya*. The party was poor. It lived on the small contributions of students, each gift rarely amounting to more than two or three rubles. Recently, however, the position had changed with the appearance of Demetrius Lizogub, who had returned to Russia from eleven years of study at Montpellier in France. Lizogub's father and mother had died in quick succession, and he was now very rich and singularly without any ambition except to serve the revolution. He was tall, pale, slim, with a long beard which gave him an apostolic appearance. His blue eyes were shaded by long lashes, and he spoke in a slow, well-modulated voice. Entirely unassuming, he wore old clothes and tried not to spend any money on himself—everything must go toward the revolution. But in August, 1878, his land agent, a certain Drigo, decided to denounce him. Lizogub was arrested at Kharkov, but succeeded in bribing a police official and escaped to Odessa, where the police again caught up with him a few days later. With Lizogub in prison, Mikhailov's task was to establish communication with him and obtain power of attorney over the few thousand rubles which remained of Lizogub's estate. There was some doubt about where Lizogub was imprisoned, and it was a long time before there was any communication between the two revolutionaries. Finally, in May, 1879, Mikhailov established communication with Lizogub in Odessa, and a few days later he met Zhelyabov.

The meeting between Mikhailov and Zhelyabov had profound consequences on the revolutionary movement. They recognized each other's strength. Mikhailov came out of the gentry, while Zhelyabov came from a family of serfs; but they had the same general attitude toward the revolution, the same distaste for what Mikhailov called "the Russian nature," and the same calm determination to free Russia from the autocracy of the Czar. Mikhailov suggested that Zhelyabov join *Zemlya i Volya*, explaining frankly that the party was a terrorist organization committed to the assassination of the Emperor. Would Zhelyabov join? Zhelyabov pondered the idea, and then said he would join on one condition: he would take part in a single assassination attempt and then retire from the scene. He had no desire to commit himself to lifelong servitude to a party, and he seems to have accepted Mikhailov's suggestion with the air of a man saying: "Well, I'll try it out once, and if it's no good, I'll get out." He knew there was a chance that he might be killed or executed and offered to divorce his wife, but Olga was still in love with him and she refused to entertain the idea. He was not very good at hiding his emotions. He told her he had come to hate her, but the words were not altogether convincing; and when he left on his mysterious errands in the north she firmly believed he would eventually come back to her.

About this time Mikhailov had decided to summon a conference of revolutionaries. The government had acted sternly after Solovyov's attempt on the life of the Czar. The death penalty was being exacted on revolutionaries even when they had merely given money to the revolutionary organisations—Lizogub was hanged in August, 1879, after refusing to defend himself at his trial. He had died bravely, smiling, very quiet, on a scaffold erected in a public square in Odessa, gazing on the crowd which had assembled in the burning heat of a summer day as though he were a priest blessing them. There had been a wave of such executions.

Mikhailov summoned the conference of revolutionaries at Lipetsk, then a famous and expensive watering place, the last place the government would expect to find them. Under false names, with false passports, Zhelyabov and Mikhailov

arrived on June 13, 1879. A few days later the other delegates arrived. These included Tikhomirov and Morozov,
two intellectuals who later shouldered most of the burden of
providing the intellectual foundation of the *Narodnaya
Volya*. Another delegate, self-appointed, was Grigory Goldenberg, who had been responsible for the assassination of
Prince Dmitri Kropotkin in Kharkov earlier in the year.
There were altogether about twenty delegates who met
secretly in the forests surrounding Lipetsk. They would go
in small groups with their picnic baskets and later meet in
some remote part of the forest. And it was in these forests
with their mineral springs and their memories of the hunt-
ing parties of Peter the Great that Mikhailov and Zhelyabov
hammered out a new statement of revolutionary policy. It
was not enough to make sporadic attacks on individual
governors, ministers, and chiefs of the gendarmerie. They
must overthrow the whole government and prepare to produce a new government in its place.

Up to this moment no one had dared to face the inevitable issues. They had played at revolution. Now, according
to Zhelyabov, the time had come to "use all possible weapons." Among those weapons was the terror which would be
brought about if the Emperor were executed. From that
moment Zhelyabov and Mikhailov were committed to killing the Czar.

The conference at Lipetsk was followed by another at
Voronezh attended by Plekhanov, Sophie Perovskaya, and
the two Figner sisters. Plekhanov had been responsible for
the abortive demonstration outside the Kazan Cathedral,
and was at that time a moderate socialist. He refused to
take terrorism seriously. Reading from one of Morozov's
pamphlets calling for widespread revolt, he asked whether
anyone in the audience could possibly believe such arrant
nonsense. He expected to hear murmurs of approval: in-

stead there was silence, and shortly afterward he left the conference, saying he had more important things to do than discuss revolutionary policy with hotheads.

Plekhanov was not alone in the view that the revolution could be brought about by discussion groups. There were more conferences. Finally it was agreed that there could be no compromise between the two groups, and the party which had originally been called *Zemlya i Volya* disbanded, to become two parties. The moderates henceforth went under the name *Chorni Peredyel,* meaning the Black Partition, the party being dedicated to the division of the black earth among the peasants. The extremists took the name of *Narodnaya Volya,* meaning The People's Will. Each party had taken one part of the original double-barrelled name for its own. During its brief existence the *Chorni Peredyel* floundered. It was never a popular organization, and its members found difficulty in obtaining recruits. It published only one issue of its newspaper. The *Narodnaya Volya* went from strength to strength, at the mercy of police spies and traitors, but never having difficulty in obtaining recruits. At its head were five resourceful and determined revolutionaries: the intellectuals Tikhomirov and Morozov, and the "bomb-throwers" Zhelyabov, Mikhailov, and Sophie Perovskaya.

On August 26, 1879, the Executive Committee of the *Narodnaya Volya* formally sentenced the Emperor to death.

The Years of Failure

The first act of the *Narodnaya Volya* was to pass sentence of death on the Emperor; the second was to draw up a charter. Zhelyabov was responsible for the sentence of death. Tikhomirov and Morozov together hammered out the charter and then presented it to the Executive Committee, which discussed it interminably and finally passed it with a few slight amendments. The charter read:

A. We are socialists and *narodniki* by conviction. We believe that it is only through socialist principles that humanity can attain liberty, equality, fraternity, general well-being, the full development of the human personality and of progress. We are convinced that the people's will alone gives sanction to the emerging social forms, and it is only in this way that freedom is incarnated in life and so enters into the consciousness of the people. The welfare of the nation and the popular will—these are our two sacred principles, never to be separated from one another.

B. When we contemplate the conditions under which people live and have their being, we observe a nation submerged in economic and political serfdom . . . We observe the present bourgeois government maintaining itself in power by the exercise of brute force: the army, the police and the officials rule, exactly as they did in the days of Genghiz Khan. We observe the entire absence of popular approval of the government. We see a government which has nothing in common with the aspirations and ideals of the people. We see ancient traditions still living among the people—the right of the people to own land, communal and local autonomy, the idea of federated states, liberty of conscience and of speech. These principles are capable of far-reaching development . . .

C. We believe that the popular will can be established by calling into existence a Constituent Assembly elected by free and universal suffrage. Though this is far from being the ideal form by which the popular will may be manifested, it is at the present time the only possible and practical solution. Our aim is therefore to remove the power from the existing government and transfer it to the Constituent Assembly.

D. While wholly submitting ourselves to the will of the people, we nevertheless as a party believe it to be our duty to put forward a program for the benefit of the people. We intend to continue making propaganda for our program up to the outbreak of the revolution, we shall continue to recommend it during the electoral campaign and we shall defend it in the Constituent Assembly itself. The program follows:

1. A popular government with full power to decide all relevant issues.
2. A wide degree of local self-government.
3. The independence of the *mir* as an economic and administrative unit.
4. The land to belong to the people.
5. All factories and workshops to be put in the hands of the workers.
6. Complete freedom of conscience, speech, press, right of assembly, and the right to agitate during elections.
7. A universal electoral law, without class or property qualifications.
8. The existing army to become a militia.

We intend to proclaim this program, believing that none of these demands can be separated from one another and only the acceptance of the entirety of these demands will bring

about political and economic freedom for the people and the
correct development.

E. With these aims in view, we believe that the party must develop along the following lines:

1. *Propaganda and agitation.*
    Our propaganda must aim to popularize among all classes
    the idea of a democratic political revolution by means of
    socialist reforms, and to popularize the existing program
    of the party . . .
2. *Destructive and terrorist measures.*
    By terrorist activity to destroy the more harmful members
    of the government, to protect the party from espionage
    and to punish the official excesses and cruelties committed
    by the government and the administration. These meas-
    ures will have the aim of weakening the strength of the
    administration and of demonstrating the possibility of an
    unrelenting fight against the government, thus strengthen-
    ing among the people a belief in our ultimate success.
    Finally, by terrorist acts we shall develop a proper and
    suitable combat strength.
3. The organization of secret societies to be centralized . . .
4. Contacts to be formed in the administration, the army,
    society, and among the people . . .
5. The organization and fulfillment of the revolution . . .
6. Electoral agitation to choose members for the Constituent
    Assembly . . .

The five paragraphs of the charter of the *Narodnaya Volya*
do not seem particularly remarkable today, but in their time
and place they came with shattering force. For the first time
there was a social program combined with a revolutionary
method. The social program was simple, the revolutionary
method direct; and there seemed every possibility that the
revolutionaries might succeed in their aims. The terrorists
stated openly that they were determined to "destroy the

more harmful members of the government and punish official excesses and cruelties." It was decided to destroy the Czar as he returned in the imperial train from his summer palace in the Crimea.

On October 1 Zhelyabov went to Alexandrovsk. It was a small town largely inhabited by Mennonites from western Prussia, slow, cautious men who spoke German, not particularly enamored of the Russians. Zhelyabov chose the place for many reasons: the lay of the land offered excellent prospects for burying land mines under the railway tracks, the Mennonites were not likely to report any suspicious activity to the government, and it was once the capital town of the Zaporogian Cossacks, and indelibly connected with the name of the Cossack hetman Tarass Bulba. Zhelyabov went under the name of Cheremisov, a merchant of Yaroslavl. He spoke of setting up a tannery. He visited the local merchants, became friendly with the chief of police and the town councillors. He thrived on his disguise, gave parties, told innumerable stories about the Cossacks and was regarded as a man who would certainly make his mark on the town. His landlord was also of Cossack descent, and they swore eternal fealty to one another. Zhelyabov possessed an inexhaustible knowledge about the workings of tanneries, and liked nothing better than discussing the operations of the imaginary factory. Afterward people remembered the endless discussions and marveled at the strange way in which they had accepted him, for no factory was ever built and there was not even any decision about its site.

Zhelyabov spent his days in the town; at night he worked on the railway track. It rained continually. With Zhelyabov were two young revolutionaries, Okladsky and Tikhonov. They worked up to their ankles in mud. The plan was to bury two land mines under the track as it wound along an embankment cut into the slopes of the mountain. When the land mines exploded, Zhelyabov hoped the imperial train would be hurled off the embankment into the valley below. Most of the work was done by Zhelyabov who suffered from night blindness, and was forced to proceed with painful slowness. There were continual difficulties. Because it was known that the imperial train would soon be returning, the line was being inspected by a patrol which passed along the embankment every three or four hours. Once Okladsky fell asleep while he was on sentry duty. Zhelyabov was heartsick. For a moment he thought of shooting the man, for were not the revolutionaries at war with the government? He told himself revolutionaries who fall asleep at their task are exactly like soldiers who fall asleep in battle. In the end he decided to say nothing about the matter to Okladsky. He was in a high fever. The embankment was a quagmire. He was afraid of being observed during the frequent lightning flashes. He had to dig out a long underground chamber, but the roof kept caving in. On November 16 he learned that the imperial train was due to pass two days later. The night of the 17th was pure nightmare. He had one cylinder in place, and he was about to insert the second in its place immediately below the rails when it slipped out of his hands, fell down the embankment and was lost in the mud below. He succeeded in finding it, placed it in its proper position, attached the wires leading to an induction coil, and returned to his house in Alexandrovsk. He was now very ill. The strain of playing a double game over a period of two months was beginning to tell on him. He had hoped for a coded telegram which would give him the order of the coaches in the imperial train: no telegram came, and he knew he would have to guess which coach the Emperor was in. It was raining when he went out in a farm cart to a place he had carefully chosen beforehand. The wires led to the cart. From the train he would appear to be a farmer driving to market. No one would suspect him. But when he pressed the switch as the fourth coach passed over the cylinder, there was no explosion and the train puffed slowly toward the north, out of sight.

Zhelyabov was downcast, and cursed his lack of mechanical ability. He knew a good deal about explosives, but he had always been clumsy with his hands. The day after the train passed through Alexandrovsk, the snow fell. In the mud he had been able to plunge about at his heart's content, but the line inspectors would easily pick up the traces of his footprints in the snow. He decided to leave the cylinders under the embankment. It might, after all, be possible to blow up the Emperor's train the following year.

The attempt at Alexandrovsk was only one of three attempts to wreck the imperial train during its northward journey. All the attempts failed. Land mines were laid under the train at Odessa and just outside Moscow. Only one exploded, and that destroyed a luggage car. With twelve revolutionaries gathered along the line, all of them armed with large quantities of dynamite, the Emperor had passed through unscathed.

On November 22 the Executive Committee published a proclamation to the people:

On November 19 near Moscow, on the Moscow-Kursk railway, an attempt was made upon the life of Alexander II by the order of the Executive Committee. Land mines were placed under the train. The attempt failed. At the present time we do not propose to go into the causes of the failure.

We believe that our agents and all the members of our party are in no way discouraged by the failure. From the present failure they have learned a lesson which will be of service to us in further attempts against his life. We shall go forward with renewed faith in our strength and the possibility of bringing our war to a successful conclusion.

Turning to all Russian citizens who honestly desire to follow the road to freedom, we affirm once again that Alexander II is the personification of hypocritical despotism, a bloodthirsty coward ever reaching out towards greater and greater deeds of violence . . . Instead of truth, justice and freedom, we are presented with a violent and warlike dictatorship . . . He has deserved the death penalty by the pain he has caused and the blood he has shed . . .

But our concern is not with the Emperor alone. Our aim is to fulfill the people's will, the people's good. Our task is to free the people and to offer them the largest possible control over their own fate. If Alexander II were to recognize the terrible evil he had brought down upon Russia, and if he refused all power for himself, and handed power over to a General Assembly chosen by the free vote of the people, then and only then would we leave Alexander II in peace and forgive him his crimes.

Until then there must be war! Implacable war!

The mood of the Executive Committee was not entirely shared by all the members of the party. The failure hurt them. A single bomb could have brought down the dynasty; and to have failed when all the advantages were on their side was to admit a fatal lack of proper organization. In a mood of profound bitterness an anonymous contributor to the journal of the *Narodnaya Volya* wrote "a story for children":

Once upon a time there was a very, very good Czar. The evil people wanted to kill him, and they even put a bomb under the railroad on which this excellent Czar was travelling. They failed to kill him. The chief of police in the very ancient capital was summoned. He made every kind of excuse for having failed to penetrate the intentions of the evil people who laid the bomb, which did not in fact destroy the Czar though it came very close to it. At the sight of his terrified entourage the Czar decided to show mercy. "None of you are guilty," he said. "I am guilty, because I am too good." Everyone was deeply moved. A triumphant and prolonged silence ensued. Everyone felt a certain awkwardness.

That night the Czar was restless, and he fell asleep only toward morning. His old servant heard him murmuring in his sleep: "The courage of a King . . . convoy . . . Providence has preserved me . . . carriages must be armor-plated."

For a long time after the event the people continued to pray for the safety of the Father of the Country, and for a still longer time the priests zealously endeavored to assure the people that this was the best of all possible Czars.

The people however don't give a damn. The people are very rough, and all they can think about is bread.

From this time onward ill-luck was continually dogging the revolutionaries. The police were alert. They succeeded in capturing the printing press, and though a new press was promptly bought, and given the name of "flying press of the *Narodnaya Volya*," the revolutionaries were continually faced with difficulty in running it. The police attempted to check their source of ink and paper supplies. It was ordinary black ink, and ordinary notepaper, moistened to take print. In December Stepan Shirayev was arrested and thrown into the Peter and Paul Fortress; there, later, Nechayev came to know him through messages circulated by the warders. Shirayev was a member of the Executive Committee and was one of those who organized the attack on the Czar's train. A more serious loss occurred when Grigory Goldenberg was arrested in November. Though he had assassinated Prince Dmitri Kropotkin the previous February and attended the Lipetsk Conference, he was not a member of the Executive Committee. He was arrested at Odessa, and found in possession of dynamite. He was a Ukrainian Jew, thin and dark, with blazing eyes and an immense wide forehead, a weak chin and a curiously shaped mouth. Though passionately convinced of the need for revolution, and with a long record of revolutionary activity, for which he had been punished by being exiled to Archangel, he was not generally liked by the revolutionaries, and in prison he talked. The police played on his vanity. They recognized him as the murderer of Prince Kropotkin, and could therefore put him on trial and execute him whenever they pleased. Goldenberg was gradually convinced that his greatest service to the state would consist of arranging a truce between the Emperor and the revolutionaries. He received assurances that no harm would come to the revolutionaries, compiled a list of their names and pseudonyms, and revealed most of the party secrets. The police found themselves in possession of a hundred names and descriptions of conspirators. Goldenberg was assiduously complimented and made to feel important. For the first time they learned the extent of the revolutionary conspiracy against the state. In the end, Goldenberg realized that the police had hoodwinked him, that there was no intention of bringing about a truce, and the police had simply used him as a stool pigeon. In utter despair, he committed suicide. The journal of the *Narodnaya Volya* announced shortly afterward in the pathetic black-bordered list which accompanied all its issues: On July 15, 1880, in the Peter and Paul Fortress, Grigory Goldenberg ended his life by suicide, strangling himself with a towel.

The harm was done. The party members grew more desperate. Another attempt to blow up the Emperor as his carriage was passing through the streets of Odessa failed. There followed a scheme to blow up the Stone Bridge over the Ekaterinsky Canal in St. Petersburg while the Emperor was riding over it. The bridge was never blown up because one of the conspirators, who had no watch, arrived too late on the scene. Altogether, in a period of eight months, six separate attempts were made on the life of the Emperor, and all failed. As the result of Goldenberg's confessions the police were hot on their trail. They had a few thousand rubles, a printing press, about twenty devoted followers, almost nothing else. Yet the *Narodnaya Volya* was headline news in the St. Petersburg and Moscow newspapers. Its manifestoes were widely read, and the power of the revolutionaries to terrorize the dynasty was slowly increasing.

In the months of despair which followed the failures, Zhelyabov and Mikhailov kept the party going by the sheer force of their good humor. Nothing daunted them. They were always on the verge of arrest, and always escaped. Occasionally Zhelyabov would fall into fits of depression, but they were short-lived. "It doesn't matter if we fail now," he would say. "We must keep on hammering. If we continue relentlessly to hammer at the same target, we shall break through." The young Sophie Perovskaya was not quite so hopeful of seeing the revolution in her own time. "It will take two generations," she said once, "and few of the terrorists will see it, but it will happen." She dressed like a workingman's wife, in a cotton dress with men's boots, her head covered with a kerchief. She would carry on her shoulders the two pails of water she had dredged up from the Neva. No one would have recognized in her the young society beauty who had once danced in the fashionable ballrooms of St. Petersburg. And gradually she was falling in love with Zhelyabov. She had half despised men in the past. "A woman's man," she had said of a young revolutionary known to Prince Peter Kropotkin, and Kropotkin remembered ever afterwards the biting tone in her voice. She had a sharp tongue, and was often strangely prim, and could not abide slovenliness. It has been suggested that she would have made an excellent school marm, but this is unfair: she was born to be a Minister of Health and Social Affairs in some revolutionary government.

By the summer of 1880 Zhelyabov and Sophie Perovskaya were living together in a small apartment in St. Petersburg off the Ismailovsky Boulevard. It was a two-room apartment with a small kitchen, very bare. The windows had muslin curtains, the cushions were stuffed with straw, and the samovar had a broken handle. Sophie did the housework and the marketing. They lived on the money coming into the party funds, and on odd jobs. Both of them called meetings among university students and among the officers stationed at St. Petersburg, and they began to extend their influence among the workmen. By the end of 1880 the party claimed some 250 members in its Workers' Section in St. Petersburg and another thousand elsewhere.

In the fall of 1880 came the great crop failure in the Volga. Prices skyrocketed. Starvation was widespread, and the peasants were flocking to the towns, away from the barren fields. It occurred to Zhelyabov that there was hope for a peasant insurrection. Himself a peasant, he was appalled by the stories of conditions in the south; and at the first meeting of the *Narodnaya Volya* he announced his determination to go south.

"I believe I have the qualities for leading the revolt," he said. "I'm convinced that this is the best way to make the government aware of the people's need for relief. You may think that by going south I have put aside all thoughts of assassinating the Emperor. No, you are wrong. I merely propose to postpone the attempt."

But the meeting broke up without any conclusion being reached, and the promised peasant rebellion was postponed indefinitely. The party had neither the physical resources nor the money needed for a peasant revolt. It was agreed that it would be best to concentrate their attention on assassinating the Emperor.

In the winter of 1880 the young revolutionaries had many things on their minds. Kviatkovsky and fifteen other members of the *Narodnaya Volya* were put on trial before the St. Petersburg Military Court in October. All of them used the court as a forum for their revolutionary views. The trial was notable for the severity of the punishments. Kviatkovsky and Presnyakov, who had taken part in the attempts to blow up the railways, were sentenced to death, and were

executed on November 4. At this trial, too, there was mentioned for the first time a phrase which was to become
only too familiar later. "The red terror of the Executive
Committee is the answer to the white terror of the government." The words were spoken by Shirayev who, though
arrested the previous year, was not brought to trial until
the police had enough evidence to convict a solid batch of
revolutionaries. The words were quoted against the revolutionaries. Worse was to follow, for a few days after the
executions Alexander Mikhailov visited a photographer to
pick up photographs of Kviatkovsky and Presnyakov. The
police had warned professional photographers in St. Petersburg that something of the kind might happen, and he
found himself trapped. Now only Zhelyabov remained of
the two leaders who had dominated the party from the
beginning.

Now more than ever Zhelyabov was determined to put
an end to the Emperor. This time he would so arrange his
forces that it would be impossible for the Emperor to escape. They had kept a close watch on the Emperor's movements. They knew that he often passed along the Malaya
Sadovaya, and when Zhelyabov learned from Sophie Perovskaya that a shop overlooking the road was for sale, he took
her along to inspect it. The landlord's agent was suspicious. The tall, black-bearded intellectual who called himself Kobozev hardly resembled the kind of man who would
normally open a cheese shop, though Zhelyabov spoke about
cheeses as fluently as he had spoken about tanneries in Alexandrovsk. The landlord's agent communicated his suspicions
to the police. They discovered the address of the Kobozevs
and learned that their passports were made out in
Voronezh; they then telegraphed to Voronezh and learned
that passports had in fact been made out to two people
called Kobozev. The police were examining hundreds of
passports a day. There seemed to be nothing wrong, the

passport had the proper number and gave the proper description. It was no more than a routine action. The landlord's agent was informed that the Kobozevs were a reputable couple. On January 1 Zhelyabov paid the first quarter's rent of 250 rubles. The next day he had a sign painted for 35 rubles. Then it was necessary to lay in a stock of cheese. Mining operations were in progress by the end of the week, with most of the revolutionaries taking part.

It was a hard winter, with sleet and snow muffling the sound of their picks and shovels. January was a month of wild excitement. This was the month when the famous letter was received from Nechayev. Breathlessly, nine or ten revolutionaries, taking turns, all consumed with impatience, were at work digging a gallery under the road. At night the lights of the cheese shop would be left burning before an ikon, while the conspirators broke through a concrete wall and pondered the problem of the iron waterpipe which barred their way under the road. They had difficulties in getting rid of the earth; and when they had settled the problem of the waterpipe by working round it they were confronted with the problem presented by an ancient wooden drainpipe. They decided to cut through it, only to discover they were cutting through a sewer. The smell was overpowering, and nearly gave them away. They were exhausted by their work in the gallery, and they lost six more of their adherents by arrest, including the handsome Kletochnikov, who had spent the last two years working at a desk in the police offices and was therefore able to warn them about most impending actions against them by the police. The strain was beginning to tell. A weary hopelessness settled upon Zhelyabov, and he would talk about the day when all the St. Petersburg terrorists were under arrest, and who would carry on? He had no great faith in the theory that terrorism would bring about swift changes in the government. Loris-Melikov had instituted the "dictatorship of the heart" and with painful slowness the government was turning toward a more liberal program. Zhelyabov was a terrorist now only because he had been a terrorist before: it had become a habit, and he was perfectly aware that it was a dangerous one. "There is something terrible about being a terrorist," he observed about this time, and added without intending any irony: "It dominates your mind so much that it affects your freedom of judgment."

That winter the wildest plans were debated. With the help of the naval officers who were secretly attached to the party they planned to bring the fleet up from Kronstadt and bombard St. Petersburg. There was more talk of peasant revolts. A writer in the party journal spoke in February of "the need to give the signal of revolt to millions of starving peasants." Nothing came of it. To friends from Moscow a weary Zhelyabov, with the exhaustion of despair written over his face, was saying: "If we fail, then Moscow must continue the fight." It was as though he knew in his bones that the revolutionaries in St. Petersburg would be wiped out.

On February 20 a meeting was held in an apartment in the Telezhnaya. Present were Zhelyabov, Sophie Perovskaya, Kibalchich, Ignaty Grinevitsky, Timothy Milkhailov, Nikolai Rysakov, and Ivan Emilianov. Grinevitsky, who was known as Kotik, was twenty-four. He was a Catholic, the son of a small landowner near Grodno, with a round, pleasant face and a studious manner. Timothy Mikhailov was twenty-one, the son of a Smolensk peasant. He had a broad forehead, eyes set wide apart, a firm chin, and could not be taken for anyone but a peasant, though he was a metalworker by trade. Rysakov was an eighteen-year-old student from a poor family, quiet and dreamy, and for a revolutionary unusually religious. He came from Tikhvin in the south; his father worked in a lumber yard and gave him a small allowance to help him to make his way through technical school. Most of the allowance went into the treasury of the party. Emilianov was nineteen. He had been brought up by his grandfather who was employed at the Russian Embassy at Constantinople, and he spoke with a heavy Bessarabian accent. These four, all of them closely attached to Zhelyabov, who had been consistently recruiting through the winter, had offered to be bomb throwers.

The meeting in the apartment in the Telezhnaya was to put the finishing touches to their plans. The gallery under the Malaya Sadovaya was now ready to receive the cylinders of dynamite. Kibalchich explained the nature of the hand-bombs. They were like heavy hand-grenades, exploding at the moment a glass vial inside them broke, and weighed five pounds. All that remained was to choose the day for the explosion. It was decided that the attack should take place on Sunday, March 1, when the Emperor made his usual morning journey to the Riding School to review the honor guard. If the Emperor's carriage passed through the Malaya Sadovaya, then he would be blown to pieces by the underground mine. If he escaped, the bomb throwers would be waiting for him. Zhelyabov himself would give the signal.

Perovskaya was unusually nervous during these last days, and seems to have suffered from forebodings. There were rumors that the cheese shop was about to be raided. They worked in an atmosphere of exhaustion and relentless pressure. Zhelyabov was usually in good humor, but the strain could be seen in his too-easy laughter. Once Sophie was observed holding his hand and looking up at him with an expression which suggested they would not be long together. There were constant conferences. Kibalchich was insisting that the bomb throwers should practice throwing bombs in a deserted quarry outside the city; he complained that they were behaving like amateurs. So far there were no arrests, and no evidence that the police were watching them. One evening Zhelyabov called a conference with Perovskaya, Rysakov, Mikhailov, and Grinevitsky. Zhelyabov looked ill, slept badly and complained of severe headaches, but his eyes were glowing. He informed them that in less than a week an Emperor would be dead. On the next day, at half past seven in the evening, when he was calling on a friend, the police pounced on him. They were too quick to give him time to draw his revolver. One of the policemen had been present at the Trial of the 193 and had recognized him.

"So you're Zhelyabov," the policeman exclaimed.

"Your very humble servant," Zhelyabov answered, "but it is not going to help you in the least."

Everything had been arranged so that the attempt could proceed without Zhelyabov. On the morning of the twenty-eighth none of them knew of Zhelyabov's arrest. Kibalchich said he was probably busy; there were a hundred possibilities to explain his absence. He took his bomb throwers to the Smolny Monastery near the Cathedral of the Redemption. They found a gravel pit and practiced throwing dummy bombs. Finally Timothy Mikhailov threw a live bomb. It was a small one, but it gave off a good deal of smoke and flame. The next morning they were to meet in the apartment on the Telezhnaya, and as far as Kibalchich knew there was nothing to prevent the attack from being success- ful.

On the afternoon of February 28 the police became once more suspicious of the cheese shop. They sent round a gen- eral from the Corps of Engineers disguised as a municipal surveyor. The general poked around. The conspirators had concealed the entrance to the gallery. There was a pile of coke in one corner of the store room. The general kicked at it. If he had kicked a little harder, he would have dis- covered the entrance to the gallery, where the cylinders were already in position. He asked about the deep layers of straw on the floor. They explained that the straw was used for packing cheese. He failed to see the earth piled under the bed. It was a perfunctory examination. Suddenly a cat came into the room, rubbed itself against the general's boots, and everyone was smiling. They talked about the cat for a while, and soon the general left.

The next morning the news of Zhelyabov's arrest was known. Alone, with two bombs on her lap, Sophie Perovskaya drove in a carriage to her appointment with Grinevitsky and Rysakov. A little while later Kibalchich, also with two bombs, drove to his rendezvous with Emilianov and Mikhailov. The last instructions were given. It was agreed that all the bomb throwers should be in their places by noon.

Shortly after Grinevitsky woke up, he wrote a letter to be given to his comrades in the event of his death:

> . . . Alexander II must die. His days are counted. I or another will bring about this last terrible blow; and the sound of the blow will be heard all over Russia and the echo of it will penetrate into the most distant corners—it cannot be long delayed.
>
> He will die, and with him we shall die, his enemies, his executioners . . .
>
> What of the future?
>
> How many more victims will our dear and unhappy country demand before we have achieved our freedom? I am terrified by the thought, as I stand now with one foot in the grave, that after me there will be many beloved sacrifices, many men killed, in the final death-struggle with despotism . . . History shows that the luxurious tree of freedom needs blood to quicken its roots.
>
> It is not my fate that I shall take part in that final battle. Fate has revealed for me an early death, and I shall not see our day, our hour of victory; and never shall I know the blaz-

ing light of our triumph. But I believe that by dying I am doing all that is in my power to do, and no one on earth can demand more of me.

A few hours after writing this letter Grinevitsky was dead. So was the Emperor.

The Death of an Emperor

At 8:30 on the morning of March 1 the Emperor Alexander II rose in his bedroom in the Winter Palace overlooking the Neva. It was a cold day with thick snow on the ground, but the sky was clear. It was Sunday. Bells were ringing. He was not oppressed by any sense of coming disaster. On the contrary he was exhilarated by the brightness of the day and by the prospect of spending the afternoon leisurely with his young wife, the Princess Yurievskaya, whom he had married morganatically after the death of the Empress. His only official task for the day consisted of reviewing a guard of honor at the riding school called the Manège, just off the Mikhailovsky Square.

Afterward his children remembered that he was in good humor when he took them for a walk in the palace gardens. Then there was divine service in the royal chapel, followed by a light breakfast. Around ten o'clock the Emperor went to his study for his usual meeting with Loris-Melikov. For some time they discussed a proposed draft law for the establishment of a commission to report on the laws passed by the State Council. It was widely believed that this draft law would herald a new constitution. The majority of the members of the State Council approved of the law, but serious criticisms had been raised against it and the Emperor had for some weeks postponed a final decision. At some time shortly after 11:30, sitting in his study with the wide windows looking out over the frozen garden, Alexander II formally accepted the draft law and ordered it published in the Official Gazette and in the newspapers. He gave the signed document to Loris-Melikov and soon afterward went to the boudoir of Princess Yurievskaya, exclaiming that he had at last signed the law and hoped the people would now believe he intended to grant everything in his power. He spoke very solemnly, and Princess Yurievskaya remembered afterwards that he made the sign of the cross as he said: "Yes, tomorrow it will be published in the newspapers—this is my order." He stayed only five minutes with the Princess. As he was leaving, she said: "I beg you not to ride along the Nevsky Prospekt. I would be so much happier if you went by the Ekaterinsky Canal."

"So I shall," the Emperor answered, and those were the last words she ever heard from him.

In fine humor, at exactly 12:55, the Emperor entered a covered carriage for the journey to the Manège. The review passed off creditably. There were no incidents. The Emperor was observed to be unusually gracious to the officers, and he complimented the troops. Afterwards he made the short journey to the Mikhailovsky Palace, where he took coffee with the Grand Duchess Catherine, the daughter of his uncle the Grand Duke Mikhail and the Grand Duchess Helena Pavlovna, who had been one of the leaders of the movement which led to the freeing of the serfs in 1861. Both uncle and aunt were dead. The Emperor was particularly devoted to the daughter. Over coffee he told her about the new draft law, smiled and seemed completely at ease. He stayed with her only fifteen minutes, then ordered the coachman to return to the Winter Palace by way of the Ekaterinsky Canal. It was now a few minutes past two o'clock.

The clear sky of the early morning had given place to heavy clouds. The streets were drab and gray, the snow turning to slush and the wind whistling. All along the

Inzhenernaya were heaps of piled up, dirty snow. The streets were crowded with worshippers returning from church. As the Emperor's carriage bowled along, Cossack outriders on either side and a Cossack guard riding ahead, with two horse-drawn sleighs filled with policemen following behind, the Emperor could reflect that he had safely avoided all the dangers Princess Yurievskaya had pointed out to him, and yet it had been an entirely memorable day: a new draft law had been formally approved, he had spent a delightful hour at the riding school, and soon he would sit over a light lunch, there would be another walk in the garden with the children, and then there would be the usual leisurely Sunday evening interrupted only by another short service in the royal chapel.

The carriage flashed down the Inzhenernaya and then turned sharply along the Ekaterinsky Canal. Fifty yards further on Rysakov threw the bomb. He lobbed it under the carriage, hoping to bring the carriage to a stop. If the Emperor survived the bomb, Rysakov was prepared to shoot him. There was a sheet of flame and a loud explosion. The carriage, however, held together: the back axle was damaged, and the seat, sides and back were torn by bomb fragments. The horses bolted, the coachmen whipping them on, and swaying a little from side to side, the carriage followed. The Emperor shouted: "Stop!" A hundred yards further on the coachman succeeded in bringing the horses to a halt. For a few moments the Emperor remained inside the carriage. Then the sleigh with Colonel Dvorzhitsky, the chief of police, drove up. Dvorzhitsky jumped off his sleigh and ran to the battered carriage and opened the door, expecting to find the Emperor wounded or perhaps dead. He was delighted and surprised when the Emperor stepped out, looking pale but unhurt. Dvorzhitsky said something about his gratitude for the Emperor's escape and advised a quick return to the palace. For some reason the Emperor wanted to return to the scene of the explosion. He could hear a child screaming in the distance. There were groans from some of the Cossacks who had been wounded by fragments. He looked strangely preoccupied, like a man compelled to move toward an inevitable destiny. By this time two marines had thrown themselves upon Rysakov. They held him, waiting for the police. The second sleigh, containing Police Captain Koch, had already veered round. The two marines shouted that they had caught the terrorist. Sulphur yellow smoke was still rising over the place where the bomb had fallen, and the Grand Duke Mikhail, who heard the explosion and saw the smoke from a nearby street, came running up. The Emperor was limping as he walked along the narrow pavement beside the parapet which overlooks the Canal. He was unguarded, for all the Cossacks except those who were wounded were still mounted, and Colonel Dvorzhitsky followed some paces behind, not knowing what to do and hardly caring, for the matter was out of his hands: the Emperor was determined to walk to the scene of the explosion.

By this time Captain Koch had searched Rysakov and found his revolver.

"Who are you?" Captain Koch shouted.

Rysakov shrugged his shoulders. He was sweating profusely. The two marines and some more policemen who came hurrying up were pressing him against the parapet, and he was almost exactly in the same spot from where he had thrown the bomb.

The crowd which had formed mysteriously after the explosion was out of hand. Everyone was shouting and screaming. Everyone was fighting for a good position to see Rysakov or to see the yellow stain left in the snow by the explosion or to see the two people who were lying in the street, wounded and writhing. One was a Cossack of the escort, the other a baker's boy, Nikolai Maximov, fourteen years old, who only a few moments before had been walking down the street with a basket of bread balanced on his head. The boy was dying. He screamed incessantly in a pool of blood. One of the few Cossacks who had not remained on horseback came running up when the Emperor was close to the boy and said: "Your Majesty, the crowd is too big. It would be safer if you didn't go among them." The Emperor answered: "You need not worry. I want to get a little closer." The Cossack then went to Dvorzhitsky and said: "My Colonel, the crowd is far too big. It's dangerous, and we must get the Emperor away." Dvorzhitsky waved the Cossack away. Suddenly one of the officers of the guard called out in alarm: "Where is the Emperor?" "I am safe, thank God," the Emperor replied, and pointed in the direction of the dying boy. At that moment Rysakov, who was being pommeled by the police and the marines, shouted: "We shall see yet whether you are safe." Afterward Rysakov denied making the statement, but it was a likely thing for him to say and it was reported by careful observers. There was a stunned silence. The Emperor walked straight up to Rysakov and said: "So you threw the bomb?"

"Yes."

"What is your name?"

"Glasov, artisan."

"A fine fellow," the Emperor said contemptuously and then moved away, calling to Dvorzhitsky to show him where the bomb fell.

Dvorzhitsky was in a strange, careless mood, his mind dulled by the excitement and the shock of the explosion. As Princess Yurievskaya complained afterward, he behaved throughout with all the simple-minded alacrity of a footman and completely forgot his duty as commander of the Emperor's security guards. It was not his task to open the door of the battered carriage for the Emperor to get out. This could have been done as well by any one of the Cossacks. His task was to protect the Emperor even against the Emperor's expressed wishes. He should have insisted that the carriage be driven to the palace and he should have prevented the Emperor from mingling with the crowd. With Dvorzhitsky hanging on the heels of the Emperor and Koch guarding the terrorist although there were a number of army officers who could have taken charge of Rysakov, the situation was out of hand. Everyone seemed to be sleepwalking. The Emperor was dragging his left leg and gazing about him with a strange, strained expression. Afterward blood was discovered inside the carriage, and it is possible that he was severely cut by shattered glass at the time of the explosion and yet did not know he was wounded.

The crowd was now so thick around the Emperor that Dvorzhitsky had to force a way along the pavement. Grinevitsky was leaning against the parapet, having come up from his position at the intersection of the Malaya Sadovaya and the Italyanskaya. Pale and smiling, wearing a fur cap, his hands crossed over his chest, he waited until the Emperor was only two feet away and then he hurled the bomb with all his strength at the Emperor's feet. Once again there was a huge yellow fountain of stone, snow, fire, and smoke. There were screams and groans, then a terrifying silence. When the smoke lifted, twenty people were dying in the snow. Dvorzhitsky was unrecognizable, blood streaming from sixty separate wounds, though they were mostly surface wounds, since he had been behind the Emperor when the bomb exploded and the Emperor's body took the full force of the explosion. All round him were pools of blood and pieces of torn flesh. Someone was shouting: "Help! Stop him! Over there, in the garden!" The words made no sense. Grinevitsky was lying close to the Emperor, and he too was unrecognizable, hardly more than a mess of bloody pulp.

The Emperor's body had been flung against the parapet. He was still alive, but the blood was pouring from his shattered legs. Lying on his back, with his head against the parapet, his eyes closed, breathing heavily, he had never looked less like an Emperor. His military cap had been blown off, his uniform was in rags, his sword had gone, and blood streamed from every part of his body. For a while he kept murmuring words which no one could understand, then he whispered to Dvorzhitsky: "Help me," and then a little later: "It's so cold, so cold." Some cadets, returning from a parade, rushed up. They threw a cadet mantle over the mangled body and put a cadet cap on the Emperor's head. The Grand Duke Mikhail, the Emperor's brother, forced a way through the cadets and bent over the dying Emperor:

"Alexander, can you hear me?"

"Yes."

"Tell me how you feel."

"Hurry. Take me to the palace."

The cadets, who seem to have been afflicted with the same tendency towards sleepwalking as the police, began to lift the body toward Koch's police sleigh. Someone shouted that it would be much better to remove the Emperor to a nearby house where his wounds could be attended to immediately.

"No, to the palace," the Emperor murmured in a voice distinctly heard by the Grand Duke, the cadets, and the two Cossacks who had taken charge of the sleigh under Cavalry-Captain Kulebiakin.

Kulebiakin ordered the cadets away. The Cossacks were ordered to drive the sleigh to the palace. There was no stretcher. Bleeding profusely, the Emperor was sitting up in the sleigh between Kulebiakin and the Grand Duke. The crowd was screaming. Now everyone knew the Emperor was dying and nearly everyone wanted to dip a handkerchief in the bloody snow. Someone was singing the national anthem. More people came running up. The Emperor opened his eyes, and saw the blood on the cavalry captain's sleeve.

"So you are hurt too, Kulebiakin?"

"It doesn't matter. We are only concerned with Your Majesty."

The Emperor made a gesture which indicated that he understood, then his head fell back and he closed his eyes. Some Cossacks had been sent on ahead to prepare the palace for the Emperor's arrival. "Hurry—the palace. I want to die there," the Emperor murmured, and then was silent. They were the last words he ever spoke.

In the palace Princess Yurievskaya was already dressed in a fur hat and a fur cloak for the afternoon promenade in the garden which the Emperor had promised her. Suddenly from downstairs there came a cry: "The Emperor is ill!" Immediately the Princess imagined he was suffering from one of his recurrent attacks of asthma, and she thought of the oxygen balloons. She ordered a servant to carry six or seven balloons to the Emperor, and she had one in each hand as she flew down the stairs. At the foot of the stairs she paused. The door was opening, and some Cossacks were bringing into the palace a strange unrecognizable object, all scarlet. She could make nothing of this until one of the Cossacks shouted that it was the Emperor. The body was taken up the marble steps, and then along a corridor leading to the Emperor's study, where it was placed on a couch near the desk. The Princess followed. When she realized at last that it was her husband lying there, she hurled herself on him, fondled him, cried out to him, kissed him, held his head in her hands, her fingers moving so frantically that she seemed to be pulling out his hair. All the time she kept screaming: "Sasha! Sasha!"

When Count Baranov murmured: "Courage, courage, Princess! He is still alive!" she let go and allowed others to attend the Emperor.

Two *valets de chambre* began to undress the Emperor, to make him ready for the doctors who had been summoned, but what remained of his uniform was in rags and sticking to

his flesh and could not be unbuttoned. They slit the uniform
with a pair of scissors down the back.

When Dr. Kruglevsky, Surgeon Extraordinary to the
Czar, arrived in the study, the bleeding was still going on. He
made a brief examination. He found that the right leg had
been torn off, the left leg was shattered, and there were
more than two hundred separate wounds. One eye was shut,
the other expressionless. The handsome head, once the blood
was washed off, was still recognizable.

"I have come too late," the doctor said. "Nothing can be
done."

"No, no, you must do everything you can to save him!" the
Princess exclaimed.

In a dead silence Dr. Kruglevsky began to bandage the
wounds to prevent the blood from flowing on the carpet. He
asked how the Emperor had been transported to the palace,
and when told of the sleigh-ride he groaned. Was there no
stretcher? Was there no way to prevent the jolting?

The Grand Duke Mikhail whispered, hardly knowing what
he was saying: "I was there! I saw it happen!"

Princess Yurievskaya turned on him sharply and said: "If
you were there, then how did you let it happen?"

"I was too late. I could do nothing."

The room was crowded. The Czarevich Alexander took
his place by the couch. The Emperor's remaining eye was
wide-open, unseeing. There was almost no pulse, almost no
breath coming from the lungs. The Princess sprinkled water
on his face and rubbed ether into his temples and put the
oxygen balloons close to his lips and nose. Dr. Botkin suggested a blood transfusion, but there were no instruments
available. Kruglevsky suggested that as soon as the Emperor
returned to consciousness, his legs, one shattered, the other
hanging to the thigh only by ligaments, should be amputated. The Princess agreed. She said later: "If God had let
him live even without his legs, he would still have been my

beloved, and he would have belonged to me all the more, for then he would have had to relinquish the throne."

The chief of police arrived, saluted smartly and said he had compiled a full report of the tragedy. No one paid any attention to him except the Czarevich who looked at him coldly, and then returned to contemplate his dying father.

The Emperor was behaving strangely. His head kept nodding from side to side. The expressionless eye was still staring fixedly. Dr. Kruglevsky had his fingers on the Emperor's pulse. Someone said: "Silence, please. The end is near."

The last sacraments were administered by an archpriest whose hands shook so violently that he dropped the golden spoon holding the sacramental mixture of bread and wine. Dr. Kruglevsky was still holding the Emperor's hand. Suddenly he let it drop.

"The Emperor is dead," he announced in a loud voice. It was 3:35 P.M.

The Princess screamed and fell to the floor, and two guardsmen were summoned to carry her to her private quarters.

The new Czar was standing by the window. Powerfully built, six feet tall, with huge hands which could tear a pack of cards in two, he alone seemed to show no signs of grief. When the chief of police strode up and asked whether the Czar had any orders to give, Alexander III snapped: "Orders? Yes, of course. The police have apparently lost their heads. The Army will take charge of the situation. I shall confer with my Ministers at once in the Anichkov palace." Shortly afterward the new Czar abruptly left the room.

Such was the end of a Czar who had ruled despotically. His murderer survived a few hours longer. Grinevitsky's mangled body was removed to a hospital. He had as many wounds as the Czar. The police kept watch by the bed, hoping he would talk in delirium. For a few moments before ten o'clock he regained consciousness. A police inspector asked him his name, and he answered in a clear voice: "I know nothing," and died shortly afterward.

When Grinevitsky threw the bomb, Emilianov was running in the direction of the Ekaterinsky Canal. He had heard the first bomb, and he was only twenty paces away from the Emperor when the second bomb was thrown. He did not act like a revolutionary, and he was puzzled by his own behavior. When he saw the Emperor fall, he ran with the crowd to help him, his bomb still wrapped in paper under his arm. He risked being arrested on the spot, and perhaps being torn to pieces by the mob, and he was one of the first to reach the Emperor's side. He stayed with the crowd for a while, and then with Timothy Mikhailov made his way to the apartment on the Telezhnaya where the conspirators had agreed to meet.

That night St. Petersburg was a nest of rumors. No official or unofficial statements were issued by the police. Rysakov refused to divulge his identity. It was widely believed that Alexander II was assassinated at the orders of high officials determined to maintain the autocracy at all costs. The mysterious behavior of the Emperor, the incompetence of the Cossack escort and the police, the silence of Grinevitsky, the strange accident by which the Emperor's death occurred just at the moment when he had signed a draft decree designed to give greater freedom to the country —all these things suggested that the assassination had been brought out by members of the "Court party;" and even when on the next day the *Narodnaya Volya* issued a manifesto to the Workers of Russia, claiming full responsibility for the murder, suspicions were not dissipated. The manifesto read:

Today, March 1, Alexander II, the tormentor of the people, has been put to death by us, Socialists. He was killed because he did not care for his people, burdened them with unauthorized taxes, deprived the peasants of their land and surrendered the workers to the mercy of plunderers and exploiters. He did not give the people freedom: he did not listen to their griefs and their tears. He defended only the rich and lived himself in the utmost luxury, while the people went hungry. The Czar's servants, from the village police to the high officials, plundered the people and barbarously maltreated the peasants; and these servants of the Czar were especially protected and rewarded by the Czar. Those who stood out for the people he hanged or exiled to Siberia. So he was killed. A Czar should be a good shepherd, ready to lay down his life for his flock: Alexander II was a ravening wolf and a terrible death has struck him. Now a new Czar, Alexander III, climbs to the throne. He must not be allowed to behave like his father. May he proceed to hold general elections in the villages and towns and in all the factories. May he recognize the sorrows and deep needs of the people, and go forward into the truth! . . .

By the time this manifesto appeared, Rysakov was beginning to crack. He had been confronted with Zhelyabov in prison on the night of the assassination, but though they quietly celebrated their triumph, neither revealed the names of accomplices to the police. On March 2 Rysakov was examined again, at greater length. Dark-faced and thick-set, with unruly hair, and a look of peasant-like stolidity, he was an easy prey for Colonel Dobrinsky, the most brilliant of the police officials in charge of eliciting information from captured terrorists. The usual promises of lenient treatment were made. The enormity of his crime was constantly repeated to him. He was told that the Czar had signed the draft law a few hours before the assassination. Rysakov said little, but what he said was enough to start the police on a singularly successful effort to round up the whole band of terrorists. From Rysakov the police learned about the apartment in the Telezhnaya, and that night they sent a detachment to the apartment. Gesya Helfman and Nikolai Sablin were asleep when the police began to break down the door of the apartment. Sablin awoke, realized he would have to shoot his way out and took up a position near the door, firing through it, so that the police were forced to scatter and find hiding-places on the landing. Then there was a long pause, followed by a single shot and a woman's screams for help. Sablin had shot himself through the head and Gesya Helfman had gone insane with grief. When the police broke in, they found Gesya Helfman standing motionless by the body of Sablin, unable to say anything at all except that she wanted the bombs to be carried to safety—she seems to have been afraid that a police bullet would set off one of the bombs. The police found two live bombs, a plan of St. Petersburg with pencil marks drawn around the Malaya Sadovaya and the Ekaterinsky Canal and another rough plan drawn on the back of an envelope. They removed Gesya Helfman to the house of Preliminary Detention, and kept watch over the empty apartment.

They did not have to wait long. Around eleven in the morning Timothy Mikhailov entered the house, climbed up the dark stairway and paused before apartment 5. The police pounced on him. Mikhailov was heavily built, and was able to shrug them off. When he explained that he was searching for a cab-driver friend, the police almost believed his story, but told him to wait and gave him a chair inside the apartment where the bloodstains were still fresh on the bed. They thought Mikhailov would break under the strain of seeing the familiar apartment deserted by the conspirators and ringed round by the police. Mikhailov did not break. He suddenly jumped up, pulled out his revolver and began to shoot his way out, wounding two policemen before being disarmed. The police never explained why they had not searched him for weapons. Rysakov's hint about the apartment in the Telezhnaya was disastrous. It led to the suicide of Sablin, the death on the scaffold of Timothy Mikhailov and the death in prison some eighteen months later of Gesya Helfman.

There remained of the major conspirators Sophie Perovskaya and Nikolai Kibalchich.

Perovskaya was on the run, hiding in different apartments each night, wandering the streets during the day. She seemed totally impervious to the danger of being abroad in a city hung with black flags, with trigger-happy Cossacks stationed at every corner, and the police embarking on a wide-scale search of all the houses where the conspirators might be hiding. She was walking boldly down the Nevsky Prospekt on March 3 when she bought a copy of a newspaper announcing that Zhelyabov had confessed to being the organizer of the assassination. She turned pale, but did not lose her self-control, and went walking down the street with the newspaper hanging in her hand, her face to the ground.

Those who saw her at the time say she was still beautiful and was full of a strange, elated tenderness. She was pale, with black rings under her eyes, and her voice, usually clear and sweet, had become a hoarse whisper, but otherwise she was unchanged. She kept talking about plans to rescue Zhelyabov. The conspirators still had secret channels in high places, and Perovskaya seems to have known exactly how far the examinations of Zhelyabov and Rysakov were progressing. Told to leave St. Petersburg and go into hiding, she refused, saying that if she left the city there would be no more hope of rescuing Zhelyabov; and thinking continually of Zhelyabov, so that the assassination of the Emperor and the arrest of Rysakov occupied only a small part of her mind, she was, according to one who knew her well, "like a bird who sees a hawk flying above her head, a hawk which has stolen her young."

We have only one clear glimpse of her in those days. One evening—it must have been March 6 or 7—Perovskaya slipped into Vera Figner's apartment on the Voznessensky Prospekt, and asked whether she could spend the night there. Vera Figner was startled. The conspirators had sworn an oath to help each other. Why, then, should Perovskaya hesitate to ask for so small a thing as a night's lodging?

"I don't understand," Vera Figner said. "Why do you ask?"

"I ask because if the police raid the apartment and find me here, they will hang you as well."

"I have a revolver, and if they come, then I will shoot, whether you are here or not."

Perovskaya was strangely quiet that night. They talked about the past, about Zhelyabov and about the correspondence they were still carrying on with Nechayev. Perovskaya smiled often, but it was a sad little smile, and Vera Figner came to the conclusion that she knew she was doomed and was not even trying to escape. On March 10th the police caught up with her, and a week later they arrested Kibalchich. All of the major conspirators were now accounted for.

In the eyes of the Russian government a conspiracy to kill the Emperor could only come out of the depths. To the surprise of the jurists at the trial, the prisoners formed a cross-section which included all elements in the Russian scene. There was Zhelyabov, born out of the peasantry, though he looked and behaved like a practiced administrator. There was Kibalchich, the son of a priest, with his black beard and dark penetrating eyes, a brilliant scientist who knew as much about explosives and jet propulsion as anyone then living. There was the weak-willed Rysakov, born out of the lower middle classes, though there was a good deal of the peasant in him. Timothy Mikhailov was a laborer, and

Sophie Perovskaya was the pure aristocrat, with the aristocrat's sense of responsibility. Finally there was Gesya Helfman, the daughter of a rich Jewish manufacturer who left her home and deliberately worked as a seamstress in Kiev during the "To the People" movement.

Under arrest, the terrorists behaved according to character. Zhelyabov assumed full responsibility for the assassination and parried all efforts to incriminate others. Kibalchich read scientific treatises, and knowing he would die, did everything possible to see that his scientific theories were carefully considered in scientific circles. Rysakov broke down completely, pled for mercy, incriminated everyone and to the very end hoped he would be allowed to lead a detachment of prison officers to the hiding places of the terrorists who were not yet arrested. Timothy Mikhailov sat quietly in his cell. Gesya Helfman, pregnant with the child of her husband, Nikolai Kolotkevich, did nothing to help the authorities arrest him, and he survived in freedom for a few more months until he was finally arrested. Perovskaya lived only for the moments when she would see Zhelyabov in the courtroom, but she was sufficiently aware of her appearance to ask her family to send her new clothes.

The fighting strength of the *Narodnaya Volya* had been broken, but the movement continued. On March 10 there appeared a long and carefully composed letter written ostensibly by the Executive Committee to the new Emperor Alexander III. The letter, which was actually composed by Tikhomirov, is an important document in the history of the Russian revolutionary movement. Many, perhaps all, of the demands made to the head of the state are applicable to the Russia of today. The letter covers six closely-printed pages in that vast compilation of revolutionary documents known as *Literatura Narodnoi Voli,* and is so important that it is here quoted at considerable length:

A LETTER FROM THE EXECUTIVE COMMITTEE
TO ALEXANDER III

Your Majesty!

While the Executive Committee fully comprehends the deep
sorrow you must feel at the present moment, it does not feel
justified in postponing an explanation simply on the grounds of
natural delicacy. There is something higher than the most legitimate personal sentiments, and this is the duty we owe to our
country, the duty to which all citizens must sacrifice themselves
and their feelings and even the feelings of others. In obedience
to the all-powerful demands of duty, we have decided to address you immediately, not waiting upon events, just as the
whole historical process now threatening us with rivers of
blood and terrible convulsions also refuses to wait upon events.

The bloody tragedy of the Ekaterinsky Canal was not an
accident, nor was it in any way unexpected. The events of the
last decade have made it absolutely inevitable; and herein lies
its deep significance for the man who has been placed at the
head of the government. Such occurrences can be explained as
the result of individual acts of malignity or as the work of
evilly-disposed "gangsters,"* but only by those who are incapable of analyzing the life of a nation. Through the last ten
years we have seen how, in spite of strong persecution and the
denial of all liberties, in spite of the Czar's total lack of interest
in his own dignity and in spite of the absolute sacrifice of
everything in order to suppress the revolutionary movement,
this movement has obstinately extended and has attracted to
itself the best elements of the country, the most energetic and
self-sacrificing people of Russia, and for three years the revolutionaries have carried on a desperate war with the administration.

You must know, Your Majesty, that the government of the
late Emperor was not lacking in energy. It hanged the innocent and guilty among us and filled prisons and remote provinces with exiles. It caught dozens of so-called "revolutionary

* Tikhomirov uses the word "sheiks."

leaders" and hanged them: they died with the courage and tranquillity of martyrs, but the movement did not cease—on the contrary, it grew and strengthened. No, Your Majesty, the revolutionary movement does not owe its existence to individual conspirators. It is a process of the social organism, and the scaffolds raised for the more energetic exponents of this process are as powerless to save the outgrown order of things as the Crucifixion of the Savior was powerless to save the ancient world from the reforming triumphs of Christianity.

The government may well be able to arrest and hang an immense number of individuals. It can suppress a great number of revolutionary groups. It may even destroy the most important of existing revolutionary organizations. But the issues remain unchanged. It is the circumstance of the age that creates revolutionaries, a whole nation's discontent, the urge of all Russia towards new social forms. It is impossible to exterminate a whole nation; it is just as impossible to stifle discontent by repression: discontent flourishes on such a soil. So, whenever a revolutionary dies, his place is immediately taken by others who come out of the people in ever-increasing numbers, but now they are more deeply angered and more energetic than before. In order to carry on the war these people organize themselves on the basis of the experience derived from their predecessors. So the revolutionary movement has grown stronger in numbers and in the quality of its men. And all this is evident from the history of the last ten years . . .

If we look back clearly and dispassionately at those grief-stricken years, we shall be able to prophesy accurately the future progress of the revolutionary movement if the policy of the government remains unchanged. The revolutionary movement will continue to grow and to extend: acts of terrorism will increase in frequency and intensity; the revolutionary organism will constantly be bringing forward new and altogether stronger forms to replace those which have been destroyed. Meanwhile there will be increasing numbers of discontented people in the country: confidence in the government will decline; and the idea of revolution, its possibility and inevitability, will establish itself in Russia more and more firmly. A revolutionary earthquake, a terrible explosion, a tremendous bloody unheaval will complete the destruction of the ancient order.

Upon what, then, depends this terrible and lamentable prospect? Yes, Your Majesty, the words "terrible and lamentable" are written here deliberately—they are not an empty phrase. We understand better than others the lamentable destruction of so much talent and energy—so many losses in bloody skirmishes and in the work of breaking down so much that possessed strength which under better conditions might have been expended in creative labor in developing the intelligence, the welfare, and the social life of the Russian people.

Whence comes this lamentable necessity for bloody conflict?

It comes, Your Majesty, from the lack in Russia of a real government in the true sense of the word. A government in the very nature of things *should give outward form to the aspirations of the people and give effect to the people's will.* But with us—excuse the expression—the government has degenerated into a camarilla and deserves to be called a set of "usurping gangsters," a title more appropriate to the government itself than to the Executive Committee . . .

These are the reasons why the Russian government exerts no moral influence and has no support among the people. These are the reasons why Russia brings forth so many revolutionaries. These are the reasons why the murder of a Czar excites in so many people only joy and sympathy. Yes, Your Majesty, do not be deceived by the reports of flatterers and sycophants—the murder of a Czar is popular in Russia.

There are only two ways out of this state of affairs—Revolution, absolutely inevitable and not to be averted by any punishments, or a voluntary transfer of supreme power to the hands of the people. In the interest of our country and in the hope of averting a useless waste of energy and in the hope of preventing the terrors that always accompany revolutions, the Executive Committee begs Your Majesty to proceed along the second course. Rest assured that as soon as the Supreme Power ceases to rule arbitrarily and accedes to the demands of the people, you may without fear discharge the spies who disgrace your administration, return the guards to their barracks, and burn the scaffolds that are demoralizing the people. At that moment the Executive Committee will voluntarily terminate its own existence and the organizations formed around it will disperse, so that the members may devote themselves to cultural work among the people.

We address Your Majesty as men who have disregarded all prejudices, setting aside the distrust created by the government throughout a century. We forget you are the representative of the authority which has so often deceived and injured the people. We turn to you as a citizen and a man of honor. We trust that no personal bitterness will cause you to forget your duty or extinguish in your mind a desire to know the truth. We too have cause for bitterness. You have lost your father. We have lost fathers, brothers, wives, children, and our dearest friends. We are ready to suppress our personal feelings if the good of Russia demands it. We expect the same from you.

We set no conditions for you: do not therefore allow these propositions to embitter you. The conditions prerequisite for a transfer from revolutionary activity to peaceful labor are not imposed by us, but by history. In our belief there are two conditions:
1. A general amnesty for all political crimes: because they were not crimes, but rather the fulfillment of social duty.
2. The summoning of representatives of all the Russian peoples to consider the existing social and economic order, and so to remodel it in accordance with the people's desires.

But we believe it necessary to remind you that the representatives of the people can come together to legalize the Supreme Power only if the elections are perfectly free. Such elections should be held under the following conditions:
1. Delegates should be sent from all the existing classes of society without distinction, and in number proportionate to the number of inhabitants.
2. Canvassing on the part of the delegates and the elections themselves should be absolutely unrestricted, and therefore the Government, pending the organization of the

National Assembly, should authorize as temporary measures:

a. Complete freedom of the press.
b. Complete freedom of speech.
c. Complete freedom of public meeting.
d. Complete freedom in election programs.

This is the only way in which Russia can return to the path of normal and peaceful development.

We declare solemnly before the people of our country and before the whole world that our party will submit unconditionally to the decisions of a National Assembly elected in this manner, and we will never allow ourselves to offer violent resistance to any Government that the National Assembly may sanction.

And now, Your Majesty, decide. Before you are two courses: you must make your choice between them. We can only beg of fate that your judgment and your conscience will lead you to choose the only course consistent with the welfare of Russia, with your honor and with your duty toward your country.

Tikhomirov had had no contact with the revolutionaries in prison when he wrote his letter to the Emperor, but he had discussed his views with them frequently. The letter, too long for effective propaganda, too short for a revolutionary handbook, and lacking in the grotesque imaginative leaps which make Nechayev's *Revolutionary Catechism* so memorable, achieved the opposite of what Tikhomirov hoped to achieve. The new Emperor read it, and was enraged. Through the whole of his reign he was determined to govern Russia with implacable absolutism.

The Judgment

With the prisoners under arrest the government set about
arranging a trial which would be brief and salutary. Now at
last, having committed their greatest crime, the terrorists
had been rounded up, and they could expect no mercy.
There would be a number of swift executions, followed by
a long silence in which the country, warned of its errors,
would realize that only obedience to the autocracy would
lead to a few small social improvements. The autocracy, instead of being weakened, had been strengthened. Hardly
anyone doubted in court circles that the main strength of the
terrorist movement had collapsed. All over Russia in those
early days following the assassination the grief of the people
was evident. Then gradually the wheel turned full circle,
and soon the memory of the dead Czar as a paternal over-
seer of his people gave place to memories of his excesses:
from being murderers the prisoners became heroes. Zhelyabov and Perovskaya especially were regarded as heroic figures. People recoiled at the thought that these legendary figures should be condemned to hang.

Throughout his life Tolstoy made many pronouncements
concerning the government, but he rarely caught the mood
of the people. One evening, two weeks before the trial, he
threw himself down on the leather sofa of his study and
tried to think out all the implications of the trial and the
inevitable executions. He was tormented by the thought that

the punishment of the prisoners would lead to a hardening of the movement for social reform. Good must be returned for evil; nothing is gained by vindictiveness; only Christian charity can dare to reap a reward. Best to forgive the Czar's murderers: give them money and send them away to America; and if they must be fought, then they should be fought with spiritual weapons. Their fate haunted him. He imagined Sophie Perovskaya standing on the little tabourette underneath the gallows, involuntarily adjusting the noose until the knot lay under her windpipe, "and then when the tabourette was pushed away and the cord pressed the soft gristle of her throat and the hard vertebrae of her neck, she felt a sudden rush of blood to her head and her whole body writhed, and then, slowly suffocating under the black cap, her face turned blue and the eyes popped out of their sockets."

For Tolstoy, as for thousands and perhaps millions of Russians, the fate of Perovskaya was so terrible, so unnecessary and so much a part of the tragedy of the times that he imagined every detail of it long before it happened. He could not forget it. Thinking of Perovskaya, he remembered how he was once attacked by a bear. "I lay under the bear and looked into the large warm mouth with the wet, white, glistening teeth. He breathed over me and I saw him turning his head to get into a position where he could bite into both of my temples at once, and then hurrying or simply because his appetite was excited, he made a trial snap in the air and again opened wide his mouth—that red, wet, hungry mouth, dripping with saliva."

Half-dozing on the sofa, in a waking nightmare, all the tragedy of the trial came to Tolstoy with terrible force: it seemed to him that it was not Alexander III, the judges, and the hangman, who were sentencing Perovskaya to death, but Tolstoy himself. As soon as he awoke he began to write in white heat a letter to the Czar.

In this letter, the most extraordinary that he ever wrote,

Tolstoy begins haltingly, deferentially, hardly knowing to what extremes he would dare to go. He began by announcing himself as an insignificant, weak and worthless person, who lived deep in the country and received news only through the newspapers, and he realized how strange and audacious it was that he should bring himself to advise the Czar. Nevertheless his conscience could not rest. He put aside all flowery introductions and demanded the right to speak to the Czar as man to man. And then he went on at once to beg for an unprecedented act of mercy—the Czar should forgive his father's murderers. There followed an extraordinary outline of the history of the revolutionary movement in which Tolstoy finds himself standing at a point midway between the autocracy and the revolutionaries, judging and excusing both. He wrote:

> There appeared about twenty years ago a group formed mostly of young people who had set their hearts against the existing government. They imagined a new social order, or even no order at all, and by all manner of godless and inhuman means, by incendiarism, robberies and murders, they attempted to destroy existing society. For twenty years there has been war against these people, but instead of dying out, this war only increases in violence, and these people have reached a most terrible state of cruelty, which is indeed harmful to the state.
>
> Those who fought against this plague have employed two methods: one method was to cut out the canker by severe punishments, the other was to allow the disease to follow its course. But there is a third way: that of Christian forgiveness, and this has not yet been employed.
>
> Today, your position is that of a sick man at the height of a critical illness. One false application of remedial measures, one mistake in diagnosis, and the patient will be dead! . . .
>
> By some fatal and terrible error these revolutionaries were the victims of a fearful hatred of your father, and so this outrageous murder was committed. The hate harbored by these

revolutionaries may die with them. As for you, though they die, you are the innocent victim of your exalted position. On your hands is no blood. Nevertheless you stand at the parting of the ways. In a few days it may be that those who believe Christianity is no more than talk, and blood must be spilled and death must reign in the political ways of life—it may be that these men will triumph; and then it will happen that you will pass for ever from that blessed state of purity and life in God and enter into the pathways of state necessity, where everything is justified, even the breaking of the law of God and man . . .

O Monarch, forgive them! Call these people to you: give them money: send them away to America, and let there be written in your hand a manifesto beginning: "I say unto you, 'Love your enemies.'" I do not know how others would feel, but for my part I would become your willing slave! I would weep with emotion every time I heard your name, as I am now weeping! What am I saying? I do not know how others . . . But I *do* know! I know that with these words love will pour like a flood over Russia.

By killing and destroying the revolutionaries you cannot contend against them. It is not only their numbers which are important, but their ideals. To struggle with them without spiritual weapons can lead only to defeat. They demand enough for all, equality and freedom. To contend against them, you must bring forward an even higher ideal. Only the ideal of love, forgiveness, and the return of good for evil is sufficiently strong to contend with them. Should you offer them your forgiveness, then I say that all Russia will melt like wax before the image of the Emperor who follows in the law of Christ.

No one had ever dared to address the Czar in these tones, and Tolstoy was well aware that he would have immense difficulty in bringing the letter to the Czar's attention. He wrote to Pobedonostsev, the Procurator of the Holy Synod, begging him to show the letter to the Czar, and to his friend Strakhov he sent another copy, asking Strakhov to see

that it was put in the hands of Pobedonostsev. But the head
of the Holy Synod, a former tutor of the Czar, refused to
have anything to do with it. Taken by devious routes the
letter was handed to the Grand Duke Sergius, himself to be
assassinated many years later. No reply was received from
the Czar. But Pobedonostsev wrote to the Czar a letter in
which he pleaded that nothing be allowed to interfere with
the executions. In reply Alexander III reassured him: "Be
calm. No one will dare to come to me with such proposals.
I guarantee that all six shall be hanged." But Tolstoy had
dared, and all over Russia there were people who hoped
for an act of forgiveness.

Some weeks after the executions Pobedonostsev wrote
a letter to Tolstoy in which he said: "My Christ is not your
Christ. Mine is a man of strength and truth, healing the
weak; yours has the features of one who is weak-willed and
needs to be cured." It is just possible that the words were
Alexander's message to Tolstoy.

Loris-Melikov originally planned to put Rysakov and
Zhelyabov on trial together. The trial would be very brief,
and followed by immediate execution. But as Rysakov gave
more and more information, and there emerged the hope
that the whole apparatus of the *Narodnaya Volya* might be
rounded up, it was decided to wait. Meanwhile the Czar took
the precaution of absenting himself from St. Petersburg;
the Ruler of All the Russias disappeared to his country pal-
lace at Gatchina, giving orders that trenches should be dug
all round the palace to guard against mining by the revolutionaries. The destruction of the dining-room in the Winter
Palace was still a vivid memory.

The date of the trial was set for March 26. On the day
before, Zhelyabov made an announcement in which he demanded trial by jury and urged that he could not be tried
by the Court of the Senate, which consisted of paid functionaries of the government. He had attacked the Czar as

the head of the government. It was up to the people to decide who was guilty. This was a warning to the authorities
of the attitude he was likely to take; they rejected his demand and discussed the possibility of a summary execution
of the criminals, and then rejected the idea only because they
were afraid of the inevitable popular clamor. A short trial
was best. The evidence must be conclusive, and the prisoners,
though they would be allowed to speak, would be given com-
paratively little opportunity to use the dock as a forum for
expressing their political views.

The prisoners were strangely subdued. They knew they
would be executed. The trial was merely a formality.
Sophie Perovskaya wrote to her mother, asking for cuffs
and collars. Her dress had been torn, presumably in the
struggle at the time of her arrest. She asked that the collars
be rather narrow, and that there should be buttons to her
cuffs. Her mother hurried from the country with the collars
and cuffs and sought from Loris-Melikov permission to visit
her daughter. After deliberately keeping her in the corridor
outside his office, Loris-Melikov at last permitted her to
enter the room. Scowling, he ordered Madame Perovskaya
to obtain from her daughter the names and addresses of her
accomplices, and the old lady answered that it was completely impossible for her to persuade Sophie against her
own convictions. Loris-Melikov was tempted to refuse the
permission she requested, but he finally allowed her to see
her daughter in two brief interviews, with a sentry and police officer in attendance. Neither the mother nor the daughter had much to say to one another. Vera Figner speaks of
how Sophie "lay with her head on her mother's knee like a
sick, tired child, motionless and speechless." Occasionally
they murmured a few words to one another, and once Sophie
said: "I am not your only child, and so you have the others
to care for." After the second interview Sophie wrote to her
mother:

My darling. I implore you to be calm and not to grieve for me. My fate does not affect me in the least and I await it with complete tranquillity. I have long expected it, and known that sooner or later it must come. And then too, my dear mamma, my fate is not such a mournful one. I have lived according to my convictions, and it would have been impossible for me to have done otherwise. So I wait here with a tranquil conscience. The only thing that oppresses me is the thought of your grief, my adored mother. It rends my heart.

The dilemma of the "sensitive murderers" has been expressed at greater length and with more subtlety by others, but until the time of Kaliayev no one ever expressed it so simply or so honestly. When Sophie entered the courtroom there was a small smile playing at the corners of her lips.

The trial began at eleven o'clock on the morning of March 26 in a courtroom packed with officials, the doors locked, the prisoners shackled, the old jurist Fuchs acting as President, sitting with a number of assessors representing the Estates of the Empire—a hand-picked rural headman represented the peasants. The assessors were silent and took no notable part in the trial. Fuchs himself had already received a message from the Czar urging condign punishment for the accused, and though he behaved with strict legality it was clear that he was prepared to obey the Czar's order to the letter.

When the six prisoners were led in, the order they were compelled to assume was significant. First came Rysakov, the weakest. He was followed by Mikhailov, Helfman, Kibalchich, Perovskaya, and Zhelyabov. One by one the prisoners were ordered to state their names, ages, religion, and occupation. At first Zhelyabov refused to answer. He declared that the manner in which the charge had been drawn up was vague and ridiculous, he denied the right of the court to put him on trial and he would refuse to answer questions put to him by hired assessors who would inevitably agree with the government's case. There was a long and involved argument between Zhelyabov and Fuchs. Finally Zhelyabov relented. He would answer questions so long as he was allowed to state his own case. Wearily, the urbane Fuchs allowed him the privilege of stating his case after he had answered the introductory questions:

"What is your name?"

"Andrey Ivanovich Zhelyabov."

"Your age?"

"Thirty."

"Your religion?"

"I was baptized into the Orthodox Church. However, I reject orthodoxy, although I admit the teachings of Jesus Christ—this teaching has an honored place among my moral convictions. I believe in the truth and justice of that teaching, and I solemnly declare that faith without works is dead. I believe that every true Christian should fight for the truth and for the rights of the oppressed and of those who are too weak to assert their rights; and I am prepared to suffer for them. Such is my creed."

The solemn admission of reverence towards the teaching of Jesus startled the assessors. The police dossiers indicated that Zhelyabov was an atheist. Then why this sudden conversion? The question was never answered. The philosopher Berdyaev later confessed to being deeply moved by Zhelyabov's tribute to Christianity. It is possible that Zhelyabov was merely paying a momentary tribute to "that moderate democrat Christ" who was worshipped by Pushkin.

Gaunt, severe, towering above the other prisoners, Zhelyabov behaved in court like an ideal witness. Unlike Nechayev, he stated his case under cross-examination simply, without rhodomontade and with no appeal to the gallery. He was occasionally rebuked by the President, but usually for nothing more serious than a misunderstanding of the law. He admitted he was an agent of the Executive Committee of the

Narodnaya Volya, spoke about the years he had spent in peaceful propaganda among the peasants and told how he had inevitably come to the conclusion that the Russian bureaucracy was the enemy of all social growth. Fuchs demanded a retraction of the statement, but none came. Zhelyabov simply shrugged his shoulders, and was then allowed to continue. He found fault with the charge. The six prisoners in the dock did not form a secret society according to the terms of the indictment, and in any event Mikhailov had nothing to do with the matter. Asked his occupation, he said that for some years his main occupation had been the liberation of his fellow-countrymen.

Muraviev, the Public Prosecutor, informed the Court that he proposed to read the depositions of Colonel Dvorzhitsky and two other witnesses wounded in the explosion. Zhelyabov countered by demanding that depositions be taken from two political prisoners, but the request was ruled out of order on the grounds that political prisoners always distort the issues. The long, involved, and often inaccurate deposition of Dvorzhitsky was read. Inevitably, Dvorzhitsky put himself in the best light, speaking about his honor, his love for the Emperor, and how he had wished that his life had been taken rather than that of the Emperor. Captain Koch was called as a witness. The captain explained at one point that he had had to draw his sword to shield Rysakov from the vengeance of the mob. The claim is unlikely. In any event he had no business defending Rysakov. Zhelyabov pounced on the captain's words and asked for further elucidation. Exactly how and where and against whom had the redoubtable Captain Koch drawn his sword? In the end the captain admitted that he had drawn his sword, but a moment later he had returned it to its sheath, for there had been no occasion to use it.

The examination of nineteen witnesses lasted most of the day. Zhelyabov could not be silenced. He was always jumping up and demanding elucidations, guidance in matters of procedure, quarreling with the President, demanding straight answers to straight questions. An artist in the public gallery made hurried drawings of him. The one reproduced here shows Zhelyabov in a mood of quiet watchfulness and the artist has drawn in the eyes with a heavy pencil, as though to emphasize his alertness, but the same artist made other drawings which emphasize the half-mocking smile, and there is one which shows Zhelyabov as the stern accuser, more like a judge than a prisoner about to be sentenced.

Of the other prisoners only Kibalchich had much to say, and most of what he said was technical. Proud of his knowledge of explosives and of Russia, he protested when the military experts insisted that the bombs were made of some substance imported from abroad, and he referred the military experts to an article in the *Russian Artillery Journal* for August, 1878. There, if they cared to read, they would find the formula for the bomb which had killed the Emperor. And when General Fedorov said that the mine in the Malaya Sadovaya would have torn a hole in the earth twenty feet in diameter, killing anyone walking on the pavement and breaking all the windows of the houses in the street, Kibalchich gave a meticulous lecture on the explosive effects of mines, proving that eighty pounds of high explosive would have done very little damage except to the carriage immediately above the mine—the only danger outside the area would come from falling fragments. The trial droned on. Muraviev was waiting for his great moment, and he could be seen drumming on his table, his eyes lifted to the ceiling. His moment came on the third day, as he launched into an impassioned plea for justice—justice for the present Emperor and for the memory of the dead Emperor "who was martyred in the Calvary of the Ekaterinsky Canal." Zhelyabov laughed at the impassioned oratory, but he would have been well-advised to keep silent, for Muraviev turned upon him, lifted an accusing finger, tossed back his head and said: "A nation mourns, but Zhelyabov laughs and mocks the greatness of the departed." It was the kind of thing Muraviev could do with considerable effect, and like another Cicero pointing to another Catiline he continued to address the Court in long rhetorical passages. He was less concerned with justice than with the majesty of his own rhetoric, until the time came for him to point once more at the benches where the accused were sitting. "Where," he asked dramatically, "shall we find the men who had the audacity to cut down the great oak under whom we all were sheltered? Who killed the Czar? I can answer in a few words. They are there, in front of you, and only condign punishment can wash away the evil they have committed. Let us then root out the venomous weeds; let us have done with them; and then breathing the air of freedom, let us follow in the hallowed footsteps of the One, the Invincible, the Sacred Hope, the August Leader who has succeeded to the Throne!"

Once Muraviev referred to Zhelyabov as a bandit chieftain, which must have seemed improbable even in that court where many improbable statements were being made. He read from Morozov's more violent editorials in the newspaper of the *Narodnaya Volya*—five copies of the newspaper had been found on Zhelyabov when he was arrested, but the Third Division possessed a complete set in their files. Yes, it was all there: Morozov was inciting all Russians to revolt. These despicable intellectuals were not expressing the great things of the soul; on the contrary, they were expounding the sentiments of murderers, thieves, the dregs of society. They were men whose lives must be snuffed out so that good citizens could sleep soundly in their beds. Against the weight of Muraviev's speeches, the defending counsel could do little, and while they spoke Muraviev watched them scornfully, as though he could hardly believe anyone could have the temerity to defend such evident scoundrels.

Gerard, who defended Kibalchich, did his superb best. He spoke quietly about Kibalchich's early years and reminded the government that the scientist had spent three years in prison for giving a harmless book called *The Tale of the Four Brothers* to a peasant. The Trial of the 193 became the major theme of Gerard's defense: the trial was put on trial. Gerard was gravely warned against his references to the police, who had gone about indiscriminately making arrests of innocent students. He was told that the actions of the police were beyond the jurisdiction of the present court.

Then it was Zhelyabov's turn to speak. He had refused the services of counsel and could therefore make a speech in his own defense. The court debated upon the validity of allowing Zhelyabov to defend himself, but he was legally entitled to the right, and Fuchs bowed to the inevitable, after explaining at length to Zhelyabov that he must keep strictly to the point, and the court would not admit a harangue in which Zhelyabov justified his actions by an appeal to political principles. And then Zhelyabov spoke, very quietly at first and then in tones of rising indignation, jerking his head sharply whenever he was interrupted by the President and glowering at the public galleries whenever the *claque* murmured in disapproval. Patiently he explained how the *Narodnaya Volya* had been brought into existence and how the excesses of the government had inevitably brought about the emergence of a terrorist party. He said:

> To understand our present use of weapons, you must understand our history. Our history—for we have a history—is short in years, but rich in experience. Gentlemen of the Court, if you will look into the records of political trials, you will find that the Russian popular parties have not always used bombs, and we too as a Party have had our days of youth and shining dreams. It is not our fault that those days have passed . . .

We have searched for means by which we could help the
people, and we chose to act as common working people propa-
gating our socialist ideas peacefully. This surely was doing no
harm. What happened? We were thrown into prison and sent
into exile. Originally we were an entirely peaceful movement,
we opposed violence, we detested the thought of revolution—
and so we were crushed . . .

Originally there was not one of us who approved of violence, but when I was thrown into prison I became a revolutionary . . . Then we saw that the "movement to the people"
led nowhere, and we looked around us and discovered that
there was much in the Russian popular tradition we could
build on . . . We took to deeds, not words. Action meant using force, but even then we were not convinced of the need
to employ force sternly. So it went on until 1878. Then it was
that we decided to cut the Gordian knot. The movement
which began with the cry "to the people" ended inevitably in
the tragic affair of March 1. Eighteen seventy-eight was the
determining year. That was the year of *A Death for a Death.*°
Circumstances were forcing this conclusion on us, but as for
myself I spent the summer of that year quietly propagandizing
in my village. That winter there was still no solution, and I
spent the next spring in the south—a time of anxiety and dis-
tress . . .

The prosecutor accuses me of killing. But our efforts were
not so narrow: we had other aims. We wanted a revolution,
and we were preparing to form a revolutionary party on the
widest possible scale . . . As for myself, my personal task
was to work for the common good, and when I found I could
not do this by peaceful means, I turned to violence. But I
would willingly abandon violence if there was the least possibility of serving my ideals by peaceful means.

Zhelyabov had hoped to be able to make his speech without interruptions, but the President was continually ordering
him to keep to the point, to speak only of his own actions, to

---

°   The pamphlet written by Kravchinsky (Stepniak) to celebrate the assassination of General Mezentsev.

refrain from any discussion of the party. Zhelyabov found himself talking more and more about the party. Indeed, he could hardly help himself, for he *was* the party.

And then at the end, the defendants were allowed to make their "final statements." Rysakov, terrified, denied that he had ever taken part in the terrorist movement. Timothy Mikhailov mumbled something about his lack of education. He was too nervous to be able to make a clear statement. Kibalchich lectured the prosecutor on the idiocy of solving all government problems by the rope and the knout. There must be social progress and there must be some way in which the aspirations of the people can be expressed. He spoke drily, professorially, and without visible emotion. Gesya Helfman spoke more passionately, but most of her speech was devoted to showing that she was in no way humbled by the prosecutor's charges. Characteristically, Perovskaya was concerned with the good name of the revolutionaries. The prosecutor had charged them with being the dregs of society, living immoral lives, and she answered:

> The prosecutor has hurled a number of charges against us. With regard to his statements of fact I will say nothing: I dealt with them all during the preliminary investigation. But I and my friends have been accused of immorality, cruelty, and contempt for public opinion. Against such charges I must protest. Those who know anything about our lives and the circumstances in which we have had to work, will not reproach us either with immorality or cruelty.

Zhelyabov was allowed to speak once more. He said only that the prosecutor had used his statements for his own ends, twisting them, and now he regretted having spoken in court. In fact, he regretted none of it, and this was his last ironical jab at his accusers.

At midnight the court rose and the prisoners were removed to their cells. At three o'clock in the morning they were brought back to listen to the verdict. All were found guilty, but Rysakov was only nineteen and there were long discussions about whether the death sentence could be applied to a minor. At last the President decided that the death sentence was appropriate even to a minor. The prisoners were then condemned to be hanged. The sentence on Perovskaya, who belonged to the nobility, would be submitted to the Emperor for his approval. The rest were given two days in which to appeal.

The news that the prisoners were condemned to death was published in the newspapers, and the government announced that a vast number of telegrams approving the sentence had been received.

Except for Rysakov who made a last desperate appeal to the Czar and Mikhailov who wrote a reasoned petition, none of the prisoners asked for mercy. After the trial they remained quietly in their cells, receiving visits from lawyers and priests. Kibalchich immersed himself in the problems of flying machines. Zhelyabov read history books and newspapers. Mikhailov read the Bible. Perovskaya was strangely calm and spent her days leaning against the walls of her prison-cell, lost in her dreams. Of the six prisoners the calmest of all was Gesya Helfman who announced three days before the hanging that she was pregnant. A medical commission was immediately appointed by the prison superintendant to examine her. They discovered that she had been pregnant since January, and as a result her death sentence was commuted to imprisonment for life. She lived only until September, 1882, dying insane.

As always in prisons where there are condemned prisoners, the guards caught the mood of quietness and were observed to be especially gentle with their charges. There were clear spring days. Once every morning and again in the afternoon the prisoners were led out into the courtyard. They were allowed to talk to one another for a few moments. At these meetings Zhelyabov and Perovskaya were always together. Afterward it was said that they rarely spoke: it was enough that they should be together.

On the evening of April 2, shortly before eight o'clock, priests entered their cells to receive their confessions and offer the Sacrament, but Perovskaya and Zhelyabov refused to see them and turned their backs to them when they insisted on staying. Timothy Mikhailov confessed, but refused communion. Kibalchich spent more than an hour calmly discussing religion with the priest, but he refused to confess or receive the Sacrament. Only Rysakov, now broken and almost unrecognizable, confessed and received the Sacrament.

According to the guards all the prisoners were asleep by midnight.

At six o'clock in the morning of April 3, when the sun had already risen, the prisoners were awakened. They were given cups of tea and told to dress, and were then taken to the prison waiting-room, where the black clothes they would wear for the execution were laid out for them. These clothes were made in the prison. Drab and shapeless, they were intended to mock the humanity of the prisoners. While putting on her black robe, Perovskaya broke down. Timothy Mikhailov found her weeping a few minutes later and said: "Keep your chin up, Sophie." She brightened, smiled, and paid no more attention to the shabby black dress which resembled a vast maternity gown. A few moments later a prison official was placing large oblong placards, held up by a string round their necks, against their chests. The placards, on which the word "Czaricide" was written in black ink which had run, so giving the appearance of dripping black blood, were made of thin sheets of wood. Exactly similar placards were tied round the necks of prisoners sentenced to death for high treason in the middle ages.

In the prison courtyard the tumbrels were waiting. They were ordinary springless peasant carts on which a kind of platform had been constructed. The prisoners were made to sit on benches on the high platform, their backs to the horses. They were handcuffed, their hands behind their backs, and their feet fettered. In the first cart were Zhelyabov and Rysakov, the man who had organized the assassination and the one who had thrown the fatal bomb. Rysakov kept looking at Zhelyabov, but though they were chained close together, Zhelyabov pretended to be completely unaware of Rysakov's existence. In the second cart Perovskaya sat between Mikhailov and Kibalchich.

The prison gates opened a few minutes before eight o'clock, and the small procession came out into the warm spring air. The two tumbrels were followed by a carriage with priests, and then in turn by a cart with five unpainted coffins. Behind these came part of the military escort. Some Cossacks rode beside the carts, and beside the tumbrels marched the drummers who were ordered to drown out any speeches made by the prisoners to the crowds in the streets. Troops lined the approaches to the vast Semeonovsky Square, where the scaffold had been erected since early the previous evening.

Many stories were told of the slow journey from the prison to the Semeonovsky Square, and the behavior of the prisoners. Vera Figner tells the story that when Perovskaya was being lifted onto the cart, her hands were tied behind her back so tightly that she complained: "'Loosen the cords a little, they hurt me." The guard is supposed to have replied: "You'll feel worse in a little while." It seems unlikely. Vera Figner also tells the story of how later in the morning she sat next to a well-dressed young man on a tramcar and noted the gleam of excitement in his eyes, and how everyone in St. Petersburg reflected in some way an awareness of the terrible joy which comes over people who have watched prisoners going to their deaths. All eyes were on Perovskaya. They watched her silently and with compassion, admiring her composure, yet admitting the inevitability of her execution. The correspondent of the *Kölnische Zeitung* noted that Kibalchich and Zhelyabov were very calm, Timothy Mikhailov was pale but firm, Rysakov liver-colored, and Perovskaya's cheeks were still rosy and she still looked beautiful. None except Mikhailov attempted to address the crowd, and Mikhailov's voice was soon drowned by a roll of drums.

That morning there was a misty white haze, and the first thaw was beginning, the streets gleaming silver with puddles of melted snow. All of St. Petersburg seemed to be in the streets along the route to the Semeonovsky Square, and in the square itself over 80,000 people were assembled.* The scaffold stood at the dead center of the square. It consisted of two uprights and a crossbeam with six hooks dangling beneath, set on a large wooden platform about four feet high and solidly built. Everything, the scaffold, the platform and the steps leading up were painted black. There were railings along one edge of the platform and three wooden posts were set securely at some distance from the scaffold, with manacles and chains already attached. Foot Guards and Cossacks were drawn up in ranks around the platform, and there were Cossacks distributed all over the square. The drummers stood immediately below the scaffold.

The executioner was a drunken ex-prisoner called Frolov, famous for bungling. He was short and squat, with a heavy red face; he resembled a punch-drunk boxer. He had been waiting there, testing the ropes with the help of his assistants, since half past seven. He had a good deal of time, for

* On a similar platform, and in the same square, Dostoyevsky with twenty other condemned members of the Petrashevsky circle were placed against a firing squad on December 22, 1849. The death sentence was read to them, they were given the cross to kiss, daggers were broken over their heads, and they were made to wear white shirts in the place of shrouds. At the last moment, after the prisoners' eyes had been bandaged, a messenger bounded up with a rescript declaring that the Czar had granted them their lives.

the tumbrels containing the prisoners did not arrive until half past eight and it was three-quarters of an hour later before the first prisoner was brought to the gallows.

When the tumbrels rolled into the square, a huge murmur rose from the crowd. The prisoners were taken down from the carts. Zhelyabov, Perovskaya, and Mikhailov were chained to the three wooden posts, while Kibalchich and Rysakov were chained to the railings. The long sentences were read out. Zhelyabov and Perovskaya were seen to be whispering together. The drums were muffled. The reading of the sentences included a summary of the crimes, and took nearly half an hour. There were other formalities to be observed: documents were signed by men in frock coats and top hats who stood beside a table and seemed in no hurry to conclude the entertainment. The five priests who had visited the cells the previous evening climbed onto the platform and held out crosses to the prisoners who kissed the crosses, received the priests' blessing and then watched the priests descend from the platform. Zhelyabov's long hair was blowing in the wind. The executioner removed their chains. It was the time for their last farewells, before the white cowls were slipped over their heads. Handcuffed, his feet fettered, Zhelyabov moved across the platform towards Perovskaya and kissed her. He was followed by Kibalchich and Mikhailov. Rysakov then came toward Perovskaya, but she turned her head away. His dark face grew darker and he was trembling with fear. Then all five were placed under the gallows, the cowls were fastened over their heads, and Frolov removed his coat.

The order of the hanging was deliberately designed: those who had committed the greatest crimes in the eyes of the government were to be hanged last.

Kibalchich was the first to climb on the tabourette, the rope already fastened round his neck through a slit in the cowl. Frolov pushed the tabourette away, and at the same moment there came a loud and prolonged roll of drums. Kibalchich died quickly, without struggling, and apparently without any pain. It was now Mikhailov's turn. He was heavily built, taller than Zhelyabov, and he may have hoped his weight would bring about a merciful quick death. He had been hanging for a minute when the rope broke. He fell on his face on the platform. He was still alive, still conscious. Because his hands and feet were tied, he could not lift himself up. The crowd screamed. Some of them were shouting: "Glory to God!" believing a miracle had occurred, for it was impossible to believe that the executioner could proceed with the hanging. Frolov lifted him up. It was observed that Mikhailov still had enough strength to mount the tabourette unaided. Then the tabourette was kicked away again, and he hung for a minute and a half on another rope until this, too, broke. He fell on his chest. The crowd was appalled. "Poor Russia!" someone shouted, and this time the crowd began to shout out to the high functionaries on the platform, saying he must be released, the farce could not be continued, it was time they showed mercy. For a few brief moments the crowd began to sway and jostle and quiver as though it was preparing to rush the protective ranks of the guards. Mikhailov was still conscious, but he could not walk any more and had to be lifted onto the tabourette. Frolov ran another length of rope to the hook intended for Gesya Helfman. With two ropes round Mikhailov's neck there was a chance that he could be hanged finally. Frolov was standing on a ladder. The ladder teetered. Among the crowd of high officials on the platform were three or four who murmured in disgust, but mostly they were silent, nervous, afraid of the crowd and still more afraid of the punishments the Czar would inflict on them if the executions were bungled. The third hanging was successful, though for some minutes Mikhailov writhed in terrible convulsions. When a military doctor protested, Frolov turned on him and began cursing.

It was then Perovskaya's turn. Because she was shorter than the others, she looked very frail even in her heavy shrouds as she was led to the tabourette. A great sigh went up among the crowd when the tabourette was kicked away. The convulsions were very brief, and she died almost as quickly as Kibalchich. Zhelyabov died slowly. Frolov had taken the precaution of tying a double knot in the noose. Zhelyabov's convulsions seemed endless.

To the very end Rysakov had hoped for a pardon. More nervous than the others he was seen to jump up and down and to hop from one leg to the other as he stood on the platform. When Frolov indicated that his time had come, he screamed and somehow dug his feet behind the railings and had to be pulled away. He was struggling up to the moment when the tabourette was kicked away, but his convulsions were brief.

By half past nine there was no longer any sign of life in the five white-hooded bodies hanging from the crossbeam. The sun burned through the morning haze, shining on the sea of faces. Then the bodies were taken down, the doctors examined them and signed the death certificates and the prefect announced that justice had been done. By 9:58 the bodies had been loaded onto two waiting carts, to be driven to the railway station, and two minutes later the prefect gave the order for the scaffold to be torn down. With a pair of scissors, Frolov was snipping off short lengths of rope to be sold to the highest bidders.

The bodies were taken to the Preobrazhensky cemetery. There, many years later, a caretaker pointed to an abandoned corner thick with rubble and weeds and said that Zhelyabov and Perovskaya were somewhere underneath. Today there is no one who knows where they are.

The history of the *Narodnaya Volya* ends with the hanging of the conspirators who brought about the assassination of Alexander II. For a few more years the party survived. There were more assassinations and more desperate attempts on the part of Tikhomirov to hammer out a policy of revolutionary action, but with the arrest of Zhelyabov and Alexander Mikhailov the party lost its two greatest leaders and never recovered its power. Mikhailov was imprisoned in the Peter and Paul Fortress: and it was perhaps no accident that he died in the famous cell number 1 in which Nechayev died. Dr. Wilms wrote in his medical report on March 18, 1884: "The prisoner Alexander Mikhailov died at twelve this morning of inflammation of the lungs and edema."

On April 29, 1881, the new Emperor Alexander III issued a manifesto in which he announced the end of all reforms:

> In the midst of Our grief the voice of God commands Us to stand bravely at the helm of government, trusting in Divine Providence and with faith in the power and truth of the Absolutism We are called upon to defend; and We are determined to strengthen the State against any attempts to weaken Our power, and this We do for the benefit of Our people.

Alexander was saying no more than his ancestor, the Emperor Nicholas I, who addressed a manifesto to Europe, beginning: "Submit yourselves, ye peoples, for God is with Us."

All power was now concentrated in the hands of the autocracy. The revolutionaries were weary and could no longer fight back with their old strength. The murder of Alexander II was like a vast explosion that had exhausted their energies. They needed time to prepare a new onslaught on the dynasty. At the end of his classic account of his life as a minor revolutionary Vladimir Debogori-Mokrievich wrote sadly that he could see no hope of any more organized outbreaks: "It seems to me that from 1881 onward the Russian revolutionary movement went into a decline. Men cannot endure to live in a state of perpetually mounting excitement. They cannot perpetually be asked to sacrifice themselves for the revolution, for such sacrifices demand spiritual resources which are not met with every day."

Twenty-two years later the Social Revolutionaries, who had inherited the program of the *Narodnaya Volya,* once more introduced the weapons of terrorism against the autocratic state.

S A Z A N O V   photographed in prison

SAZONOV

The savages are coming into their own. For ourselves there is only one task: to stand up to them, to fight every act of human degradation and every dishonor.

The Attack Renewed

In the early spring of 1904 a wealthy "Englishman" settled in a small apartment in St. Petersburg with his mistress, valet, and cook. The apartment was on the first floor of a house in Zhukovsky Street owned by an elderly German widow who lived on the floor above. The "Englishman" had selected the house with considerable care. It had a wide view of the street, and there were two separate ways of escape from the back. He called himself Charles Harley, carried himself well, wore immaculate clothes and spoke Russian with a pronounced English accent. Every morning the porter brought him his mail, and the landlady, who was sometimes able to thumb through the mail before it reached him, observed that it consisted of business letters from abroad and catalogues containing announcements of the latest models of bicycles and automobiles. The landlady was well content with her tenants, and she would talk delightedly to her neighbors about the satisfaction of serving an Englishman who had answered her advertisement in the *Novoye Vremya.*

Every morning at the same hour the business man set out with his portfolio to his office in the center of St. Petersburg. Every evening he returned to the supper his mistress had prepared for him. The landlady, who spent half her life on the stairs eavesdropping on her tenants, observed their affectionate greeting. They were evidently deeply in love with one another. During the day she occasionally found a pretext for entering the rooms and would talk to the girl about the handsome Mr. Harley who spoke Russian with a formidable accent. She was a little puzzled. Mr. Harley possessed all the virtues—he was rich, suave, and dignified—but he was living in sin. She wondered why he refused to marry the girl. Had Mr. Harley given her any jewelry? Had he deposited money in her name in the bank? When the girl replied that he had done none of these things, and she was deeply in love with him and wanted nothing except his love, the landlady began to speak of a German wine-merchant who might be inclined to offer her marriage, jewelry, and a safe-deposit box. Then the girl laughed and explained that she wanted nothing in life but "my Charles" and the freedom to continue her singing lessons.

The landlady made inquiries about the valet and the cook. The cook, Daria Kirilovna, was an old, bent, peasant woman with a deeply lined weather-beaten face. She hovered between the kitchen and the porter's lodge, rarely going out. She liked warming her old bones by the kitchen stove; the porter spent most of his spare time with her; she had a fund of old jokes and stories, and suffered from heart trouble. Jacob, the valet, also spent a good deal of his time in the lodge, though in the mornings he would often accompany his mistress on shopping expeditions. He was tall, red-cheeked, dark-haired, and he laughed easily. He was twenty-five, but looked twenty. He treated the "Englishman" with the exaggerated respect required of valets and spoke of "the great affairs which my master is accomplishing in the business world." He hinted that very soon factories producing bicycles and automobiles would be built in St. Petersburg and he hoped his master would allow him to work in the factories "because it is necessary that men should improve themselves." The landlady had a particular fondness for Jacob. Skilful with his hands, he could be called upon to mend a leaking pipe. He had bushy eyebrows, and when he laughed his eyebrows would shoot up and he gave an impression of extraordinary enjoyment of the world around him.

Sometimes in the evenings the "Englishman" dismissed his servants, who went off on their own errands. A *droshky* would be waiting for him, and soon he would come down the narrow stairway with his mistress on his arm, explaining that he was attending a dinner given by one of his business associates or a ball offered by one of the princes he had met in the course of his business affairs. When the *droshky* had passed down the street, the landlady let herself in the apartment with a pass-key. It amused her to wander through the deserted apartment. There were photographs in silver frames, the piano stood near the window, English books filled the bookcases, and on Mr. Harley's desk in a corner of the living room lay the neat piles of his correspondence, and in the drawer below lay his British passport stamped in blue and gold. Once when the police called and inquired about Mr. Harley, the porter replied: "Are you fools? He is a rich English business man, and if you annoy him you'll hear about it from the British Embassy."

The British Embassy knew about the existence of Mr. Harley, but they would not have recognized this particular Mr. Harley. At the moment the passport had been borrowed by the revolutionary Boris Savinkov, who was being hunted by the Russian secret police. There was a price of ten thousand rubles on his head. Savinkov was a little alarmed by the price. He thought he was worth at least a hundred thousand rubles.

In the ménage which he kept at 31 Zhukovsky Street, nothing was what it seemed to be. His twenty-four-year-old mistress was not his mistress. She was an expert on explosives, a student of medicine, and a dedicated revolutionary. Her name was Dora Vladimirovna Brilliant, and she was the daughter of a rich Jewish family from the Chersonese. Pale and slight, with dark hair and enormous black eyes, she had been studying obstetrics with the desire to serve as a registered midwife in a remote village until she decided she could serve the world better as a terrorist. She had been living in a student garret in St. Petersburg when Savinkov found her, undernourished, earning a precarious living by singing at the café-concerts, absorbed in terrorist activities which never came to anything, with sticks of dynamite and gelignite in her battered suitcase. She had worked with passionate intensity in her garret; she worked with the same passionate intensity in her fashionable apartment.

As for the old cook with the kerchief round her head, she was better known among revolutionaries as Praskovia Ivanovskaya. She had been sentenced to long terms of imprisonment, had been exiled to Siberia and had spent forty of her sixty years in revolutionary activity. She was the link with the past, with the great days of the eighties when the nihilists had first emerged to threaten the government with terror. No one seeing her as she clambered slowly up and down the stone staircase would have guessed the power she still wielded in revolutionary circles.

The landlady was always trying to find a legitimate husband for Dora Brilliant. She was also concerned to find a good wife for Jacob, the valet, who was well paid and remarkably pleasing to women. Half the servant girls in the house were finding excuses to go to the porter's lodge, where Jacob could often be found sitting round the wood fire.

Jacob's real name was Yegor Sergeyevich Sazonov. He was twenty-five. He had already spent a year and a half in the Butyrky prison, had been exiled to eastern Siberia for five years, and escaped to Switzerland. He was eighteen when he came to Moscow to study medicine at the University. Like

Dora Brilliant he had hoped to become a village doctor, serving the peasants.

As a student Sazonov showed no interest in revolutionary activity. A monarchist, deeply religious, he hung ikons and portraits of the Czar on his walls in Moscow. His father was a rich lumber merchant, eminently respectable, a future town councillor. "Pay no attention to the young hot-heads at the University," his father warned him. He was an obedient son. He argued with the hot-heads and demonstrated a lofty indifference to their discussions of the coming revolution. During his second year at the University he called himself an "aesthete" and proclaimed that he was interested only in the good and the beautiful. But in 1901 the students declared a strike. Several hundred were herded into the huge courtyard of the Riding School and turned over to the mercy of mounted Cossacks who flogged them with knouts. Some girl students were outraged. Sazonov was caught up in the strike, thrown into prison, expelled from the University and banished to his native town, where he was held under police surveillance. In prison he read revolutionary literature for the first time. He was seething with hatred, his mind made up. "My friends know well," he wrote, "with what difficulty I have reached my present conclusion. It is not easy to reject the fundamental laws of humanity, but I have been forced to it. From now on I dedicate myself to open warfare with the government and I know that once decided upon my course, I shall go on to the end." In Ufa he instituted study classes in his home. The police swooped down on him. The man dedicated to revolution was once more in prison. As he sat in the porter's lodge, his hair cropped short, his red face and his hazel eyes merry with laughter, he sometimes paused and stared into space. At such times he was thinking about Siberia and the desperate deeds he was determined to accomplish. By his own calculation he had only a few more weeks to live.

The four revolutionaries living in the heart of the fashionable quarter of St. Petersburg were surprised by their luck. No one had penetrated through their disguise. They spent long hours hiding behind the curtains and looking out on the dimly-lit snow-covered street, and they discussed at interminable length the problem of maintaining their disguise. Savinkov would discuss with the instinct of a master the exact way in which Sazonov was to accept the tips which he, Savinkov, would grandiloquently toss into the porter's lodge the next day. Dora Brilliant had no liking for finery—she liked to wear black cotton dresses and low-heeled shoes—and Savinkov, as part of his revolutionary duty, set about teaching her to wear perfume and to put curlers in her hair. He was the same age as Sazonov, but looked older. He wore a small dark mustache under a long aristocratic nose, and there were pouches under his eyes. He wore a monocle. His hair was brushed straight back from the forehead, and he walked a little stiffly and pompously, as befitted a young Englishman with so many business interests. One evening he saw some plain-clothes men standing on the opposite side of the street. He gave the signal for immediate evacuation and then relented. There was something strange about the behavior of the plain-clothes men. They stood there in the snow, very brazen, making no effort to conceal themselves. They remained there for a week. Savinkov wondered whether the police had invented a new form of torture. Then one evening, while Sazonov was sitting in the porter's lodge, he saw the familiar face of the lawyer V. V. Bernshtam coming through the gate, followed by the plain-clothes men. Sazonov's heart went to his mouth. He was sure they had come to make an arrest. Later he learned that the lawyer was simply visiting another lawyer in the house. Both lawyers were under suspicion, because they were visited by students and were known to possess considerable libraries. But the police seemed satisfied after a desultory inspection, and soon they left. The conspirators breathed a sigh of relief.

The main task assigned to the band around Savinkov was to kill the Minister of the Interior, Count Von Plehve, then at the height of his power. Von Plehve was responsible for the *pogrom* at Kishinev, the arbitrary arrest of thousands of young students, and he was identified with the actions of the secret police. With his heavy bland Germanic face, his thick eyebrows, his heavily-lidded eyes, his *pince-nez*, and his horde of mistresses, he represented the accumulated power of the reaction. Kill him, and the whole power of the reaction might be destroyed.

The conspirators went about their work quietly. They were in contact with half a dozen other revolutionaries in St. Petersburg. These others were mainly scouts. The conspirators regarded themselves as the striking force. Dora Brilliant and Sazonov were each determined to be Von Plehve's murderer.

Savinkov had no illusions about the difficulty of killing the Minister of the Interior. Von Plehve was surrounded by armies of police spies and special agents, and had spent many years combatting terrorists. Behind his bland face he concealed an extraordinarily quick mind and unusual cunning. When he drove through the streets, it was always at a reckless speed.

"The only way we shall ever kill him," Sazonov suggested one day, "is by throwing ourselves under the carriage with the bombs."

The idea was characteristic of Sazonov, whose hatred of the Minister had increased from the moment when he was sentenced to Siberia. He told himself he could not live in the same world as Von Plehve, and spoke of hearing voices which whispered: "Strike him, strike him!" during those long days when he made his way back from his Siberian prison. He said: "I could not live in peace any more. When

I thought of all the things he had done to Russia, I felt that any ordinary life would be alien to me. I must kill him or be killed by him."

Savinkov quickly rejected the idea of allowing Sazonov to throw himself under Von Plehve's carriage. He wanted to move cautiously. The scouts reported on all the Minister's movements. They knew at exactly what hour he left his house on Aptekarsky Island in the north of St. Petersburg. They knew when he arrived at the Ministry of the Interior on the Fontanka. They knew every detail of his Thursday morning journeys to the Czar at Tsarskoe Selo. They knew when he attended cabinet meetings at the Marinsky Palace. Savinkov, Sazonov, Dora Brilliant, and Ivanovskaya acted as their own scouts, and were helped by three resourceful assistants, Dulebov, Kaliayev, and Matzeyevsky; to this group the young Borishansky was added a little while later.

Of these assistants the one closest to Sazonov was Yegor Dulebov, a twenty-four-year-old peasant from the railway shops in Ufa. He had already made his mark in revolutionary circles, for in May, 1903, he was one of the two members of the Socialist Revolutionary Party who shot and killed Bogdanovich, the Governor of Ufa. Bogdanovich had given orders to his troops to fire on strikers. Twenty-eight had been killed, and some two hundred wounded, and it was inevitable that the Terrorist Brigade should order his execution. Dulebov had been chosen for the task because of his sense of dedication. He had written a long letter on the night before the killing, justifying the action, saying that he had prayed all his life for an opportunity to do good to his fellow men, and now at last he had been given the privilege he desired above all others. At Ufa he had worked as a locksmith, but after the assassination he wandered around Russia, always in hiding, and sometimes the revolutionary organization lost track of him. There was talk of sending him abroad, but he explained that he was a peasant and there was nothing he could do for the revolution while abroad. He talked the same language as Sazonov, whose workingmen's study circles he had attended at Ufa. Both were determined, relentless, and experienced revolutionaries.

Yosip Matzeyevsky and Ivan Kaliayev had less experience. They were both excitable, and at first sight lacked the heroic qualities of Dulebov and Sazonov. Matzeyevsky and Dulebov acted as drivers. They had cabs and were continually driving through the streets of St. Petersburg in the hope of coming upon the Minister's carriage, while Kaliayev acted as a peddler, wearing drab clothes and carrying a tray slung over his shoulders. In the tray there would be apples, pencils, writing paper. As a peddler, in full command of the peddler's jargon, Kaliayev was more useful to the organization than the two cab drivers. He could go anywhere, join any crowds, wander right up to the edge of the Minister's palace. He grew a beard. With his shambling gait and his burst of quick laughter whenever he made a sale, he was popular among the other peddlers. It was Kaliayev who usually learned first about any change in Von Plehve's movements. Writing about him later, Savinkov said: "He would observe the most minute changes in the streets. He could tell just by a change in the atmosphere, whether Von Plehve was on his way. He could see whether the Minister was coming by the way the policemen were standing, by the way they grouped themselves together, or simply by the way they looked at one another. He had an almost mystical understanding of what was passing through Von Plehve's mind. He described everything: the footboards, the door handles, the harness, the lamps, the coach box, the axles, and if there was any change in these, he would deduce the reasons for the change. And he knew the names and the appearance of the police spies who always congregated around the Minister."

In all this Kaliayev had an advantage over the other scouts. The cab drivers were always being moved on by the police or having to accept fares. Savinkov himself had to be careful. He was the businessman interested in automobiles and bicycles, and therefore kept close to the business part of the city. Ivanovskaya hobbled around, too old and too ill to help them watch Von Plehve's movements. Dora Brilliant spent most of her time in the apartment on Zhukovsky Street, though she would make occasional forays abroad.

Life in the apartment on Zhukovsky Street continued as before. None of the minor conspirators ever visited it. They lived at widely separated places in St. Petersburg. Kaliayev, for example, lived with four other young peddlers in a single room in a tenement. But occasionally life in Zhukovsky Street was disturbed by the arrival of important visitors from abroad. Among them was Evno Azev, who stayed there for ten days in the early spring. To the landlady it was explained that he was a distant relative who was visiting the city on matters of business.

Of all the revolutionaries the plump, round-shouldered Azev, with his gray eyes and swarthy yellowish cheeks, thick lips and large square teeth, was the most unprepossessing. In theory he was in command of the Terrorist Brigade, receiving his powers from the Executive Committee of the Socialist Revolutionary Party. He leaned heavily on the advice of Savinkov, but no attempt at assassination took place unless he was fully warned, and unless the full details of the attempt were explained to him. He selected the targets and decided which revolutionaries should take part in the attempt. He supplied money, revolvers, and dynamite. All the time he was a paid agent of the Czarist police, his sympathies divided between the autocracy and the revolution. For no reason which anyone has ever discovered, it pleased him to play with the hunters and the hunted. He disliked Von Plehve, and therefore put no obstacles in the way of the as-

sassination attempt; he seems to have liked Stolypin and
Dubassov, with the result that attempts on their lives failed,
for the police received prior warning. Power amused him;
he had the conjuror's delight in performing continual
miracles, standing in front of the mirror, admiring himself,
knowing that a single mistake would mean death.

Gorky described Azev in a short story called *Karamora* as a
man who played the double game "simply for the sake of
variety," and so it may have been. When Azev visited the
house in Zhukovsky Street, he was already a legendary character, a man who had supervised a host of attacks upon government officials. Sazonov and Savinkov trusted him completely. It was Azev who insisted that bombs must be thrown,
and he refused to tolerate any plan which involved knives or
revolvers. He dismissed out of hand Sazonov's idea of throwing himself with the bomb under the carriage. No, the
proper way was the simplest: four terrorists walking forty
paces apart. The first was to cut off the Minister's retreat,
the second was to throw the bomb, the third would throw
another bomb if the other failed, the fourth was to throw
his bomb only in case of dire necessity. With luck the first
and fourth would survive the attack and be able to report
to headquarters. They must come to the help of a terrorist
if he was attacked, but it was unlikely that they would be
needed for throwing bombs. Azev explained that he would
send the bombs just before the attack. Shortly afterward
nearly all the conspirators left St. Petersburg. Their plans
were laid. It was necessary that the enemy should be
unconscious of their existence. Azev and Sazonov went to
the Volga. Savinkov went to Sestroretsk, a watering
place along the coast northwest of St. Petersburg, where
there was a small armament factory and immense rolling
parks laid out in the English fashion. Ivanovskaya made her
way to Vilna, and there soon afterward all the conspirators
came together for their last reunion before the attack on the

Minister. Here Azev would give them their final instructions.

The terrorists spent a week in Vilna. "In a small dimly-
lit room," Ivanovskaya recalled, "sat thoughtful men whose
fate was already sealed, exchanging trivialities. Azev alone
seemed calm, attentive, and unusually kind." When it was
time for them to return to St. Petersburg, Azev kissed them
farewell. Years later, when the terrorists placed him on trial
and accused him of being an *agent provocateur*, Azev said:
"Believe me, when I kissed Sazonov, it was not the kiss of
Judas."

The house in Zhukovsky Street had been given up. All
the details were agreed upon. The terrorists knew where to
meet and how to dispose of the bombs immediately after
the attack and where they should go if they survived. Azev
had vanished, but everyone else was back in St. Petersburg. It was decided that Von Plehve should be killed on
July 8, 1904, when he was on his way early in the morning
to the Baltic Station for the journey to Peterhof, where the
Czar had his summer palace on the shores of the Gulf of
Finland. Three days earlier they had been joined by
a new recruit, a young leather worker from Byelostok called
Schimel Leiba Vulfovich Sikorsky. He spoke Russian badly;
he was awkward and thin-boned; he had a shock of dark hair
which fell over his small forehead; but he had long ago decided to offer his life for the revolution. As a Jew he detested
Von Plehve; as a Pole he detested the Czar. Borishansky
knew him well and vouched for his courage. He was to be
given the fourth place in the line. Kaliayev was to go first,
followed by Sazonov and Borishansky. Dulebov was placed
in charge of the bombs and would distribute them at the
proper time.

For some reason which was never made clear Sazonov
failed to receive his bomb in time. Von Plehve's familiar
carriage drove past on its way to the Baltic Station, no one

suspecting that an attack had been averted by a failure in timing. It was decided to repeat the attempt a week later on the occasion of Von Plehve's next journey to Peterhof. There was another meeting in Vilna, another leavetaking with Azev, and then the conspirators returned to St. Petersburg.

On July 15, a few minutes before nine o'clock, on a bright summer's day, Sazonov hurled the bomb.

The Death of a Minister

In those days the streets of St. Petersburg always seemed to
have an air of emptiness, except in the evenings and the
early mornings when people hurried to their business. But
this morning the streets were crowded with policemen. Some
were disguised as beggars, others as officials. There were policemen on horseback, in uniform, and in plain clothes. At
every turning in the road a plain-clothes man was waiting.

Savinkov was appalled by the number of policemen in the
street. Someone had evidently warned the police of an imminent attack on Von Plehve. He caught a glimpse of Sazonov's beautiful quick loping stride as he hurried along the
Ismailovsky Prospekt, his brass buttons shining, his peaked
cap a little to one side over an expressionless face. Sazonov was carrying something in the crook of his elbow. For
a moment he disappeared from sight, then Savinkov saw him
again, still striding along in the direction of the railway
station—a railwayman late for his work, and no one would
ever have guessed otherwise. He did not look worried,
though in fact he was more perturbed than he had ever
been. He was afraid someone would nudge him. A quick
shove, and the bomb would fall to the ground. He was forever making little dancing steps to avoid contact. Once
he saw a plain-clothes detective bearing down on him, but
he quickly disappeared into the crowd.

Savinkov was still keeping a close watch, trailing behind.

By now the police were alert. In the sudden excitement two things were evident: someone had warned the police, and the Minister's carriage would soon be coming down the road. People were being searched. At street corners especially the police were watchful. They asked questions and motioned people down alleyways where they could be searched more efficiently. There was that trembling in the air which announced the coming of an important personage. It was as though even the buildings were suddenly alert and watchful. Savinkov caught a last glimpse of Sazonov hurrying over the bridge which soars over the Obvodny Canal; there was the gold band round his railway porter's cap glinting in the sun, and then he was gone.

"We're too late," Savinkov muttered. "We should have come out earlier, and prepared better."

A moment later Von Plehve's black carriage with the two black horses came bowling down the street. The liveried coachman, wearing a top hat and a cockade, sat in the driving seat. The coach, like the coaches of all the Ministers and Court officials, was armored with thin steel plates. The coach was heavy and possessed remarkable momentum. The police were saluting smartly. Occasionally Von Plehve would bow at the people in the street, but mostly he held himself stiffly, very stern and upright, his white face gleaming in the dark interior of the coach. Near the back wheel a secret-service man on a bicycle was peddling furiously. Another cab came up in the rear, filled with detectives. The police were saluting smartly and the Minister's coach was slowing down because a *droshky* had swung into the road.

Kaliayev was crossing the bridge when he saw Sazonov disappearing in the crowd. Savinkov had already lost track of him.

It was impossible to imagine that Sazonov would ever emerge from the crowd to toss the bomb. Intoxicated with failure, Savinkov decided that there was nothing further to

be done; he would meet Sazonov according to arrangements
in the Yusupov Gardens and he would himself kill the Minister on his return from Peterhof. But a few moments later he
saw, as in a dream, a tall man in the blue uniform of a railwayman darting out of the crowd in front of Von Plehve's
carriage. Sazonov's timing was fantastically accurate. He
stood in the middle of the street with the bomb poised in
his hand and he waited for the carriage to swerve past him.
In that brief instant he recognized Von Plehve, and it seems
that Von Plehve recognized that he was about to be attacked, for he suddenly changed his position. Then Sazonov
flung the bomb straight at the carriage-window. It seems to
have exploded on Von Plehve's lap. There was the sound of
a steel plate shuddering under a hammer blow. Sazonov remembered nothing more, for he was thrown ten feet in the
air by the force of the explosion.

From his vantage point on the brow of the bridge Kaliayev watched a thin sulphur-yellow cloud, black at the edges,
rising from the place where the carriage had been. He heard
the clatter of broken glass from a thousand neighboring
windows. There was no sign of Sazonov or of Von Plehve;
the carriage itself had been shattered into fragments, with
only some sticks and fragments of the wheel-hoops still attached to the shafts. The crowd was screaming. Everyone
was running away. The horses, wounded in the explosion,
were driving madly across the street, dragging the smashed
wheels with them, and soon they made straight for the
bridge. The thin column of sulphur-yellow smoke puffed
out and filled the width of the street; it was like a curtain
drawn over the death of the Minister.

Savinkov was inquisitive. He wanted to see exactly what
had happened. If he went straight up to the place where the
explosion had occurred, he would be reasonably safe, for
hundreds of curiosity seekers, who at first had run away,
were now returning to look for souvenirs. Someone was

shouting: "Don't run up there! There may be another explosion!" The words suggested that Von Plehve had escaped. Everyone knew that the terrorists worked in pairs, and if the first bomb failed, there was always a second in reserve. There was a stiff wind and the smoke was being winnowed away. Passing the Warsaw Hotel, Savinkov observed that the crushed remnants of the carriage were burning fiercely. This, too, was unexpected: from the force of the explosion he had hardly expected to see anything of that massive carriage. There was no sign of Von Plehve, but Sazonov was lying in the roadway, about four feet from the sidewalk, his left arm flung out on the cobblestones, his face rigid and pale with little streams of blood trickling over his forehead and cheeks. His cap was blown off. His thick hair lay wet and tangled over his brow. His eyes were half-open, and he was breathing with difficulty; and as he lay there, spread-eagled in the road, not moving nor stirring in any way, Savinkov assumed he was dead or dying. There was blood streaming from a wound in the abdomen, forming a huge widening pool at his feet. Savinkov bent over and studied the unconscious face, and then he heard a voice saying: "Well, they say the Minister has escaped." The voice belonged to Police Captain Perepelitzin. Savinkov recognized him, as he recognized all the other police captains because it was his business to recognize them, and together with the other conspirators he had formed a complete mental dossier of their behavior and characteristics and personal appearance. Perepelitzin seems to have thought Savinkov was just one more curiosity seeker. His jaw was working, he was deathly pale and he kept fluttering his white-gloved hands. "Move along, please," he said. "It's none of your business, sir. Keep moving."

For Savinkov it was all a nightmare, and he made his way to the Warsaw station hardly knowing where he was going. He had brought the nightmare on himself, but when he

remembered Sazonov, the tangled hair, the dark blood welling out of the abdomen, the head strangely bent toward
the right shoulder as though in his last moments Sazonov
was turning his face toward the bomb he had held so pre-
cariously, he was overcome with a feeling of inexpressible
grief. Some bricklayers, covered with dust, ran screaming
past Savinkov. All he could think of was: "The Minister is
alive, Sazonov is dead." In his excitement he had failed to
observe the body of Von Plehve lying close to Sazonov
among pieces of the carriage furniture. The body was terribly mangled, without arms or legs, the face crushed and
unrecognizable. When Sazonov awoke to consciousness the
first thing he saw appeared to be a red cloak such as those
worn by generals. It was lying near the gutter, and for some
idiotic reason people were staring at the red cloak from
the sidewalk. The red cloak was Von Plehve.

Savinkov wandered through the city until he came to the
Technological Institute. Dulebov, Sazonov's closest friend,
was waiting outside in his cab. Savinkov climbed in.

"What happened?" Dulebov whispered.

"They say the Minister escaped."

"And Yegor?"

"Dead or dying."

There was a long pause. The cab was racing over the
cobblestones.

"What do we do now?" Dulebov asked, tears streaming
down his cheeks.

"We carry out the plan. The Minister will be returning
from Peterhof at four o'clock. At three o'clock I'll hand the
bomb to you. You'll be waiting for me outside the Technological Institute."

At a busy cross-street Savinkov climbed out of the cab and
made his way on foot to the Yusupov Gardens. Once he had
to hold on to a wall for support. He had almost fainted
when the thin sulphur-yellow cloud rose, and then again

when he was bending over Sazonov. He hoped Kaliayev was safe and had not thrown his bomb away, but even if Kaliayev had panicked, or been caught by the police, there was always the hope that with Dulebov's assistance he would be able to kill the Minister in the afternoon. He expected to find Kaliayev in the Yusupov Gardens, but there was no sign of him. There was no sign of Sikorsky, either. Savinkov was perturbed. If Von Plehve was alive, both Kaliayev and Sikorsky might well have been arrested by now. Savinkov wandered in the empty gardens for a while, and then made his way to a bathhouse in the Lane of the Cossacks, where he rented a room, stripped, bathed, and stared at the ceiling. It was now ten o'clock. When he emerged at noon, he bought a newspaper. The front page had a thick black border, a portrait of Von Plehve and an account of the assassination which had occurred, according to the correspondent, "at the hands of an unknown terrorist who was critically wounded in the explosion." Savinkov could make little of this. It had never happened to him before that he had been so deadly wrong in his interpretation of a terrorist action. He slipped the newspaper in his pocket and walked straight back to the Ismailovsky Prospekt, determined to discover exactly what had happened by talking with people who had witnessed the explosion.

A few moments after Savinkov was told to move on by Captain Perepelitzin, Sazonov awoke from his stupor, gazed around and breathed a deep sigh of relief, and this was followed by a terrible groan, for as he looked across the empty street and saw no sign of the carriage or the two black horses, he assumed that the Minister had escaped. He remembered everything vividly. It astonished him that he was still alive. He tried to get up, but he seemed to have no body. He saw that one of his feet had been smashed and the blood was running out of a great wound in his stomach, and then he turned his head a little and saw what appeared to be a general's cloak. He succeeded in raising himself on his elbow and thinking he was about to die he shouted: "Long live freedom!" He had the feeling that his enemies would soon be after him and it was necessary to make an escape. He thought: "I must be careful. I may get delirious. It would be much better to commit *hari-kari* like the Japanese than to fall into the hands of the filthy policemen." He tried to remove his revolver from his pocket, determined to defend himself or shoot himself through the brain. He had not observed Captain Perepelitzin, who had been studying him carefully. When the captain saw Sazonov making an effort to take the revolver from his pocket, he knew he was face to face with the assassin. Perepelitzin knew a great deal about wounds. He knew that this terrorist was far from being dead. There was still a possibility that the terrorist would escape. He removed the revolver. Sazonov, recognizing a plain-clothes policeman, screamed and tried to get to his feet. Perepelitzin pressed him down. More policemen came running up. They had recovered from the shock and like Perepelitzin they had come to the conclusion that they had found the assassin. Enraged, they began to beat him up. They used their fists, boots, and the butts of their revolvers. It did not occur to them that Sazonov was dying, or at least desperately wounded. He must be made to pay for his sins. And it did not occur to them that Sazonov was beyond suffering and could not feel the butt-ends of the revolvers which fell across his face, until his face was no more than a mass of blood and both eyes were badly damaged. Sazonov heard someone shouting: "Be careful! Where's the bomb—the other bomb?" Weakly, while they were still flogging him, Sazonov said: "Please leave me alone. I haven't got another bomb." There was a brief discussion between the policemen. It was decided to take him off the street.

"Where the devil shall we take him?" someone shouted. "Take him to a hotel—anywhere."

There was a hotel a little way down the street, and after some more discussion it was agreed to take him there until official instructions were received from headquarters. A messenger had already been sent to inform Muraviev, the Minister of Justice. There was a further discussion about how he should be taken, until someone decided that the simplest way was the best: they dragged him by the feet with his head bumping against the cobblestones, leaving a long gleaming smear of blood behind him. At the hotel he was told to climb up the stairs to the only vacant room on the third floor, but he was now too weak even to stand, and with a blanket thrown over him he was carried up to the hotel room and thrown down on the floor, where his clothes were torn off and he was again beaten. None of this beating affected him. He watched it all drowsily, as though from a long way away, in the peace of approaching death, noting that the room seemed to be unaccountably filling with smoke. More and more policemen and officials came in, until there was hardly room to move about. They were all talking in loud voices. Someone came up to Sazonov, knelt down, felt his head and murmured: "He'll live. Better not hit him any more." Then he was taken down the blood-stained staircase, and he remembered nothing more until he woke up in a hospital.

At the hospital one of the policemen remembered that Sazonov had made a curious gesture, putting his hand quickly to his mouth. They were not sure, but it was possible that he had taken poison. Sazonov woke up just as a tube was being pushed down his throat. This, too, seemed to be happening to someone else, in some other place. No poison was dredged up by the stomach-pump. It was agreed that he was still too weak to be questioned. He was put under chloroform while the doctors probed in his body for bomb-splinters, sewed up the gash in his stomach and amputated two of his crushed toes.

It was evening when he came round. Once again he remembered what had happened on the Ismailovsky Prospekt. He wanted to sing for joy. He heard strange voices coming from a long way away. The voices were soft and faint. He felt hideously thirsty and asked for water. Someone was saying: "Tell me your name." Sazonov kept asking for water. "We'll give you water if you tell us your name. Just tell me your name—"

"Why?"

"We have to know. You're in a hospital. We're nurses."

Sazonov laughed deliriously. It was incredible that they should talk like that.

"If you're nurses," he said, "then why aren't you at the front? It's an absolute scandal, eh?"*

The nurses had to shout to make themselves heard. The savage kicks in the head had made him deaf.

Soon water was brought to him. Another voice, deep-toned, said: "We want to help you. We have no other aim. Let us start by being friends."

About this time Sazonov was aware that he had either gone blind or his eyes were bandaged. He lay very still. He refused to talk. He kept telling himself: "Whatever happens I must not let them know my name."

The voice said: "I am the examining magistrate. You are charged with the assassination of Minister Von Plehve. You are required to tell me your name and the reasons for your act."

"I can tell you nothing," Sazonov answered softly, "except one thing—"

"And what's that?"

"I am a member of the Terrorist Brigade."

* Russia was at this time at war with Japan.

There was a long silence. He heard the doctors whispering, and then the heavy footfalls of the examining magistrate as he left the room. Soon the examining magistrate returned; presumably he had received new instructions.

"I must know your name."

"I can't tell you."

"And the names of your accomplices?"

"You are an idiot if you think I will tell you."

The examination went on for two or three hours. When Sazonov fell asleep he was prodded awake. The doctors were still afraid he would die before being brought up to trial. Once he asked the name of the examining magistrate. There was no answer. He learned later that the magistrate was the Minister of Justice, Muraviev, and when he left the room it was presumably to contact the Czar. The Minister shrugged his shoulders and said: "He may speak better in prison," and gave orders that everything the prisoner said in delirium should be written down.

The next morning Sazonov was removed from the Alexandrovsky Workmen's Hospital to the prison hospital attached to the Kresty, a large and recently modernized prison overlooking the river. Here there began the long battle to extract information from a singularly silent prisoner.

The man placed in charge of the incessant cross-examination was a police official named Gurovich, who later became an important functionary under the Bolsheviks.

Sazonov knew what to expect. He had slept well, and some of his old *braggadocio* returned in the prison hospital. Gurovich had a friendly voice as he bent over the bed. Sazonov was in sharp pain, for the effects of the chloroform had worn off, but the pain kept him awake and helped to distract him from the investigation.

Gurovich began pleasantly with a long speech full of phrases about the misdirected heroism of the terrorists, how it was possible to honor them and at the same time regret their foolish extremism. He explained patiently that the government would always be stronger than the terrorists. The prisoner had been prepared to sacrifice himself for his beliefs, however wrong-headed, and "to a certain degree" had behaved in a praiseworthy manner. Then the tone changed. There were hints that Gurovich was in a position to help.

"I am a doctor," Gurovich explained. "Doctors are concerned with the welfare of humanity. Like you, they want everyone in Russia to be happy. I shall look after you to the best of my ability, but you understand I shall need your cooperation. You have committed terrible crimes. It is a small thing perhaps to have killed Minister Von Plehve, but what about the others—the man who was just standing nearby, and the old woman and the two-year-old child? There were very many people killed. These are the only ones we have been able to recognize."

Sazonov told himself this was a trick, but the doctor went on relentlessly, talking about the old woman and the child, mentioning casually that altogether twenty-nine people had died in the explosion and there were many others who were not expected to live. He mentioned their names and spoke of how all Russia was in mourning for their deaths. People had sometimes praised the terrorists in the past; now they were universally execrated.

"You must have known it would happen," Gurovich went on. "At half past nine in the morning, on the Ismailovsky Prospekt, it is always crowded—people going about their affairs, shopping, taking the air. And so you chose the very worst time of the day, and the most crowded street. That's why people are calling you 'traitor.' I don't altogether share their view. They say the two-year-old child was very beautiful."

For an hour Sazonov listened to these lies. Every few minutes Gurovich asked some pointed question about the terrorists' organization, saying: "You must help us—it is so shameful," or "You have already mentioned many names in your delirium. Why don't you tell me the rest?"

Gurovich had a long experience in dealing with prisoners. He was probing the wound. The torture continued. He discovered that whenever he talked about the dead child, the prisoner stiffened and sweat poured over the bandaged face. Sazonov's calm *braggadocio* gave place to terror. He held onto the doctor's hand and screamed: "Don't call me a traitor! Call me anything, but never a traitor!" Then he lost consciousness. When he awoke Gurovich was still there. When Gurovich began to speak, Sazonov said quietly: "It's no use. I won't listen. Go away, or I'll shout for help. You're not a doctor. You're a police agent."

When Gurovich left the cell, a real doctor took his place. There were intervals of quiet when new bandages were put on or the bed-sheets were changed. The new doctor explained the nature of the wounds and said there was hope of a complete recovery. Then, though Sazonov was aware that others were in the cell, the doctor bent low and whispered: "We're absolutely alone. Let me help you. Would you like messages sent to your friends? Just tell me who to send the messages to." Sazonov half-believed him until he said: "The police already have a great deal of information about you. They know one of your comrades threw a bomb in the Neva. They say the boatman who took him out on the Neva was a terrorist, too."

This was the first time the police had shown they knew anything positive about the plot. The comrade who tossed his bomb in the Neva was probably Sikorsky. Presumably the boatman had also been arrested. Sazonov was afraid he had mentioned Sikorsky's name during his ravings. Gurovich had spoken of a second explosion. When he was alone, Sazonov tried to dovetail the pieces together. Two bomb explosions? Sikorsky and the boatman arrested? Twenty-nine people killed? He was still feverishly attempting to understand what had happened from the limited information which reached the cell in the Kresty Prison when Gurovich came and told him there was bad news: Ten more people had died as a result of the explosion, bringing the death roll to thirty-nine. Sazonov refused to believe him. Gurovich gave details, names, addresses, occupations, the kinds of wounds they had received, until Sazonov screamed himself into delirium.

Long before the attack on Von Plehve the terrorists had discussed the possibility of their arrests. They had promised to believe nothing the police told them. They had sworn an oath to reveal nothing to the police. In prison they would have to fight the same silent deadly war they had fought outside. There were long intervals in which Sazonov remained extraordinarily calm—calm even in delirium. He wrote afterwards: " I believe I can remember everything I said in delirium, and this is not at all difficult if you take the proper precautions." He did not reveal what precautions he took, but he seems to have steeled himself to unusual feats of silence. But he could not always remember his ravings and he was not always silent. He wrote in another letter: "My sufferings from wounds were nothing compared with the moral torment of the investigation. Heaven knows what I may have said in delirium. I cried out for death to deliver me, death which had touched me so closely and then so terribly betrayed me. Better not to have been born than to bring disgrace and ruin on our cause, betray my comrades and disturb their faith in me." Gradually a deep sense of guilt was awakened in him: guilt because he may have betrayed the revolutionaries, guilt because he may have been responsible for forty deaths, and then the guilt which came when he faced his own inadequacy in parrying the relentless questioning of the investigators.

The Russian secret police were past masters at extracting

confessions. Even in these early days they employed moral torture almost to the exclusion of physical torture. The policemen who attacked Sazonov on the ground had acted in hot blood and in anger: most of them knew they would be punished for not having guarded Von Plehve against assassination. Prince Peter Kropotkin mentions in his reminiscences the shock of horror when he heard that Karakozov was physically tortured in the last days before his execution, and how even though there seemed to be no bones in his body, and his head and hands hung loose, he made strenuous efforts to climb the scaffold unaided. Torture had not prevented Karakozov from dying well. There is no evidence that Nechayev was ever tortured. Sazonov had no fear of physical torture, but he was beginning to be desperately afraid he would talk too much.

For three weeks he remained in his cell in the hospital, bandaged and blind. From the moment he awoke to the moment he fell asleep there was an interrogator by the bedside. He heard no voices except the voices of the young assistant doctor and of Gurovich. Gurovich's hard bluster would be followed by the soothing sermons of the doctor, the tough and the soft, an age-old technique still pursued by the police. In the end it usually succeeds. Gurovich announced that Sikorsky had confessed and told a strange tale about a meeting with an old woman in Vilna shortly before the assassination, and then he went on to say that another Jew, "whose name I do not have to acquaint you with, for you must know it already—he is a man who wears an English coat," had also confessed under arrest, and this man was another comrade from Byelostok. By this time Sazonov realized that Sikorsky, who was once a leather worker in Byelostok, must at least have stated his name and place of residence. There were few other consolations to be derived from listening to Gurovich. He was in great pain, and though the thought of having killed Von Plehve gave him, as he declared later, "a moral satisfaction so great there is nothing in the world to compare with it," the thought of the thirty or forty innocent people who might also have been killed remained to torment him, so that he had no desire to live and wished desperately he could put himself out of his misery. "Everyone has heard of your revolutionary mottoes," Gurovich said one day. "I applaud them! What noble sentiments! Truth through Blood. Joy and Pride. Beautiful mottoes, until you think of the young mother cut down in her womanhood and the small child still holding a doll, though there is a bomb splinter as large as your fist in her throat."

There were other things that tormented Sazonov. He remembered dimly that when the examining magistrate questioned him in the Alexandrovsky Hospital about whether he had known Pokotilov, killed when experimenting with a bomb in his room in the Northern Hotel, he had replied that he knew Pokotilov well; and when asked about the aims of the Terrorist Brigade he had launched out in semi-delirium in a long, militant discourse, describing these aims in detail. This was weakness, though no harm had been done. In talking at all about a member of the Brigade, he had disobeyed a cardinal rule of the organization: the terrorist must be silent when faced with his accusers. When he tried to rationalize his own weakness, he put it down to the terrible thirst which must have arisen as a result of shock. He asked for water. They refused to give it to him. In the end, when the thirst became a raging fever, he had thrown out these tid-bits of entirely useless information. But what if it should happen again? He told himself he must beware of giving information away when in a state of shock, for they could produce a state of shock whenever they wanted to. He was at their mercy, fed by strange hands and with a bandage over his eyes. He thought they might be able to induce shock by drugs mixed with his food, but the shock came three weeks and five days after the arrest when the bandage was taken from his eyes. He had thought he had been alone with Gurovich or the doctor. Now he saw, arranged along the four walls, the silent impassive gendarmes who had stood guard in the cell throughout his imprisonment.

"Why don't you tell us your name?" the young assistant doctor asked. "What harm can it do?"

In a weak moment Sazonov answered: "All I can tell you is that my name begins with S."

Two days later he was told: "We know who you are. We have discovered everything. You are Yegor Sergeyevich Sazonov."

During his trial which began on November 30, four and a half months after the assassination of Von Plehve, Sazonov smuggled a letter out of prison addressed to the surviving members of the Brigade. At the time he thought he would be sentenced to death, and the letter was at once an apologia and a final farewell to his friends. He wrote:

> Believe me, the enemy is contemptible without limit. One should never surrender oneself to them alive. Please tell this to all our comrades. Farewell, dear ones! I salute the dawn of liberty! . . .
>
> Let me tell you of my unpardonable crime. I cannot tell you why, after three weeks of silence, I revealed my name. Comrades, I beg you not to judge me too harshly. If you knew how much I suffered, and how I still suffer, remembering how I sometimes talked in my delirium. I was helpless. What could I do to save myself? Bite off my tongue? But I had not even enough strength for this. I was terribly weak. I wanted only to die or to recover quickly. And then too I remember how I sometimes spoke about the aims of the party, and then I remember that I may not have explained them adequately. As you know, my conception of terror springs from the *Narodnaya Volya* and so to some extent I disagree with the program of the Terrorist Brigade. When I appeared before the court I felt I was in a false position. I should not have

spoken of my personal views. I should have spoken exclusively of the views of the Brigade. Did I commit a sin against the brigade? Please forgive me. Tell the party to announce my errors publicly, tell them to say they are not responsible for the words spoken by individual members, especially one who is ill. I have still not recovered. The blow on my head was too strong. So I am weighed down with a sense of sin, and I want to confess my errors to you, my dear comrades. And if I am the only one who has wronged our cause, let this too be known. I have tried so consciously to lessen the importance of my errors.

At the trial those who had known Sazonov could hardly recognize him. The youthful apple-cheeked face had gone forever. He was pale and nervous, and had difficulty in collecting his thoughts. His brow was deeply furrowed, and he seemed to have aged by twenty years. He walked on crutches, complained of intolerable headaches, and sometimes stared round the court with a vacant expression. It was whispered that he had been drugged, but in fact he was still suffering from a sense of his own intolerable guilt.

Sikorsky was placed on trial with him. The twenty-year-old leather worker from Byelostok who spoke Russian so badly that his replies had to be translated in court had behaved with remarkable incompetence. He had been ordered to hire a boat in Petrovsky Park, row out across the lake and then drop the bomb carefully in the water. Instead he had hired a boat on the Neva and in full view of the workmen building a battleship in a dockyard overlooking the river he had hurled the bomb into the river. The boatman was alarmed, and when Sikorsky stuffed a ten-ruble note in his hands, he grew still more alarmed. When he returned to the shore the boatman took his prisoner straight to a police station. Sikorsky denied everything. For some days he held out, refusing to give his name; then he told the rambling incoherent story about the meeting with the woman in Vilna which was communicated to Sazonov. Some time in the autumn some fishermen found the bomb in their nets and handed it to the authorities. It was assumed by the police that at least six people must have taken part in the assassination, but neither Sikorsky nor Sazonov revealed the names of their associates.

During the trial Sazonov learned for the first time that the assassination of Von Plehve had completely altered the atmosphere of Russia. The Liberal statesman Prince Svyato-polk-Mirsky succeeded Von Plehve and announced a program of liberal reforms and a relaxation of the censorship. The Holy Synod proposed to convene a Church Assembly to discuss the restoration of the Patriarchate, a sign that the Church was already aware of a change in the weather of the autocracy. Vast plans were afoot for altering the basic structure of government. While the trial was in progress, plans to assemble a Council of Ministers to introduce a legally-appointed government and to abolish the extraordinary powers of the Czar were being widely discussed, and in fact the Council of Ministers met shortly after the trial was concluded. Unknown to Sazonov, his deed had been applauded over large areas of Russia, and when the Liberal lawyer Kazorinov who defended him said: "The bomb was loaded not with dynamite but with the tears and sufferings of the people," there was general assent. Sazonov, who had expected to be tried by a military tribunal and hanged immediately after sentence was handed down, found himself the hero of the hour.

The trial was the quietest of all the trials in which the terrorists took part. There were no loud declamations. The judge treated Sazonov with considerable respect. Though the judge laid down the rule that Sazonov could make no apologia at the trial, Sazonov was in fact allowed to speak at some length. He spoke badly, often lost the thread of his ideas, paused lengthily and sometimes seemed unaware that he was in court. He had, however, written out a statement which he intended to produce at the trial. In this speech, which was never delivered, he said:

I wish to explain that our party cannot be described as one which acts by violence. It is by its very nature inimical to every kind of violence . . . We are not forcing our ideals upon the people: we wish only to speak the truth . . . We hate and despise violence, and we are convinced that violence is powerless against ideals. But all our attempts at peaceful activity have been met by ruthless persecution on the part of the government. We are subjected to the humiliation of corporal punishment, beaten by knouts, trodden upon by horses, and shot down as soon as we declare our desires and our purposes. We are deprived of the protection of the law and declared to be enemies of the people . . .

Yes, the government made me a revolutionist and a terrorist, though originally I prayed only for peace. When I escaped from Siberia, I felt that red ghosts were creeping behind me, never leaving me all day and all night, and they whispered in my ear: "Go and kill Von Plehve!" Since I began to understand the work of the Ministers of Russia, I felt I had no right to enjoy a peaceful and happy life. So in killing Von Plehve I acted according to the dictates of my conscience.

Sazonov had so completely confessed his crime that the jury had no alternative but to judge him guilty. He was sentenced to life imprisonment with hard labor and deprivation of all rights and property. Sikorsky was sentenced to fifteen years' hard labor. The same day the two prisoners were removed to the Schlusselburg Fortress.

Like Nechayev, Sazonov in prison was almost more formidable than when he was plotting assassination. He was already a legend. In the five years that remained to him he became a more formidable legend and in the end he sealed the legend with a fantastic suicide.

The Sense of Guilt

In Czarist Russia there were two completely different kinds of prisons. There were the great fortress prisons of Moscow, St. Petersburg, and the provincial capitals, with high stone walls, great courtyards, and small damp cells. These prisons were governed by iron laws and were under continual scrutiny by the officials of the Minister of the Interior. From the most important of these prisons went daily or weekly reports to the Czar. Such prisons were for the aristocrats among prisoners, those who had most dangerously offended the autocracy, and very few had ever escaped from them. In these prisons most of the prisoners were lifers and they could expect to die in their cells.

The fortress prisons were made of stone; on the other hand the Siberian prisons, though often surrounded by a high stone wall, were made of wood. The Ministry of the Interior had little influence in these remote regions. The prison governor was a law to himself, and if he chose, he could make the lives of his prisoners tolerable and even pleasant. Usually the Siberian prisons resembled immense cattlesheds. They were very long one-story buildings set down in some isolated place far from civilization, two or three hundred miles from any cities or railroads. The cells were arranged against the long prison wall and the corridor between the two rows of cells was the common meeting-place. Quite often there was little formal discipline. The prisoners took their meals in their cells which they shared with three or four others. They were locked into their cells at night. But they were generally allowed to walk whenever they wanted in the prison courtyard and they could talk and study. In summer they were allowed to wander in the woods under guard or on parole. They could receive newspapers and could send as many letters and telegrams as they pleased. The prisoners' families lived in villages which grew up around the prisons, and the men were occasionally allowed to spend the night with their wives, while children and wives could enter the prison at will. Political prisoners sentenced to hard labor rarely performed hard labor; nor—after 1900—were they shackled. The young revolutionary Maria Spiridonova tells how she arrived at Akatui prison and thought she was in "a guest-house under republican management." The prison governor spoke to her kindly, and she was invited to attend a welcoming party in the prison courtyard: there were speeches at a long table set with flowers and loaded with food. Under the liberal regime of Prince Svyatopolk-Mirsky prison life in Siberia became a holiday. But Sazonov lay in the Schlusselburg Prison, and hardly hoped to be sent to Siberia.

The assassination of Von Plehve heralded a vast change in the climate of Russia. Two months after Sazonov was sentenced to life imprisonment, on January 9, 1905, "Red Sunday," a solemn procession of working men with their wives and children marched in procession through St. Petersburg, singing hymns and bearing ikons. Led by the priest Gapon, they made their way to the great square facing the Winter Palace, intending to lay a petition at the feet of the Czar. At the approaches of the Winter Palace they were met by armed police and Cossacks who took fright and fired into the procession and then proceeded to exact a formal massacre. This was only the beginning. There followed a series of disasters so violent that by the end of the year Russia was within an ace of being a republic dominated by soviets. In February there were widespread strikes in the universities and high schools, and the peasants were coming out in open rebellion. Kuropatkin's army was defeated at Mukden, and in May Rodzhestvensky's Russian fleet was destroyed at Tsushima. In June came the mutiny of the cruiser *Potemkin*. In August the peace treaty with Japan was signed at Portsmouth. By October the whole country was caught in a general strike, and the first Soviet, the St. Petersburg Council of Workers' Deputies, had already emerged with Trotsky as its presiding genius. On October 17 Count Witte issued a manifesto promising far-reaching reforms. It was almost too late. The sailors revolted at Kronstadt; the Soviets defied the government; for ten days the streets of Moscow were littered with barricades, and Nikolai Lenin addressed mass meetings. But the Manifesto of October broke the cutting edge of the revolt and by the new year the fire had burned itself out. A scorched and shuddering Russia faced a burning future.

Through all that year Sazonov remained in the Schlusselburg. His wounds healed, he was treated well and recovered some of his old jauntiness, but he had been close to death and the thought of death was never far from his mind. Guilt still plagued him. In the letters to the Terrorist Brigade which he smuggled out, doubt and grief and exaltation can be seen struggling together. Toward the end of the year he wrote:

> Dear comrades! A year and a half has passed since I was removed from your ranks, but though physically separated from you, I have not for a moment ceased to live with you in my thoughts. While the thunder of the revolutionary storm has swept across the country, I have listened for the authentic voice of the Terrorist Brigade, and have not failed to hear it above the great chorus of revolutionary voices. The terrorists know the proper answer to life. With what exaltation have I

greeted your victories, and with what sorrow have I grieved over your failures; and yet all these must be expected by the nature of our work, which is truly great and living. With immense humility, with love and adoration I bow before the graves of the fallen.

The end is not yet. I believe the terrorists have still great things to accomplish on the historical scene. Remembering the tasks which still remain for us, and the sacrifices which are still demanded of us, it pleases me to remember, dear comrades, how happy I am when I recall the trust you placed in me on July 15. It would have been a thousand times worse than death if I had betrayed your love . . .

I feel the need to repeat again and again that there must be no misunderstandings between me and those who may one day be called upon to sacrifice themselves. It is absolutely necessary for my happiness to feel identified with you on all matters pertaining to the life and the program of our party.

To those doomed to die I send a special greeting, and it is my prayer that they will go out and honor the banners of our party in firmness and in good health. I greet you, dear comrades, with the knowledge that your courage will be crowned with success. And let us soon arrive at the time when it will no longer be necessary to employ terrorism. Let us pray that the time will come soon when we can foster our socialist ideals under conditions more commensurate with our human strength.

In the early spring of 1906 Sazonov learned that he was to be sent to Siberia. His mood changed. The letters of this period are no longer concerned with death and thoughts of betrayal. In March he was moved secretly to Moscow and lodged in the Butyrky prison, the clearing house through which political prisoners passed on the first stage of their exile to Siberia, Turkestan, or the Arctic. He was placed in the Pugachov Tower, reserved for the most important prisoners and there, to his intense delight, he found Gershuni, another member of the Terrorist Brigade. On the Trans-Siberian Railroad they made the journey together.

Arkatui lay then, as it does now, at the end of the road, ten miles from the Mongolian border and some two hundred miles from Serensk, the nearest railhead. The village lay in a barren landscape, bald hills overlooking marshy earth and the endless bare steppes where everything made by man looked unbelievably small against the vastness of sky and earth. There were two rows of ragged wooden huts clinging to the side of a hill—this was the village. Beyond the hill, in an immense grove of beeches and birches, lay the white-walled prison with its red church. Flowers grew everywhere. There were flowers at the foot of the birches, and in the courtyards. The tall wooden gateway was smothered with flowers. "I did not believe I had come to a prison," wrote Spiridonova, who reached Akatui a month after Sazonov. "To me it was like something seen in a dream, and I gazed upon it with wide uncomprehending eyes." There were children in gay clothes, dancing and singing. There were welcoming committees—the words "We welcome you, dear comrades" were painted in bright red letters across the prison-gate, but you could hardly see the words for the flowers. Banners and ropes of flowers were strung between the trees. There was almost no sign of any prison guard. And here, for some reason no one understood, a scented wind came over the steppes.

At the beginning Arkatui was as near paradise as any prison could be. Gershuni and Sazonov were its most distinguished inmates, and they rapidly took charge. Gershuni, with his bright blue eyes and trim beard, organized classes in history and law. Prosh Prozhian, an Armenian revolutionary who later became a member of the first Soviet only to fight a relentless battle with the Bolsheviks until his early death in 1919, taught science. Sazonov taught medicine, literature, and law; he also taught in the elementary classes given to young workmen. Gershuni's lectures were the most avidly attended. The warders and prison-officers listened and

took notes, discreetly standing in the corner. There is no
evidence that they ever showed their notes to higher authority; they had come to learn, not to spy. There were choir-
practices held in the prison courtyard and round-table discussions, and anyone who wanted to deliver a lecture had
only to scribble a note and pin it on a notice-board. Arkatui
resembled a junior university even to its code of manners
and its strict morality: no drinking, card-playing, fighting,
or sexual irregularities were allowed. Prisoners sentenced
to a lifetime of hard labor could be heard bitterly complaining that their bodies were wasting away because they were
never allowed to perform any physical labor. In winter it
was bitterly cold; in summer the heat came in waves against
the wooden walls of the prison cantonment; spring and fall
were idyllic.

For a year and a half Sazonov enjoyed a calm carefree
existence. There was an atmosphere of intellectual excitement, of intense and puritanical striving after the perfect
life. Gershuni, with his immense learning, his determination
to sacrifice himself for a cause, his deadly logic, and his air
of casual superiority over his guards, was a pillar of
strength. Born to riches, Gershuni entered the revolutionary struggle from above; and like Lenin, who belonged to
a family of the minor aristocracy, he possessed a relentless
will and the intellectual mastery which enabled him to
exert his will to the uttermost. He had organized the assassinations of Sipyagin and Bogdanovich, Von Plehve's two predecessors in the Ministry of the Interior. He was one of the
original founders of the Social Revolutionary Party, and had
been sentenced to death. He was determined to escape from
the prison. Two early attempts failed because the rendezvous in the forests north of Arkatui was somehow mis-timed.
There was no great difficulty in escaping from Arkatui provided a rendezvous was carefully arranged. All that was necessary was to slip past the guards and then vanish in the

birch forest and make contact with friends who had ridden secretly from Serensk or Chita. Once Gershuni escaped for several hours, but failed to find his friends. At another time, when the prisoners were temporarily forbidden outside the walls, a tunnel was dug. Unfortunately a guard pacing outside the walls tripped over the soft earth where the tunnel was coming to the surface; the secret was out; and the beautiful tunnel with its floorboards and birch wood supports and wooden panels along the wall had to be abandoned.

Finally the prisoners decided that Gershuni should hide in the cabbage-cellar under the prison-governor's house. From the cellar there was the usual corridor-like tunnel leading to open ground outside the walls. Guards kept watch on the cellar. Gershuni was placed in a cabbage-cask liberally sprinkled with brine, and left there toward nightfall. He wore a metal helmet to protect him from a bayonet thrust by one of the guards who were on the lookout for just such adventures, and he breathed through two rubber tubes which led to two holes cut in the bottom of the cask. The cellar was ice-cold, and Gershuni suffered from cramps. The space between the cabbages was poisoned with carbonic acid gas from the brine. It was a small cask, and he was doubled up like a snake, and in considerable pain, because it was necessary to avert suspicion by tossing the cask roughly into the cellar. Over his head a sheet of leather had been fastened, and he had to cut through the leather with a knife to free himself. He was almost unconscious when he emerged, his face and clothes torn by the nails inside the cask. He had a revolver, a small bottle of ether, and a knife—he only lacked a bomb to have the four essential pieces of a terrorist's equipment. When he climbed out of the cellar at last it was nine o'clock on a bright October morning with thick snow on the ground. By chance one of the prison officers' children came running past him, chasing a dog. Gershuni froze. The child ran past, but the dog kept sniffing the brine and started barking; he thought the game was up, but soon the dog went wandering away. He had to pass close to the small wooden houses where the prison officials lived. He pretended to be making snow-balls and then ran across the road which led to the birch forest. No one saw him. Then there was the long journey through the silent forest, along the banks of a river, into deep valleys, and over the bald mountains toward the place where friends with a small cart were waiting for him. A storm came up. Blue-black clouds raced low over the earth, and the wind was so cold that Gershuni nearly abandoned hope of reaching his rendezvous. Even when he found his friends, Gershuni had little hope of completing the journey. For hours they were lost in the storm. He was running a temperature. The wolves howled. He was sure the prison officials were already pursuing him, and they must by now have given warning by telegraph to the neighboring towns. There would be road-blocks and police investigations at the hotels. But some of the telegraph wires had fallen in the storm and they passed through three towns unharmed. Within twenty-four hours he had reached his friends' house. He was given some beggar's rags to wear and put on a coach bound for the Far East. Once a gendarme struck him for pushing his way onto the coach, contaminating the fine gentlemen there with his beggar's rags, and Gershuni commented afterwards: "No one will ever know the pleasure I derived from that hard blow." Five days later he was on his way to Japan, and from there he reached the safety of Switzerland.

Gershuni's escape on October 13, 1906, heralded a change of policy toward the prisoners, and Sazonov, who had been Gershuni's intimate friend, received the full force of the rigors of the new administration. The prison governor at Arkatui was dismissed. In his place there came a more

hardened governor called Subkovsky. New orders came to
the prison. All prisoners must henceforth be chained, they
shall sleep on straw and not on bed-linen, their money must
be taken away, and for the least infraction of discipline the
most rigorous punishment must be meted out. The prison
governor had orders to shoot at the first sign of disturbance,
and he was warned that his resignation would be demanded
unless the terms of the new orders were carried out. He
was ordered to transfer the women at Arkatui immediately
to another prison at Malzev, forty miles away. It had been
a bad winter and now a blizzard was raging. Many of the
women were ill. They had no heavy clothes to protect them.
Spiridonova was ill, suffering from tuberculosis, in no state
to make a winter journey. The women prisoners decided to
defy the authorities by barricading themselves in their cells.
Subkovsky was terrified by the women's display of ruthless
determination, and telegraphed to the governor of the local
prison system: "Cannot obey order because of lack of clothing. Please name my successor." He invited a medical commission to examine the prisoners. Spiridonova and some
others were pronounced unfit to travel. Subkovsky might
have prevailed against his superior if another prison governor had not appeared on the scene. This was the infamous
Borodulin, governor of the Algashi prison, which lay some
thirty miles to the west. A heavy-set man with a brutal
humor he invaded the women's section of Arkatui at the
head of a column of soldiers and ordered them to leave
immediately. If they were cold, they could wear blankets.
Spiridonova was all for obeying the order. The alternative
was bloodshed and rape. She succeeded in arranging a meeting between Borodulin and Sazonov, who was too stunned
to say anything except that he entirely disagreed with her
acquiescence to the new orders. The prison was seething
with revolt. Sazonov had merely to give the order and at the
cost of perhaps a hundred lives the soldiers might be over-

whelmed. In the end Spiridonova's insistence won him over. "As the sledge drove us away from Arkatui," she wrote, "I could not forget Sazonov standing at the door of his cell, tall and thin and his shoulders bowed down a little. His face was not pale but gray, and his features were strangely fallen and his eyes were closed."

A few days later Sazonov wrote to his mother:

> The worst is happening. Borodulin has taken over; the prison is full of his armed soldiers. We heard Borodulin saying: "Be utterly merciless. Shoot at the first sign of protest, and be careful not to hit the guards." In the presence of one of our representatives he kept toying with his revolver. He said: "I am an expert at cleaning up prisons. I know, of course, that I may be killed. I'm not afraid of death as long as I can first walk over your dead bodies."

It was believed that a closer watch could be kept on the prisoners if they were at Algashi. So Sazonov and fourteen others, regarded as the most dangerous elements in Arkatui, were sent off to Algashi, Borodulin's private preserve. They were put into prison uniform, their heads were shaved, and they were forced to take off their caps and stand at attention whenever they were spoken to. Borodulin was out to break their spirits. He threatened mass floggings, endless tortures. Some of the prisoners refused to have their heads shaved. At the time Borodulin said nothing, but at midnight they were summoned into a large bare room, soldiers with bayonets standing guard against the wall. Afraid the prisoners would fall upon him, Borodulin concealed himself behind the soldiers, and while the prisoners were half-blinded by glaring lights, he shouted: "Remove their caps, strip them naked, then shave their heads by force." Prisoners who refused to obey had their clothes torn from them and were clubbed over the head, while Borodulin kept shouting: "You're not at Arkatui any longer! Before we have finished with you even your bones will have been lost sight of."

From the very beginning there had been a demon of rebellion in Sazonov, but when he assassinated Von Plehve he was pitting himself against the powerful symbol of autocracy. In his Siberian prison he could only pit himself against mindless brutality. There was no glory to be won from Borodulin, who attempted to reduce everyone to his own mindless level. There had been brutality in the Siberian prisons before, but mostly it had been the aroused brutality of frightened guards. With Borodulin the inhuman, mechanical monster of punishment appeared for the first time. He was the ancestor of the prison officials of our own day in Nazi Germany and Soviet Russia, determined to stamp out the recognizable features of the prisoners, impatient of all common humanity, in love with death. Sazonov saw the menace and determined to pit his whole strength against it.

There was little he could do. He could only make his protest and then die under the blows of the executioners. He seems to have guessed that prisons were to become even more anonymous and infinitely more destructive of human honor. He was enraged because the prisoners were addressed in the second person singular. Borodulin treated everyone like vermin, even his own soldiers. Prison, Sazonov thought, had become an intolerable offense against human dignity, and it was time this offense was punished.

On the first night at Algashi, March 4, 1907, Sazonov urged the prisoners to embark on a campaign of nonviolent resistance. They would refuse to obey commands, refuse to remove their caps when addressed by Borodulin, and when addressed in the second person singular they would refuse to listen.

That night the prisoners were in a mood of somber defiance. Some burst out singing. For some reason these melancholy defiant songs nearly unnerved Sazonov, who buried his head in a mattress and prayed for the singing to end. They were all locked up in a large common cell. They expected Borodulin to enter, order them to their feet, and flog them when they refused. They would go on refusing, and soon some would have been flogged or clubbed to death. They were desperately determined upon rebellion. All night they took turns standing on guard. Sazonov could not sleep, and, after debate with himself, decided to commit suicide in the hope that his voluntary death, which would be immediately known in Moscow, would save the others. He had a phial of morphine sewn in his clothes. He swallowed it. He awoke some hours later with a feeling of nausea, a bad headache, and that was all, save the knowledge that he had now lost the last of his possessions.

All day they waited, but Borodulin made no appearance. On the second day a young terrorist called Rybnikov encountered Borodulin in the corridor. Ordered to remove his cap, he refused. Borodulin ordered him to be led to a dark cell. A few moments later pandemonium broke loose. The prisoners shouted and threatened to batter down the door unless Borodulin appeared with Rybnikov, and when Borodulin arrived with an escort but without Rybnikov and ordered the prisoners to stand at attention, they refused sullenly. In a rage Borodulin ordered two prisoners selected at random to be removed to the dark cell. "Club them over the head if they disobey!" he shouted. Then began the slow deadly game of passive resistance, with the prisoners linking their hands and forming a human chain, while the soldiers struck them over the head with rifle-butts. Soon three prisoners were wounded: one with a broken skull, another with a smashed face, and the third clubbed in the chest. The soldiers surrounded one prisoner and led him off to the dark cells, and Borodulin, still hiding behind his soldiers, announced that the prisoners would be punished by being deprived of hot meals, bed covers, and exercise. As a further punishment, the pots filled with excreta would remain in the cell throughout the day.

Sazonov wrote in a letter:

> Evidently he can do anything he likes with us: there is no limit to his tyranny. Borodulin is attempting to curry favor with the criminals, hoping to set them against the politicals, but their sympathy is with us. The only way out is to force this butcher to kill us. Yet a prison revolt would cost too much blood. As for ourselves, we dare not hope for a happy outcome, but we are at peace with ourselves—the peace with which condemned men await their deaths. But to die in an active war is not the same thing as falling beneath the tyranny of a Borodulin.

That Sazonov was able to write a letter in which he recounted the whole incident at length and smuggle it out of prison with the intention that it should be read in the Duma shows that the administration and atmosphere of prisons in Russia has since changed vastly. No such thing would now be possible. What he described was a small incident, which has since been endlessly repeated. The public conscience was still tender. Uspensky, a Social Revolutionary member of the Duma, read portions of Sazonov's letter to the tribune. There was a storm of protest; the government was compelled to make a special investigation about the three obscure political prisoners who had been clubbed with rifle-butts, and a month later the Duma received the results of the investigation in an atmosphere of derision. The government maintained that the prisoners had behaved so contemptuously toward the prison governor that he had been compelled to use a minimum of force. All over Russia Borodulin's name was now ironically identified with "those who use a minimum of force." On May 28 the military governor of the Nerchinsk Katorga, who had been responsible for the original orders, was shot at Chita by a young terrorist.

Borodulin's days were now numbered. He was not the worst of prison governors. Taunted by the revolutionaries, he had behaved stupidly and brutally, but his brutalities compared with those of our own day were of small consequence. There is no record that anyone was killed during his administration. But the revolutionaries had recognized the machine-like inhumanity of the man, all the possibilities of prison terror and murder latent within him, and they were determined that the government should take warning. In half the provinces of Russia young students were busily plotting ways to assassinate him.

It was a deadly game, played for high stakes. In the end the Borodulins won, but in 1907 the revolutionaries still believed that victory was in their grasp. They had two weapons, assassination and civil disobedience, and it never seems to have occurred to them that these weapons were incompatible.

One day Borodulin invited Sazonov to the governor's office. Sazonov kept his cap on his head, and Borodulin was careful to address him in the second person plural. According to Sazonov, who wrote down the conversation immediately afterward, they talked roughly as follows:

BORODULIN: It occurs to me that I shall soon have to ask the political prisoners to perform repair work in the prison. I accept the fact that they will probably resist my orders. Then I will have to punish them, and that probably means force.

SAZONOV: You must understand one thing—political prisoners have never nourished the false hope that their lives are safe.

BORODULIN: I insist that their lives are in no danger. You completely misunderstand me. If we go on living together, you will learn I am not a beast. Why are you so bitter against me? I merely carry out orders.

SAZONOV: You give orders.

BORODULIN: No, I carry them out. I obey my superiors, and I take the consequences. I do what has to be done, so that the prison can achieve its purpose.

SAZONOV: Then there is nothing more for you to say—

BORODULIN: Yes, there is one thing. I know quite well that the revolutionaries are now determined to kill me. I am not afraid. But before I die, I would like to know what my crime is.

SAZONOV: All Russia knows your crime, and so do you.

BORODULIN: Very well, then. Why don't you write to the revolutionary authorities and ask them to kill me soon? It's distressing to have to wait. Much better to get it over with. Write the letter, and I give you my word of honor that it will go through.

SAZONOV: All you are saying is that you consider you deserve to die. My letter will change nothing. You know you are guilty. You chose to commit a crime, and the consequences follow. As to whether you will be killed, this is a matter for the people outside and does not concern the prisoners.

BORODULIN (*with a faint smile*): Then I understand. I suppose it is time I ordered a coffin and dug a grave behind the hill.

There was no answer from Sazonov, who left the governor's office shortly afterward. A few days later Borodulin journeyed to Irkutsk, where an attempt was made on his life. Barely escaping, he asked for a month's leave of absence, presumably to put his affairs in order, and traveled to Pskov in western Russia. The terrorists were hot on his heels. His movements were carefully watched, and it was decided to assassinate him on the last day of his holiday. He was leaving the house of the local prison governor when he observed two strangers making their way to his carriage. One leaped up and caught the horses' reins, bringing the carriage to a stop. The coachman shouted: "What's the matter, eh? Let go, you little fool!" Then the coachman heard a single shot. It was fired by another terrorist who had jumped onto the carriage step, aiming at Borodulin's heart from a distance of twelve inches. The prison governor died instantaneously. Only one of the terrorists was caught.

He was tried summarily, sentenced to death and hanged the next day.

By using terror the terrorists had hoped to alleviate the miseries of Russia. Singularly successful when they murdered Von Plehve, they were less successful at all other times. The assassination of Borodulin resulted in the appointment of a still harsher governor. Ismailov, the new governor, was the worst kind of Cossack officer. He enjoyed brutality, whereas Borodulin had merely placed himself at the service of brutality. It was rare for a prison governor to beat a prisoner with his own fists, but when a prisoner refused to remove his cap in the governor's presence, Ismailov struck him repeatedly. It was July, 1907. The reaction was in full swing. When the politicals protested, Ismailov ordered them all to be flogged. He ordered that he should be addressed as "Your Excellency." When they refused they were carried to the dark cells. He regarded attendance at church services as imperative. Those who refused were forced into the chapels at the end of bayonets. The old penalties were revived: the prisoners must sleep without bedding, they could receive no visitors from outside, and no food could be sent to them from the neighboring villages. Ismailov introduced a refinement of torture: a prisoner locked in a dark cell could see through the narrow eye slit a whip hanging in a brightly-lit corridor.

"There is absolutely nothing we can do against him," Sazonov wrote in a mood of profound dejection. "He is like some huge and elemental force of nature. One must submit to him, or die."

More and more Sazonov found himself thinking of death. There came to him at times a desperate need to expiate his own crime. He had failed to kill himself with morphine; then he must kill himself in some other way and by so doing attract the attention of the world to the plight of the prisoners. On July 25, largely on Sazonov's pleading, the prisoners decided to go on a hunger strike. It was a hopeless gesture. No one believed it would succeed in changing Ismailov's attitude. Sazonov sent a message to Ismailov: "You have beaten us with rifle butts and flicked your whips over our heads. Now we have nothing to hope for except death. We have resolved to starve until conditions are improved or death frees us from our torturers."

The news of the hunger strike reached Moscow five days later. There were newspaper editorials. Was Russia, a civilized country, to be known throughout the world as a place of barbarism? In England there was uproar; and Cunningham-Graham, speaking in Trafalgar Square, pointed to the imprisonment of Spiridonova and Sazonov, and the beatings they had received, as symptoms of the disease of autocracy. It was the time when governments were still tender-hearted. On the seventh day of the hunger-strike Sazonov, who had fallen into a waking stupor, was awakened by a heavy knock on the door. One of the guards entered the cell. He said: "His Excellency the prison governor has been relieved from his post." It was not quite true. Ismailov had been given extended leave of absence, and returned to his post at Algashi some months later. But the government had bowed before the fury of the newspaper editorials, at least temporarily, and from Moscow there came orders to send Sazonov to the prison at Gorny Serentui, where the regime was less harsh and where it was hoped the rebellious prisoner would be forgotten.

The government might have known better. Sazonov had found in the prisons the Archimedean point where a lever could be inserted, and he continued to throw all his weight upon the lever to the end.

The Protest

In a mood of prophecy Sazonov wrote to his father: "I have a feeling I shall never leave this prison alive. Everywhere about me there is only death. The truth is I am not a good prisoner and I doubt if I shall ever accustom myself to this slow maniacal existence in which every effort is made to destroy the personality of the prisoner."

Sazonov wrote often in this strain, but he also wrote many letters in which he described the occasional delights of prison life. On sunny days fresh air and sunlight streamed through the four large windows, through which he could see the bare blue hills in the distance. There were interminable discussions with prisoners who lived together in a large cell—Sazonov said it was ten paces wide, thirteen paces long and only six feet high, but he was a tall man with a large stride and other prisoners have described it as being the largest cell in the place, and the most comfortable. Then there were the new arrivals, and he found most of them delightful—"They are so good, my dear father, that I am altogether lost in brotherly affection for them"— though he complained that the cell was filled to overflowing. The walls were whitewashed, very clean. There was a table set across the whole length of the room where the prisoners studied. Along the walls were benches heaped with bedding. On sunny days the prisoners fought for places near the windows, but they did this with good humor. Though they were half-famished and lived on broth, tea, black bread, and three or four lumps of sugar a day, they were remarkably full of animal spirits and as noisy as schoolboys, so that Sazonov, whose deafness had given place to an acute sense of hearing, complained that "they keep howling all day long, so that it is completely impossible for me to work during the day, and as you know my best times for working are late at night and early in the morning, but these are precisely the times when they are most noisy." But he liked these people even though he was always shouting to them to keep quiet, and he wrote to his mother:

> It is impossible for me to tell you how much I admire them. In spite of walls and imprisonment, in spite of the terrible diet and the knowledge that every one of us has friends and relatives in the outside world pining for him, there is so much resilience of spirit, so much human strength, that whenever you contemplate it, it strengthens your hopes for the future. Your own sufferings disappear when you realize how much they are suffering with you. If you only knew how splendid it is to feel part of this living whole; to be completely without possessions, having no gold and no bread entirely your own. Best of all, we have lost the sense of our own separateness and all our joys and sorrows are held in common. If you would really understand and feel this, then you would know the secret which keeps us so fresh and green.

Gorny Serentui was the headquarters for the whole complex of prisons on the Mongolian border, and was something of a show-place. The prison governor lived there in a large house, outside the white walls of the prison. Here, too, was an excellently equipped prison hospital. Intended for 300 prisoners it contained three times as many, but for the prisoners in their cramped quarters there were advantages in numbers. The governor was lenient. From August, 1907, to July, 1909, there was only one incident which alarmed Sazonov, and for this he could hardly blame the prison governor, who was a model of fairness.

In December, 1907, Spiridonova fell ill at Malzev. She had been ill ever since her arrest, but the illness took a turn for the worse. Sazonov was attached to her. He had admired her when they were fellow prisoners at Arkatui, and by smuggling letters they had kept up a continual correspondence. At Malzev there were almost no hospital facilities. A young medical assistant, Sarra Dantzig, herself a prisoner and in the last stages of tuberculosis, was the only person allowed to treat the prisoners. The governor was in no mood to deal leniently with his prisoners and refused to allow Spiridonova to be transferred to Gorny Serentui. He wanted her under his own eyes. Once he suggested that he would willingly allow Spiridonova to be transferred on condition that two sick prisoners now in the hospital were brought back to Malzev. One of these prisoners was the Social Revolutionary Dora Kaplan who later made a determined attempt to kill Lenin. Spiridonova refused. She had no desire for special treatment, and seemed resigned to her approaching death. She had not counted on Sazonov.

As soon as he heard that Spiridonova was so ill that she was thought to be dying, he demanded an interview with the prison governor at Gorny Serentui. The governor was sympathetic and immediately offered to have Spiridonova transported to the hospital, provided that the officials at Malzev agreed. The officials at Malzev refused. Prosh Prozhian and Sazonov debated the matter and decided upon a hunger strike. Once more they hoped to reach the headlines of the Moscow newspapers. At the threat of a hunger strike the governor at Gorny Serentui used his wide powers to bring Spiridonova to the hospital, only to learn that the governor of Malzev had appealed directly to the provincial government headquarters at Chita. A telegram was received from Chita demanding the immediate return of Spiridonova to

Malzev. Reluctantly the governor of Gory Serentui was compelled to send her back.

Sazonov was now convinced that the authorities at Malzev
were determined to kill Spiridonova. He wrote to his father: "She is going out like a candle, and every day she is approaching closer to death. They want her to die, and they
are deliberately provoking her death. As for us, what can we
do? Must we be indifferent spectators of her murder? Our
hands may be tied, and we are powerless to rescue her, but
at least we can die with her!"

Before leaving Gorny Serentui, Spiridonova was allowed a
last interview with Prosh Prozhian and Sazonov. The interview was stormy. Sazonov kept talking about "those murderers at Malzev," and Prosh Prozhian with his mastery of
argument almost convinced her that she would be a rene-
gade to the revolution if she moved an inch from where she
was standing. She was suffering from hemorrhages and fever, but the excitement was worse. She wanted to be left
alone, and hardly cared whether she was at Malzev or at
Gorny Serentui.

"You are making it a matter of tragic importance,"
Spiridonova said, "but it is really not very important. I want
to rest, and I don't care where I rest. I'm too ill to become a
bone of contention. Please leave me alone."

Sazonov and Prosh Prozhian exchanged glances. Sazonov
was now for silence, but Prozhian resumed his dialectical arguments, insisting that the revolution needed her presence at
the hospital and it was above all necessary to fight against the
officials at Malzev.

"We absolutely insist that you see the matter in its revolutionary aspect," he said, and he would have gone on to in-
vent more arguments if Spiridonova had not conveniently
fainted.

She was allowed to rest. By nightfall she seemed better
and on the next day she returned to Malzev. When the pris-

oners discussed a new hunger strike, Spiridonova wrote that they were behaving foolishly and she urged them to safeguard their health.

In July, 1909, orders reached Gorny Serentui from Moscow, demanding that the prisoners should no longer be treated in the old lenient way. Prisoners must be warned that if they approached the windows in the evening, they would be shot by the guards stationed outside. They must no longer smoke cigarettes or receive food from outside. The number of books they were allowed to receive must be severely curtailed. Punishments must be severe. Chemodanov, the prison governor, was warned that he had behaved too leniently and was now under the watchful eye of inspectors sent by the government. The governor obeyed the new orders reluctantly for nearly a year and a half. He respected and liked the prisoners, and had a particular fondness for Sazonov. He was a humane man and had nothing but contempt for guards who humiliated the prisoners. "I am doing my best to hold on to my post," he told Sazonov, "for the man who replaces me will be an infinitely worse task-master." Sazonov half guessed the terror would begin the moment Chemodanov was replaced.

Early in November, 1910, it was announced that a new governor, General Vissotsky, was on his way. Of all the prison governors Sazonov had known by reputation, Vissotsky was the worst. As governor of the prison in Perm, he had an unenviable reputation for ordering prisoners to be beaten at the slightest provocation.

A few days before Vissotsky arrived Chemodanov went to see Sazonov in his cell. Usually Sazonov would rise to greet the governor with a quick smile. This time there was no smile. Sazonov was pacing the cell, his brow furrowed, his eyes glazed with suffering.

"You're foolish to give way to anxieties," the governor said quietly.

Sazonov halted. He turned on the governor sharply.

"Why foolish? Don't you know that the hangman of Perm is on his way?"

"Why do you say that? It's only a rumor—"

"Rumor! Do you think we don't know these people? When he comes here, he will flog us and murder us—there will be no end to his floggings and murders."

"But not for you, Sazonov. After all you have only three more months' imprisonment since your sentence has been reduced. I have given you a separate cell because you have been a model prisoner, and I shall point out your good behavior to my successor. The three months will pass quickly."

Sazonov smiled and shook his head.

"No, they will be very long," he answered. "I don't believe they will ever let me leave here. I know, as well as you do, that there's some connection between Vissotsky's arrival and the fact that I am shortly to be released. I've seen the newspapers. They talk about the unpardonable laxity of our treatment here. Well, there will soon be an end to 'unpardonable laxity.' "

On November 21 Vissotsky arrived with an escort of soldiers and with his own trained warders.

Sazonov had discussed the possibility of a reign of terror in the prison ever since the previous July. In interminable talks with the prisoners he had outlined a course of action to combat the terror. If the new governor refused to treat the prisoners as human beings, he must be killed, and if it was impossible to kill him, then the only alternative for Sazonov was suicide. A message was sent to Spiridonova, asking for her opinion. She argued that it was better to buckle under temporarily. The important thing was that the lives of the revolutionaries should be preserved for the sake of the coming revolution. Nothing was so important as to preserve a nucleus of revolutionaries ready to take over when the reaction had exhausted itself in fruitless punishments and killings. Sazonov replied: "They have an enormous appetite for these horrors and they will go on indefinitely unless we stop them in their tracks. More decisive measures are needed." Spiridonova disagreed, and when Sazonov wrote about "the insults they offer us," she replied: "Remember, they cannot insult us." These letters were exchanged during the later part of 1909, when it was rumored that Chemodanov was about to be removed. Now in November, 1910, they were confronted at last with the enemy they had long feared.

For the first few days Vissotsky kept out of sight. He was in conference with Chemodanov, arranging the last details for taking over the prison. Three days after his arrival the prisoners learned from the chief warder that Vissotsky had despatched two of his lieutenants for two cartloads of whips. Chemodanov sent messages secretly to the prisoners, warning them of what was in store, begging them to behave towards the new governor with exaggerated respect, and he confirmed the story that the two cartloads of whips were on their way. Henceforth all prisoners must wear the drab prison uniform supplied by the government and have their heads shaved. These were two of the ordinances which Chemodanov had refused to enforce. An atmosphere of hysteria and terror settled over the prison.

By this time Sazonov had already decided that, if a single brutal punishment was inflicted on a prisoner, he would take his own life.

On November 23, he wrote three letters: to his parents, to his brother Zot, and to his fiancée Maria Alexandrovna Prokofieva. In his letters he explained that he could see no other way out. Henceforth the prison was to be given over to "a wild beast, who has no respect for the human person." From Vissotsky nothing could be expected except death, humiliation, and torture. It was true that he could probably outlive the remaining three months of his imprisonment by toadying to the new governor, but he had decided against this course for reasons which should be perfectly clear. He wrote:

> I believe that my suicide, deliberately committed, will arouse the attention of the public to the horrors of the Siberian prisons, and from the better members of society there will come a shout of protest. My comrades in prison will then know that voices are being raised against a government that makes torture and death common occurrences in prison life.

In the same letters Sazonov wrote of the kindnesses he had received from Chemodanov, and he insisted that he was not acting so much against Vissotsky as against a whole system. Above all, he hoped to justify his life by his death.

These letters were the end-product of a long process of self-examination. Ever since the attack on Von Plehve, Sazonov had been afflicted by a towering sense of guilt. He wanted desperately to expiate his guilt, which sometimes embraced the guilt of others, so that when he met the young revolutionary Karpovich, who had assassinated the former Minister of Education, Bogolepov—the least defensible of all the assassinations committed by the terrorists—Sazonov wrote: "The thought frightens me that in some way I too am morally guilty of murdering Bogolepov." At another time he wrote of himself as "one who has committed the greatest of all crimes," and went on desperately to try to fathom why he, who had dreamed of striving peacefully for the sake of suffering humanity, should have the mark of Cain on his brow. "We took up the sword," he wrote in extenuation of his conduct, "because the enemy compelled us, and only after terrible struggles and agonies and under the pressure of tragic necessity." Now the pressure of tragic necessity was driving deeper, and against Spiridonova's advice he resigned himself to suicide.

On the night of November 25 the prison was formally handed over to Vissotsky by Chemodanov.

In a low room reached by an iron staircase the prisoners were introduced to the new governor. Behind a table heaped with documents and complete lists of the prisoners and their prison records sat Chemodanov and Vissotsky. Chemodanov was nervous, flicking over the pages of the documents in front of him. Vissotsky, small, wiry, with a face that was strangely gray and with small waxed mustaches, gazed hungrily at the prisoners as they were brought before the table. A paraffin lamp hung over the table and a prison clerk stood a little to one side. A prisoner shuffled to the table.

"The prisoner Akimov," shouted the clerk.

"Well, what are you sentenced for?" Vissotsky said, glaring. He had used the familiar second person singular.

There was no answer from Akimov.

"Why don't you speak?" Vissotsky said, jumping up, his small eyes gleaming with light from the paraffin lamp.

"I don't choose to speak when I am addressed in that way," Akimov answered, and then he felt a blow over his heart.

"Take him away!" Vissotsky said. "Throw him in the dark cells!"

Then he turned toward Chemodanov and said: "They're all vermin! You have to know how to deal with them."

More prisoners were brought up. Vissotsky talked to all of them in the same way. He roared and thumped the table and made speeches. When a prisoner explained that he was a political, Vissotsky said: "I make no distinction between criminals. Believe me, I shall stop at nothing to make you obey my orders." Half way through the interrogation Chemodanov could stand it no more, remembered that his coach was waiting, made his abrupt farewells to the new governor and departed. He wrote later that he went away with the absolute certainty that the prison would be a holocaust by the next day. Also, he knew that the prisoners were in possession of a revolver and three steel files sharpened to a razor's edge.

By midnight nine prisoners were in the dark cells, but no one had been flogged.

Sometime during the night Vissotsky visited the special cells where the more important prisoners were guarded. Sazonov was waiting for him, his hands behind his back.

"So you dare to have your hands behind your back when I come to your cell?" Vissotsky barked.

Sazonov placed his hands at his sides.

"I see I am going to have trouble teaching you obedience," Vissotsky went on. "I have heard all about you. Make no mistake, you will soon be screaming for mercy."

"I have survived Borodulin," Sazonov answered, and Vissotsky was perfectly aware of the threat. He marched out.

Two days later a small incident precipitated the holocaust. The long debate was nearly over. The carefully-laid plans to murder Vissotsky were abandoned. Vissotsky ordered a criminal to pose as a political in one of the dark cells. The subterfuge was soon recognized, and Mikhailov, a Social Revolutionary, objected firmly. Vissotsky had expected such objections and marched up to the cell, flung open the door, flicked his whip and ordered Mikhailov out. Mikhailov refused to step out. Vissotsky grew more threatening. He barked that Mikhailov was to receive twenty strokes for impertinence and for refusing to obey orders. Before the warders could jump on the prisoner, he had taken strychnine, and a moment later, because the strychnine had no immediate effect, he took morphine. Even then he was conscious. He asked for some nitric acid. This was given to him, and at last he fell to the floor. When he reached the hospital there was a gaping hole in his stomach. He died shortly afterward.

All Sazonov's fears were now seen to be well-founded. Vissotsky regarded the politicals as instruments for the exercise of his sadistic desires. Slomyansky, a former soldier, refused to eat the black bread which was thrown to him in his dark cell. Knowledge of the hunger-strike was brought to Vissotsky, who ordered Slomyansky to receive thirty strokes. When Slomyansky was stripped and bound to the whipping bench, a doctor was sent for. The doctor declared that Slomyansky was suffering from heart disease and would probably die under the blows.

Vissotsky said: "I'll give him something to cure his heart disease."

Slomyansky was beaten until the blood ran, and he was unconscious when he was taken to the prison hospital.

The doctor who had said Slomyansky should not be beaten was ordered to receive thirty-five strokes "for showing his ignorance of medicine." Manacled, the doctor thrust out at the guard with his chained hands. By a new law any attack on a guard could be punished by summary death. Vissotsky decided to prolong the agony. He ordered that the doctor should be given a thrashing with rifle-butts and then beaten.

Sazonov had come to the end of his resources. Ahead there stretched unending years of brutality in Siberian prisons. He counselled the others to remain alive; for himself he chose death in a supreme act of protest. He had written once to Spiridonova: "The savages are coming into their own. For ourselves, there is only one task: to stand up to them, to fight every act of human degradation and every dishonor. Unless we do this, the savages may summon from the depths of our unconscious the ancient habits of slaves and kill the revolutionaries in us." Now had come the time to make the only effective protest he knew against the savages. Shortly after three o'clock on the morning of November 28 he took morphine, blew out the lamp and prepared for death. It was exactly three months to the day when he was due to leave prison.

An hour later the night-guards heard him coughing and moaning. They rushed in, but he was already dying. The warders discussed whether to awaken Vissotsky and tell him the news. There were long discussions about whether the hospital doctor should be informed. Nothing was done until six o'clock, and it was half an hour before the doctor arrived. By then it was too late, and by seven o'clock Sazonov was dead. *

Told about the suicide Vissotsky remarked: "It's nothing at all to worry about. I don't mind how many of them commit suicide. Suicides by day, suicides by night! Well, there's no point in nursing them. Tell the assistant doctor on duty that neither he nor anyone else is allowed to attend the prisoners at night. He can see them well enough during the day."

Three other prisoners took poison that night, but the prison doctor gave them antidotes and their lives were saved. Petrov, the young doctor who had gone to the help of Slomyansky, attempted to kill himself by pouring paraffin over himself and then setting light to it. He, too, survived.

Except for a letter smuggled to Spiridonova at Malzev, none of the letters written by Sazonov during the last days of his life were ever received. They were confiscated, sent to police headquarters in Moscow and gathered dust until the revolution. But though the prison officials did everything possible to conceal his death, it was known the next day in Moscow. Russia was reeling with the death of Tolstoy, which

---

* Whittaker Chambers has described in *Witness* the reasons which brought about his conversion to Communism. He recounts his overwhelming admiration for three revolutionaries: Felix Dzerzhinsky, Eugen Levine, and Sazonov. Of the third he writes:

"The Russian was not a Communist. He was a pre-Communist revolutionist named Kaliayev. (I should have said Sazanov.) He was arrested for a minor part in the assassination of the Tsarist prime minister, von Plehve. He was sent into Siberian exile to one of the worst prison camps, where the political prisoners were flogged. Kaliayev sought some way to protest this outrage to the world. The means were few, but at last he found a way. In protest at the flogging of other men, Kaliayev drenched himself in kerosene, set himself on fire and burned himself to death. That is also what it means to be a Communist. That is also what it means to be a witness."

It is doubtful whether a more muddled and inaccurate account of Sazonov has ever been written.

had occurred mysteriously at Astapovo only a few days before. To the 30,000 students who came out on strike, the two deaths were strangely symbolic. For three years the revolutionary movement had been dying. Now the ghosts of Tolstoy and Sazonov arose to give a new, strange and peculiarly lasting vitality to the movement. The strike lasted three weeks, and the movement did not collapse until 1918. For years afterward it became a legend that the two apostles of passive resistance had died at the same hour and on the same day.

From Ufa, Sazonov's father sent a telegram to Stolypin, the Minister of the Interior:

> I learn with sorrow that my son, Yegor Sazonov, has died in the prison at Gorny Serentui. I most humbly request permission to go to Siberia and bring his body home for Christian burial. The mere permission to bring his body to Ufa, to be buried according to the unchanging rites which have come down from our ancestors, will bring consolation to his grief-stricken parents.

Stolypin's reply was brief:

> Minister of Interior regrets impossibility to comply with your wishes received in letter dated December 5th—Stolypin.

Vissotsky remained in charge of the prison at Gorny Serentui for some years. But after Sazonov's suicide he received an official reprimand, the power to inflict corporal punishment on political prisoners was removed from him, and most of the political prisoners were sent to outlying prisons. From then until the Bolsheviks came to power, political prisoners were generally treated with remarkable leniency.

During the October Revolution of 1917 the Social Revolutionaries made their bid for power. The surviving members of the party met in St. Petersburg under an immense banner which showed the young Sazonov in the prime of his life. From the rostrum Spiridonova made a speech against the Bolsheviks:

> They talk all the time of terror, but we who have known terror and practiced terror know that the time of terror is over. We have taken power from the old feudal autocracy and the Revolution has been won. Let us talk now of love.
>
> We stand under the banner of Sazonov, who proved in his life that love has its own laws. We honor him as one who struggled for the happiness we all desire. In prison most of us were inhumanly bitter, but Sazonov knew how to create joy in the midst of suffering.

Eight months later the headquarters of the Social Revolutionaries were captured by the Bolsheviks and its members were scattered to the winds.

KALIAYEV at the age of eighteen in high school uniform

KALIAYEV

Everything is beautiful. The stars and clouds and flowers and people and— death is beautiful, too.

The Poet

He had a long and delicate face, a broad forehead, a firm chin, bright blue eyes which would smoulder and change to a darker blue when he was excited and an almost feminine mouth which curled easily at the corners. He was more Polish than Russian, and to the very end he bore traces of a soft, musical Polish accent. Savinkov called him affectionately "our poet." Sazonov described him as "a precious iridescent stone," and wondered how so slight a person could conceal such power. Shy, incurably quiet, given to long periods of silent meditation, Ivan Kaliayev came to terrorism by way of a luminous faith and a desperate desire to sacrifice himself for the salvation of mankind. He joined the Terrorist Brigade in 1903; two years later he was hanged for the assassination of the Grand Duke Sergius, and no one ever died more gladly.

With Kaliayev we are confronted with the revolutionary in the purest form. Believing in the infinite value of each human life, he was prepared to kill, but only on condition that he sacrificed his own life, his death at once an offering to the revolutionary cause and the sign of an overwhelming love for his fellow-men. He found no particular delight in terrorism. He regarded murder as inexcusable and at the same time necessary, and he never escaped from that tragic dichotomy. Nechayev, and Lenin after him, embraced violence with passionate conviction: it was the air they breathed, the atmosphere they carried with them, the stimulus which kept them alive; it was, almost, their food. Kaliayev detested violence. He would go out and kill because he hoped that with one single clean-cut blow he could force the enemy to surrender. He killed scrupulously, plagued by doubts, never entirely convinced of the need to murder but wholly convinced of the need to sacrifice himself. Like Sazonov, whose sense of guilt he shared, he was determined that the war should be waged chivalrously according to the rules he was always having to make up because there were no guidebooks for sensitive murderers. Once, talking to Mikhail Gotz, the most practical and least visionary of the revolutionaries, Kaliayev said: "You understand, when we offer ourselves as a sacrifice, then it is necessary that we should be absolutely pure and chaste. We should not offer up a life we have already grown weary of." For him the terrorists who were prepared to abandon their lives for the sake of others were "knights of the spirit" (*ritsari dukha*), employing a phrase beloved of Kierkegaard, though Kaliayev must have found it among his memories of his Polish ancestors.

In his brief revolutionary career Kaliayev demonstrated so little wilfulness and was so transparently dedicated that when he was dead it seemed inconceivable that he had ever existed. Even when he was living people felt he was too unreal, too good, too virtuous altogether to be included among the revolutionaries. He dressed elegantly. He wrote superb poetry. He liked the fine things of life. He had a strange deep rolling laugh which would come on at the most unexpected moments. He had a habit of looking at you with his deep-set penetrating eyes in a way which made you reveal things about yourself you were prepared to tell no one but yourself. He was a Shelley set loose in the tortured world of midnight conspiracies, a Shelley who not only wrote poems against Castlereagh but set out to kill without compunction, violently, quickly, and cleanly, the man he had already murdered in his poetry.

What was his secret? Perhaps we shall never know, but occasionally he hints at it. He belonged to the past. He spoke a language his fellow revolutionaries did not always understand, a language in which the words chivalry, knighthood, purity, were not just counters but possessed depths of meaning so real to him that he could hardly understand why they were meaningless to the other revolutionaries. He complained of the boredom of revolutionary discussions. For him there was only one problem—to kill cleanly. A revotionary must regard himself as a soldier, but one overwhelmed with a sense of honor. He must have a conscience of a knight-errant, giving all the advantages to the adversary, and he must explore every punctilio of conscience before infringing on the lives of others. It is the matador's code, the delicate swerve of the veronica, the impulse to live close to death only in order to value life more highly. "He is more like a poet than a revolutionary," Sazonov said when he first set eyes on Kaliayev. In fact Kaliayev was more like a knight-errant whose only desire was to serve his princess to the end, and for him the princess comprised all suffering humanity.

When Kaliayev arrived in St. Petersburg in 1903, he was already fully formed. His past tells us little. He was born in Warsaw on June 24, 1877, his father a small landowner and a former officer in the Kiev Regiment, his mother a Polish beauty known for her charities and her love for the poor. His father seems to have been one of those stern, impractical, retired officers who are the commonplaces of Russian novels. From his mother he learned about the Polish uprisings against the Czar, the blood spilled on the streets of Warsaw.

He was eleven when he was sent to the Apukhtinsky Gymnasium in Warsaw, then celebrated because it produced Polish students fanatically loyal to the Russian crown. In 1896 he left the gymnasium. He had immersed himself in Polish and Russian literature, and already regarded himself as a poet. The next year he went to Moscow, attending lectures in philology and history at the University. By chance he came upon a thin pamphlet written in Polish and printed in London describing socialism. He immediately joined the Polish Socialist Party, but apparently without any intention of leading the life of an agitator. He had still no idea how he would earn a living. Abandoning philology and history, he left Moscow and in the fall of 1898 became a law student at the University of St. Petersburg. In the spring of 1899 student disorders broke out, directed against the excesses of the regime. Kaliayev suddenly found himself in the midst of political activity. He made speeches, wrote manifestoes and helped to organize the students. Almost inevitably he was arrested. He spent three months in prison and was then exiled to Ekaterinoslav in Southern Russia, where he lived under police surveillance. His interest in a law career had by now completely vanished. He decided to become a teacher of history and philosophy, and one night he slipped out of Ekaterinoslav and made his way to Lvov, where he attended courses at the University, gave lessons (but not enough to stave off hunger), read subversive political magazines and kept up a tremendous correspondence. During a journey to Berlin he was arrested. Several copies of the revolutionary magazine *Iskra*, which had first appeared on December 21, 1900, were found on him. He was summarily arrested and thrown into the Warsaw Citadel, but was released soon afterward, though once more he was sent to live under police surveillance at Ekaterinoslav. In 1903 he went abroad again. By this time he was in close touch with the Terrorist Brigade. It was Savinkov's influence which propelled him into the revolutionary movement, for Savinkov too was born in Warsaw and they had known each other since childhood.

Kaliayev did not look like a revolutionary; nor for that matter did Savinkov, who resembled with his high forehead and sharp, intelligent face, the sharpness occasionally masked by an appearance of polite boredom, a member of the minor aristocracy. Victor Chernov, who was to become President of the Constituent Assembly which the Bolsheviks dissolved in January, 1918, knew them both, and for him Savinkov always resembled a kind of Mephistopheles, while Kaliayev reminded him of "young green leaves still sticky from birth." There was in Savinkov the weariness of the conspirator who sees every incursion into the landscape of danger as an incentive to still closer brushes with death, until death became a commonplace, something he knew so well that he rarely paid it the tribute of fear. For him conspiracy was a kind of intellectual game. He had no deep convictions. He became a terrorist for the joy of watching himself playing, admiring his own expertness, delighting above all in assembling around himself the disciples whose lives he gambled with, as he gambled with his own, for the highest stakes. And Kaliayev with his pale feminine face with its delicate lines, the bright eyes which would sometimes lose their fire and smoulder with a strange sadness, the slim figure in the clothes that were always a little too tight for him, the boy who resembled nothing so much as a young prince, in love with life and death at their sharpest points, was the perfect foil for Mephistopheles. Chernov said it was the most extraordinary sight to see them together. They seemed in some strange way to belong to one another, and yet when you saw them together you were aware of irreconcilable differences. Nearly all the terrorists, when they met Kaliayev for the first time, found him wonderfully strange; he was always talking about the symbolist poets, Blok, Balmont, and the rest, and he was always carrying dog-eared copies of the poets with him. One cannot imagine Nechayev reading any poet with pleasure, unless it was the terrible little poem written by

Ogaryov in honor of the enlightened personality of Nechayev himself. Kaliayev wrote poetry because he had to. It was revolutionary poetry, reminiscent of Shelley's revolutionary poems, but a Shelley who had read Pushkin:

> *So now my soul blazes in a fierce tempest*
> *And my heart shouts with a fierce courage!*
> *Soon we shall see the purple fire of freedom*
> *Piercing the darkness of an ancient violence.*
> *The mask of lies will be torn from the face of evil,*
> *And from ourselves we shall tear our deathly fear . . .*

In translation, of course, the poetry loses nearly everything, and Kaliayev's peculiar vibrancy, his talent for introducing trumpet-notes in poetry is completely missing in any English version. Zhelyabov had a fondness for poetry and liked to roar out the verses of Lermontov, whom he considered a greater poet than Pushkin, but most of the revolutionaries had a defective ear. Like Pisarev they were prepared to agree that a pair of shoes was worth more than all Shakespeare.

Kaliayev belied his name, for in Russian *kalit'* means "to temper"; but like all poets he was intemperate. He could not understand why everyone in Russia was not a revolutionary, and half-pitied the millions of Russians who did not have the good fortune to belong to the Terrorist Brigade. Once, talking to Savinkov, he said: "I wish to heaven I was in Macedonia. They say everyone is a terrorist there. And with us? Five or six, no more. How on earth can one be a revolutionary, and not be a terrorist?" And then a little later: "Soon enough we shall see the flames! The peasants will get hold of the bombs, and then—the revolution!" For him the revolution was a white flower which would suddenly burst open, and nothing in the world could be as exciting as the opening of the flower. Though he thought in this way, a deep unconscious striving of religious feeling stirred within him,

and Savinkov was probably right when he spoke of
Kaliayev's "completely religious" attitude to terror.

When Sazonov was stalking Von Plehve through the streets
of St. Petersburg, Kaliayev, dressed in a railway porter's uniform, was only a little way behind him, carrying a bomb
wrapped in a handkerchief. They had all paused briefly in
the square which faces the Church of the Protection and In-
tercession of the Virgin, and while Sazonov sat on one of the
benches, explaining quietly to Sikorsky how he should get
rid of the bomb if the attempt failed, Savinkov had caught a
glimpse of Kaliayev solemnly crossing himself before the
ikon which hung on the church gate. Kaliayev had removed
his hat. He was still holding the bomb as he crossed himself.
Savinkov went over to him and told him it was time to go. It
was now twenty minutes to ten. A few moments later they all
left the square, Savinkov cutting across the Sadovaya, while
the others went in the direction of the Warsaw Station.
Borishansky went first, followed at a distance by Sazonov,
Kaliayev, and Sikorsky. Kaliayev was smiling and walking
with an easy, beautiful gait.

To reach the Warsaw Station it is necessary to cross the
bridge over the Obvodny Canal. The bridge swung high over
the canal. Kaliayev was on the bridge when he saw the great
clouds of smoke rising from the explosion. The blood-stained
horses, dragging the remnants of the carriage, came racing
past him, and he knew Von Plehve was dead and there was
no need for him to throw his bomb. Sikorsky was behind
him. He decided to turn round, explain what had happened
and then get rid of the bomb. As he slipped down a side
turning a janitor stopped him. Nearly all the janitors in St.
Petersburg were police-spies, and for a moment Kaliayev
thought he would be arrested.

"Well, what happened?" the janitor asked.

"I don't know."

"Didn't you come from there?"

"Yes."

"Then why don't you know?"

"How could I know? They say someone fired a gun."

The janitor seems to have been satisfied with the answer. It had been a peculiarly dull explosion, the sound absorbed by the high houses on the Ismailovsky Prospekt, and soon Kaliayev was racing away, hoping to find a pond where he could sink the bomb before someone asked him what he was carrying in his handkerchief. Then he took the noon train to Kiev.

It was all much simpler and far more terrible than he had imagined. The horses ripped with bomb splinters, the mangled carriage rushing past, the heavy sulphur-yellow cloud rising out of the street, the sudden frightening appearance of the janitor—all these things were to haunt him for the rest of his short life. He had had no time to see whether Sazonov was dead, but he had already lost hope of ever seeing Sazonov alive. Savinkov, too, was convinced that Sazonov was dead. It was more than a week before the news leaked out that Sazonov was alive.

With Von Plehve dead, the conspirators planned to meet in Geneva and hold a conference to decide the next step. They had all fled from St. Petersburg in different directions —all except the unlucky Sikorsky. Savinkov took the night train to Warsaw, hoping to meet Evno Azev, but there was no sign of the arch-conspirator there. It occurred to Savinkov that it was unlikely that the search was being extended to Kiev, and he decided to join Kaliayev. There were disturbing rumors that Sikorsky had been arrested, and together they decided to make the journey to Byelostok, which was Sikorsky's birthplace and the place where accurate news of him was most likely to be found. But at Byelostok there was no news at all, and in despair they decided to make for Geneva, traveling through Germany. At Eydtkuhnen on the German border there was usually a quarter of an hour's

pause while passports were examined. Savinkov had no passport. When the German frontier-guard asked for his passport, Savinkov thrust the little green book which all Russians
must carry when they are traveling inside Russia into the
guard's hands. The guard seemed satisfied; the train rolled
on; and within three days they were in Geneva, basking
quietly in the sun, while newspapers all over the world were
commenting on the death of the Russian Minister, who was
now no more than a memory to the conspirators who had
killed him. According to Savinkov the Terrorist Brigade had
proved itself, and there remained only one problem: who
was the next to be shot down?

One by one the conspirators made their way to Geneva.
Schweitzer, Borishansky, Dulebov, Dora Brilliant, perhaps
three or four others. Savinkov was so proud of the recent exploit that he demanded autonomy for the Terrorist Brigade.
It should have its own treasury, its own high command, its
own power to make decisions. There were excellent reasons
for this. In theory the Brigade was no more than the fighting
arm of the Social Revolutionary Party. In fact it was the
most widely known revolutionary movement in Russia, and
though comprising only a handful of men, was the most
feared and the most respected. It was waging war against
the government itself while the other revolutionary parties
were waging war among themselves; and though Savinkov's
claim to autonomy was rejected by the Party, he seems to
have convinced all the members of the Terrorist Brigade that
henceforth they must behave autonomously, whatever the
opinion of the Party. In this he was aided by Mikhail Gotz,
the foreign representative of the Terrorist Brigade, then lying ill at Geneva. It was Gotz's task to provide finances,
high explosives, shelter for escaping terrorists, and whatever
intellectual sustenance the brigade needed. Unassuming,
with penetrating dark eyes, a thin high-pitched voice, a
manner of almost excessive gentleness, Gotz acted as chief of

staff to Evno Azev. There was no sign of Azev in Geneva. As usual, Azev was on one of his mysterious journeys. Except for a brief account of the killing of Von Plehve, which was written by Kaliayev, nothing of importance seems to have been done by the terrorists during the summer. They rested, compared notes, fussed over Gotz, and prepared for the party conference in Paris in the autumn. Azev's absence was perhaps the reason why no program was agreed upon. Mysterious, remote, never present when his presence was necessary, Azev was still in the eyes of the party the chief of the Terrorist Brigade, and no one yet suspected that he was an *agent-provocateur.*

In Paris, at conferences over which Savinkov presided, it was decided to destroy the main stronghold of the monarchy. Those who were most fervently loyal to the Czar were to die. Among those who were marked for death were the Grand Dukes Vladimir and Sergius, Kleigels (the Governor-General of Kiev), Trepov (the Governor-General of St. Petersburg), Buligin (the new Minister of the Interior), and his assistant, Durnov. For this purpose the Terrorist Brigade was split into three groups: Schweitzer was to go to St. Petersburg, Savinkov to Moscow and Borishansky to Kiev. Schweitzer knew that in the Peter and Paul Fortress there would be a memorial service in March, 1905, commemorating Alexander II, killed by the revolutionaries twenty-four years earlier. During the service he hoped to kill the Grand Duke Vladimir, Buligin, Durnov, and perhaps Trepov. In fact the two expeditions to St. Petersburg and Kiev failed, and in the long list of people on the death-list only the Grand Duke Sergius, Governor-General of Moscow and uncle of the Czar, paid the penalty.

The conspirators left France and made their way back to Russia by roundabout routes, with false passports, in November.

In that desperate winter the revolutionary fires were

burning high. Never had there been a time when Russia was so ripe for rebellion. In the Far East the Russian army had suffered one reverse after another. On January 1, 1905, it was learned that Port Arthur had fallen. On January 9 Father Gapon led his famous march of unarmed men, women, and children to the gates of the Winter Palace. It was a bitterly cold day, with snow and piercing winds. When the Cossacks fired into the crowd, the die was cast. From that moment there could never be any doubt that the autocracy would fall. In a manifesto to the Czar written shortly after the shooting, Father Gapon wrote:

The innocent blood of workers, their wives and children lies forever between thee, O soul-destroying Czar, and the Russian people. Now is the time for bombs and dynamite, terror by individuals, terror by the masses, and this must be, and so it shall absolutely come about. An immense sea of blood shall be shed, and because of thee, because of the evil wrought by thy family, Russia may perish! Understand and remember: it would be better if thou didst abandon the throne of Russia and suffer thyself to be placed on trial before the Russian people. Do this, and pity thy children, thou who hast offered peace to other countries but drinkest the blood of thine own children.

Now is the time for bombs and dynamite, terror by individuals, terror by the masses . . .
Since they were determined to kill the Grand Duke Sergius, the most important problem facing the conspirators was to discover his whereabouts. They knew he had three palaces—the Governor-General's official palace on the Tverskaya, another official palace set in the gardens of the Neskuchny Park, far away in the southeast of Moscow, looking over the Moskva River, and a small private palace, the gift of the Emperor, within the Kremlin walls. Which one was he living in? There was only one way of finding out. The conspirators, disguised as coachmen and street-peddlers,

wandered about the city, made inquiries, stationed themselves outside the various palaces of the Governor-General,
and, in general, kept discreet watch on all his movements.
They found to their astonishment that the Grand Duke was
visiting all his palaces, but usually spent the nights in the
palace in the Neskuchny Park. This was surprising, because
it meant a long journey to the official residence along
roads that could be easily watched. It was as though everything was being made easy for them.

Kaliayev wore the disguise of a coachman. Over his coachman's livery he wore a heavy fur coat with a red silk belt.
He looked prosperous, his horse had a sleek coat, the sleigh
was well-kept. In the livery stables he deliberately assumed
the air of a young coachman determined to fleece his cus-
tomers, miserly, proud, a little pompous and more than a
little pious, always crossing himself. It was an odd character
for him to assume, but he played it to the hilt. He would
tell the coachmen in the stables long stories about his early
life as a waiter in St. Petersburg—mercifully few of the
coachmen knew St. Petersburg, and he was never questioned. Moiseyenko, who was also under orders to keep
watch over the Grand Duke's movements, played the role
of a coachman too poor to care for his horse. His sleigh
was second-hand, falling apart at the seams. Where Kaliayev
was garrulous, Moiseyenko was mute. He rarely spoke to the
other coachmen, and simply refused to answer questions
about himself. Strangely calm, inscrutable, methodical and
completely reliable, he was probably the most determined
and most courageous of the small band of conspirators
around Savinkov.

There were three other members of the group. There was
a young, recently recruited schoolteacher from Baku called
Peter Kulikovsky, who had no experience of terrorism but
possessed a desperate desire to show himself as a resolute
revolutionary. There was Tatiana Leontyeva, the daughter

of the Vice-Governor of Yakutsk Province, a blond-haired and statuesque young woman who moved in court circles, dined with Grand Dukes, and observed the decay of the Czardom from close quarters. Tatiana Leontyeva was also a recent recruit, and if they had been in touch with her earlier they would have had less difficulty in discovering the Grand Duke's movements. Finally, there was Dora Brilliant, who posed as Savinkov's mistress.

Savinkov was so busy planning the attack on the Grand Duke that he did not learn until long afterwards that just before the famous day when Father Gapon led the procession to the Winter Palace, the Grand Duke had resigned from his post as Governor-General, and was gradually arranging for his furniture to be transferred to the small Nicholas Palace in the Kremlin. He had resigned ostensibly on the grounds that he did not believe he had acted firmly enough during the strikes and the student riots, and he was losing his interest in politics. He had been Governor-General since 1891. He was tired, and wanted a rest. Not knowing all this, Savinkov was puzzled by the visits to the three palaces. In fact the Grand Duke Sergius was simply collecting his papers, disposing of his furniture and training his successor.

Through the newspapers it was learned that the Grand Duke would attend a performance at the Bolshoy Theatre on the night of February 2. It was decided to throw the bomb as he drove up to the theatre. Kaliayev was to take up his position with a bomb on Vozkressensky Square, and Kulikovsky was to stand at the entrance to the Alexandrovsky Gardens. From the Kremlin to the Bolshoy Theatre was only a short ride. The Grand Duke would have to pass through the Nikolsky Gate, past the Alexandrovsky Gardens on the left, and then swing into the Vozkressensky Square. The conspirators would therefore be on both sides of him as he passed through the gate.

Kaliayev was overjoyed. Now at last he would be able to demonstrate his faith in terrorism. He wrote to a friend a few days before the attack: "Today I am as carelessly happy as the joyful sun, which calls to me from the blue canopy of a tender and gracious sky. I wander aimlessly in the streets. I gaze at the sun and at people, and I marvel how all my wintry anxieties have fled." To Savinkov he said: "I do not believe there is a past—only a present. It seems to me that Zhelyabov is still alive, and Sazonov is not shut up in the Schlusselburg Fortress. They are with us. Surely you feel their presence! They are here, all round us!"

In a mood of wild elation, Kaliayev waited on the Ilynka for Savinkov to deliver the bomb into his hands. All that day a storm had been threatening, and by six o'clock in the evening there were flurries of snow in the air and the wind whipped the walls of the Kremlin. Just after seven o'clock Savinkov drove up in a sleigh, handed him a bomb wrapped in a handkerchief, and then vanished down the dark street, to give another bomb to Kulikovsky, who was waiting at the corner of the Varvarka. From the Ilynka Kaliayev walked to the steps of the Duma. It was only a five-minute walk, and he took his time. He was in no hurry. The square outside the Duma was empty. There were no carriages in sight, no sleighs, only the vast emptiness of the square with a few peasants wandering in the direction of the Kremlin as they did at all times of the day and night.

Kaliayev repeated to himself all the details of what had to be done. He must get close enough to the carriage to recognize the Grand Duke, but of course there would be no difficulty. Really, it was not necessary to recognize the Grand Duke at all. It was enough to have recognized the bright green carriage lights, the imperial crest on the carriage door. There was still no one else in the square. It was absurdly cold, and he felt lost and lonely.

"It's impossible," he murmured. "Absolutely no sign of

him. Of course he may send someone else to represent him at the theater. Anything may happen—"

He stamped his feet in the snow. The moon was shining. He looked at his watch. He heard shouting coming from some other part of the city. He was strangely at ease, strangely calm. He knew exactly how he would throw the bomb when the carriage came in sight. He had practiced it a hundred times, and he was quite certain he would be able to hurl it through the window, darting out of the shadows so quickly the driver would have no time to swerve, no time to jump down from the driving seat, no time to grapple with him. He was sorry for the driver, but there was a possibility that the driver would only be wounded. And if the Grand Duchess Elizabeth was with the Grand Duke, then he would have to kill her too. He was sorry, but so it had to be. She was after all the sister of the Czarina, and by killing her he would put terror in the heart of the autocracy. But best of all if the Grand Duke was alone in the carriage! Then there would be no guilt on his hands. It was a few minutes past eight o'clock.

Suddenly Kaliayev stiffened. A carriage was coming through the Nikolsky Gate. He smiled, gripped the bomb a little tighter, and waited for the carriage to come closer. He was sure it was the Grand Duke's carriage. It was a large, old-fashioned closed carriage, with bright green lights and white harness, an astonishingly heavy vehicle. When the carriage was half-way across the square, Kaliayev darted out. He thought he recognized Rudinkin, the Grand Duke's coachman, but this was not so important as the fact that he had already recognized the Grand Duke, a tall, heavy, broad-shouldered man with a small beard trimmed close, wearing a dark blue uniform, his chest covered with medals.

"The time has come," Kaliayev whispered, and he dashed across the path of the carriage and he was already whirling the bomb over his head when he saw the Grand Duchess

Elizabeth sitting beside the Grand Duke, while facing them
were two dark-haired children—the son and daughter of the
Grand Duke Paul, who had left Russia in disgrace when, after
the death of his wife, the Grand Duchess Alexandra, he
married morganatically and without the permission of the
Emperor. The children were extraordinarily handsome.
Kaliayev whirled the bomb above his head, paused and let
his hand fall. The coachman had seen Kaliayev, and he now
whipped the horses to a faster gallop, shouting at the top of
his voice, but there were no policemen in sight and Kaliayev
simply disappeared into the shadow of the Duma before
making his way to the Alexandrovsky Gardens, where Savinkov was waiting for him.

"What happened?" Savinkov asked.

He had expected to hear an explosion. Kaliayev was sweating and trembling, and he was still carrying the bomb
wrapped up in a handkerchief.

"I couldn't throw it," Kaliayev said. "I think I've done the
right thing. How can one kill children?"

"What children?"

"The Grand Duchess Maria and the Grand Duke Dmitri.
They were traveling with the Grand Duke Sergius. I couldn't
kill them."*

There was a long silence. Kulikovsky, who had been waiting in another part of the Gardens, came to join them. He
had seen the carriage passing in the distance. He was almost
out of his mind with anxiety. Until he was face to face with

---

* In Savinkov's novel *The Pale Horse*, which describes the incident in fic-
tional terms, Kaliayev (Vanya) is made to say: "A woman and children!
Children! Do you understand that? But now you must sit in judgment. You
must believe me. I could not then, and I cannot now— Tell me what I did
was right! Let them live! They're innocent! I ran straight up to the carriage!
I saw them, and I saw him, and I wanted to throw it, but I couldn't! My
hand stayed me!"

The present account is based on Savinkov's memoirs and Kaliayev's own
recollections of the event.

Kaliayev he believed that Kaliayev must have been arrested.

"It's astonishing," Savinkov said. "We never once raised the question, never brought it up before the Committee. You understand, you might have been arrested with the bomb in your hand. It was terribly dangerous. The whole organization is endangered. You understand, if you had been arrested, the whole attempt would probably have to be postponed indefinitely."

Kaliayev nodded miserably. He believed now that he had done wrong. He had placed the terrorist organization in jeopardy.

"Let the Committee decide," he said. "Let us decide now between ourselves. If you agree, I'll throw the bomb when the Grand Duke leaves the theatre. It all depends upon whether you decide to kill the whole family. Tell me what you want me to do."

"Killing the whole family is quite out of the question," Savinkov answered, and he went on to ask Kaliayev whether he was absolutely sure he had recognized the Grand Duke, the Grand Duchess, and the children. It was just possible that the Grand Duke had traveled alone in one carriage, and the Grand Duchess with the children and some high officer of the court had made the journey in another. It was known that the Grand Duke and Grand Duchess had their separate carriages. It was decided that Kaliayev should prowl outside the theatre and see whether there were two carriages, while Savinkov made inquiries at the theatre. Then they learned, as they had suspected, that the Grand Duke and his whole family had arrived at the Bolshoy in a single carriage at exactly the time corresponding to the passage of the carriage across the square. Kaliayev sighed with relief. He was more than ever convinced that he had done the right thing.

They waited outside the theatre until the performance was over. Once they went for a stroll along the embankment of the Moskva. Kaliayev was depressed. He walked with his head bowed, still clutching the bomb. When the performance came to an end, they returned and silently watched the Grand Duke and the family entering the carriage.

Half the night they discussed their failure; they were sick at heart, intensely excited, and aware that they might be followed. Years later the Grand Duchess Maria, who was fifteen and could remember many details of those terrifying days, said she could remember nothing about this first attempt. It seemed to her that they had simply raced in the carriage through the darkened streets of Moscow. Savinkov was still perplexed. He was not completely convinced of the rightness of Kaliayev's actions. Dressed as an elegant Englishman, he was accompanied by two bearded peasants. He thought of taking them to the apartment, but it was necessary to keep the police off their tracks, to disappear entirely into the vast night of Moscow. There were some disreputable bathhouses open all night, but these were often watched. He settled on a restaurant called *The Alpine Rose* on the Sofiyka. The restaurant was closed. Savinkov summoned the porter, gave him a large tip and begged him to bring down the manager, who could make nothing of the studiously insolent Englishman accompanied by two peasants who seemed to be drunk. At last a warm room at the back of *The Alpine Rose* was prepared for them, and once more in hushed whispers Kaliayev recounted how he had jumped across the loneliness of the immense square and had already whirled the bomb high above his head when he saw the two children. They warmed themselves over the stove. Kulikovsky was ashen-faced, shivering. Once, when they were wandering along the banks of the frozen river, Kulikovsky faltered and almost lost consciousness as he leaned back against one of the granite pillars which supported the embankment wall. Savinkov and Kaliayev had passed on ahead. They heard a rustling sound, and turned just in time. Kulikovsky, the sweat streaming down his face, was moaning: "Take the bomb. I'm going to let it fall." Now he shivered uncontrollably. They had entered *The Alpine Rose* shortly before twelve o'clock. By four o'clock in the morning Savinkov decided it was time to leave, and by this time all arrangements were made for the next attempt on the life of the Grand Duke. They were too weary to make the attempt immediately. They decided to wait. It was the early morning of Thursday, February 3, and by the end of the week they confidently expected that the Grand Duke would be dead, and his death would be followed by the revolution.

"I am sorry I shall not live to see the revolution," Kaliayev said a few weeks earlier. Now with the knowledge of his approaching death and the thought that almost single-handed he would bring about the end of the dynasty, he walked out of *The Alpine Rose* into a snow-storm, saying over and over again that he was ready to do the work entrusted to him and rejoiced in the thought of laying down his life for Russia. He would rest in the country for a day. On Friday he would return refreshed.

That night Savinkov returned to his apartment alone. He had darted back once before to return the bombs to Dora Brilliant, who was responsible for connecting and disconnecting the fuzes, a task at that time of quite extraordinary danger and difficulty. When asked her opinion about the failure, she said, lowering her eyes: "The poet did what he had to do." Dora Brilliant's words comforted him. It was after talking with Dora Brilliant that Savinkov felt absolutely convinced that Kaliayev had behaved rightly.

For the rest of the night Kaliayev and Kulikovsky, who had separated, tramped the streets of Moscow. Early in the morning Kaliayev set off by train for a small village in the outskirts of Moscow. Kulikovsky went to another village. They had agreed upon a meeting-place for the 4th. It was expected that the attempt would take place some time in the afternoon while the Grand Duke was driving between his palaces. Throughout Thursday Savinkov rested. The strain was beginning to tell. He remained alone in an obscure hotel. Dora Brilliant was staying at the Slavyansky Bazar Hotel on the Nikolskaya. It was the best hotel in Moscow, and outrageously expensive, but no one would pay much attention to a woman coming out of the hotel carrying a blanket in her hands. She would even be expected to be carrying a blanket, to wrap round her knees when she entered a sleigh. At exactly one o'clock Dora Brilliant stepped out of the hotel and gave the blanket to Savinkov as he dashed up in Moiseyenko's sleigh. The bombs were concealed in the blanket. It was a clear winter day, the frost sparkling. There was no hitch. All the previous night Savinkov had been afraid Dora Brilliant would have an accident with the bombs. Pokotilov had been killed; Schweitzer would be killed later; the trouble was that none of the revolutionaries really knew very much about bombs. But as he drove off in the sleigh, Savinkov was well-pleased with himself. It was a pleasant sensation to be driving through the brilliant frosty streets, holding the bombs on his lap. Suddenly Moiseyenko was saying: "Tell me, have you seen our poet today?"

"Yes," said Savinkov, remembering that he had met Kaliayev briefly during the morning.

He was puzzled by Moiseyenko's tone: there was something ominous in the way he put the question.

"But you haven't seen Kulikovsky?" Moiseyenko went on.

"No, of course not. I made no arrangements to see him."

"How's the poet?"

"He's perfectly all right."

"I'm glad, but Kulikovsky is in bad shape. He's breaking up. He came back this morning, and told me he hadn't the strength to take part in the assassination. After what happened the day before yesterday, he says he will have to give up terrorist work."

Savinkov frowned. It meant that all their plans would
have to be revised. The plan had always been to have two
men ready to throw bombs, in case one was wounded or
failed to hurl the bomb. Dora Brilliant desperately wanted
to throw the bomb, but Savinkov was determined to refuse
her wish. As for Moiseyenko, who wore the uniform of a cab-
driver and whose papers were all written out with an
imaginary cab-driver's name, his arrest would only lead to
the discovery of their methods. It would be necessary for
Moiseyenko to sell the sleigh and acquire new papers before
he could be entrusted with the bomb. As Savinkov explains
all the reasons which made it impossible for him and for
Moiseyenko to assassinate the Grand Duke on that day, we
are aware of hesitations, excuses, somber *arrière-pensées*, and
concealment of motives. It would have been perfectly possible for both of them to discard their disguises; throw the
bomb; vanish; but if they did this, the small tightly-knit organization would probably evaporate. At the moment Savinkov was commander-in-chief, a position he delighted in.
Dora Brilliant was the Chief of Staff, and the two soldiers
remaining were Moiseyenko and Kaliayev. There was no
Sazonov, who gave meaning to the struggle by his mere
existence. One by one the incompetents had been discarded.
As Savinkov turned the problems over in his mind, he saw
only one recourse: postponement.

He had not counted upon Kaliayev, who wanted nothing better than the single glory. He would throw the bomb
alone. To all Savinkov's strained arguments he had a counter-
argument. Had he not been alone on the night of February 2? Kulikovsky had chosen the least likely of the two
places from which the bomb could be thrown, and now
Kulikovsky had failed them, and so it was right and proper
that Kaliayev should complete what they had begun. Savinkov raised the question of a premature explosion. Well, that
was something that they had to face at all times; why stress

it now? As for employing two men, that surely increased
the danger—there were no advantages to be derived from
posting two men in different places, when it was quite certain that the Grand Duke would make the journey from the
Nicholas Palace in the Kremlin to the headquarters of the
governor-general on the Tverskaya. No: enough of these
arguments. "Failure is quite impossible," he said. "I shall
kill the Grand Duke, and that's certain." He was blazing
with enthusiasm, with the imminence of self-sacrifice. They
were standing on the road beside the sleigh, and Moiseyenko turned and said quickly: "It's getting late. Hurry up,
and make up your mind."

"Very well, Ivan Platonovich," Savinkov addressed himself to Kaliayev. "You shall do it alone."

Kaliayev smiled. It was a moment he remembered afterward with acute precision, the moment of his triumph.
They walked on for a while, embraced and separated. Kaliayev was now strangely calm. In front of him, he thought,
there was only the moment of death, calmly considered and
deliberately chosen. He did not think he would survive the
explosion. If he did, he was sure to be hanged. It never
seemed to have occurred to him that he might be wounded
in the explosion or that he might be sent on one of those
green prison trains with cross-barred windows to a peniten-
tiary in Siberia, where Sazonov was already installed. Two
o'clock had struck while he was talking to Savinkov. Now
Savinkov was walking slowly to the Nikolsky Gate, passing
under the Spassky Tower and so into the Kremlin with its
red walls and piles of golden cupolas blazing in the winter
sun, the black Romanov eagles outstretched against the sky.
For a while Savinkov paused before the statue of Alexander II. From there he could see the Nicholas Palace where
the Grand Duke Sergius was living; he could see the
coach, a closed brougham, and he thought he could recognize the coachman, Rudinkin. Soon the Grand Duke would

be making the usual afternoon journey to the governor-general's palace, and in fact, at that moment the Grand Duke was solemnly discussing with the fifteen-year-old Grand Duchess Maria the purchase of a mandolin. Someone suggested that it was dangerous for the Grand Duke to make the journey alone; it would be better if he did not go alone. The Grand Duke was a man of violent prejudices, insanely autocratic in temper, but he possessed considerable physical courage. Brusquely, he refused the offer of a companion and stepped into the carriage. Savinkov, walking casually, had already passed the Grand Duke's palace and was now making his way to a pastry-shop on the Kuznetsky Bridge where he had an appointment with Dora Brilliant.

The Grand Duchess Elizabeth was preparing to spend the afternoon in her workshop in one of the remote palaces of the Kremlin where the titled ladies of the Court rolled bandages and prepared dressings for the soldiers of the Russo-Japanese War. She had already called for her sleigh to be brought closer to the steps. The children were in the schoolroom which looked out over the square. In one corner of the schoolroom Fraülein Hase, the Grand Duchess Maria's German teacher, was quietly reading a book. Time passed slowly. The sounds of Moscow were muffled by the snow. For the children it was an afternoon like all the winter afternoons in Moscow, when dusk comes early.

Suddenly there was an explosion; all the window-panes rattled, and at the same moment a flock of crows began to wheel madly around the painted steeple of St. Ivan's Cathedral. Fraülein Hase rushed to the window. She was followed by an old professor of mathematics, and then by the fifteen-year-old Grand Duchess Maria. The snow-covered square was filling with people. It was impossible to see what had happened. Dmitri came running into the schoolroom. Maria imagined that one of the old Kremlin towers must have fallen in under the weight of snow. She sent a servant to see whether her uncle had left the palace. The servant returned, saying he thought the Grand Duke was still there. He spoke solemnly and evasively, and went away, while the children crept again to the window.

Across the square two sleighs were driving through the crowd. The Grand Duchess Maria was already reconstructing in her mind the whole incident. It seemed to her that the sleighs were filled with policemen and a good number of struggling young terrorists, their clothes in disorder, hair blowing in the wind. These terrorists seemed to be haranguing the crowd, but the windows were closed and she could hear no words. Everything seemed to be happening as though in a dream.

Down below they saw the Grand Duchess Elizabeth, wearing a blue dress, a fur coat flung loosely over her shoulders, jumping into her sleigh, followed by Mlle. Hélène, the governess of the children. In her haste Mlle. Hélène had picked up a man's coat, and like the Grand Duchess she wore no hat. The sleigh drove at a wild gallop and disappeared into the crowd. The children waited, their noses pressed against the window.

After leaving Savinkov, Kaliayev made his way to the chapel of the Iverskaya Madonna and for a long while he gazed at a colored poster set in a glass frame. Reflected in the glass frame he could see the road leading from the Nikolsky Gate and every detail of the Grand Duke's progress from his palace. As usual he wore peasant clothes, high boots, a long coat, and a thick fur hat. His beard was uncombed. Then he walked slowly through the Nikolsky Gate in the direction of the court house. He had already seen the carriage driving away. He waited. The road once again was deserted. When the carriage came past, he hurled the bomb at a distance of four paces straight into the window. He was caught up in the explosion, the wild spray of snow and smashed timber and broken flesh. The heat of the explosion seared his face. For a moment he was stunned. When the cloud lifted he could see only the twisted rear wheels of the carriage. His cap was torn off. Splinters stung his face. Curiously, he was still standing, and at the moment of the explosion he had the presence of mind to turn his face away. Of the carriage almost nothing remained: the twisted wheels, a little heap some eight or ten inches high, mingled with pieces of clothing and scraps of flesh, and that was all. Of the Grand Duke Sergius' body there was almost nothing recognizable except one hand and part of a leg which had been broken in half, with the foot torn away. The right arm still clung to part of the torso, but the head, neck, and most of the chest were smashed to pulp. Kaliayev was dazed by the fumes. About ten feet away he saw his cap lying in the snow. He went to pick it up and put it back on his head, and then he saw that his coat was seared in places and there were little slivers of wood hanging on it. Blood was streaming from his face. There was still no one else on the square. He thought of escape, but he knew it was useless, and he was not surprised when a police sleigh bore down on him from behind. A policeman called Leontiev jumped off the sleigh and pressed down on Kaliayev's shoulders. More policemen hurled themselves at him. A man whom Kaliayev recognized as a police spy, with a small ugly face, kept shouting: "Hold him! See whether he is armed! Glory to God, I wasn't killed!" Kaliayev was aware of a growing feeling of nausea which had nothing to do with the naked lumps of Grand Duke Sergius's flesh lying in the snow. The nausea was directed at the police spy. He had not brought a revolver, but he wished now he could kill the little plainclothes police spy. He said: "You don't have to hold me. I won't run away. I've done everything I wanted to do." As he said this, he realized that he was still deafened by the explosion. Someone was shouting for a cab. At last a cab drove up, and Kaliayev was thrown into it, shouting: "Down with the damned Czar! Long live freedom! Down with the accursed government! Long live the Social Revolutionary Party!" At the police station in the Kremlin Kaliayev walked up the stairs with surprisingly firm steps. He was wildly excited, brazen, and insolent, and laughed at the policemen. When a little later he was transferred to the Yakimovsky police station he fell at once into a profound sleep.

While the policemen in the sleigh were hurling themselves upon Kaliayev, the Grand Duchess Elizabeth was making her way through the crowd. She knew what had happened. She was hysterical and at the same time icy cold. She saw people standing around, gazing at the bits of flesh which were sacred to her and she began to gather them up and make a neat pile of them. Most of the people standing around still wore their hats. It seemed to her an unpardonable affront to the dead, and to herself as a member of the imperial court. She began to shout to them to remove their hats, and soon Mlle. Hélène was ordering everyone to doff his hat in the presence of the Grand Duchess Elizabeth Feodorovna. Mlle. Hélène's face, usually scarlet, had turned blue. Her eyes were glazed. Because she wore a man's coat, people said afterward that the Grand Duchess was accompanied by her valet. There was a strange silence. Once the Grand Duchess looked up and said: "You ought to be ashamed to be standing there. Go away." No one paid very much attention to her. There was confusion everywhere. At three-quarters of an hour after two o'clock a bomb had exploded, and this was the only fact that could be generally agreed upon. The sleeves of the Grand Duchess's blue gown were gleaming with blood, there was blood under her fingernails. She found the medals her husband wore on a chain round his neck, and clutched them, and carried them about with her as she picked up the mangled fragments of flesh. From her own workshop someone brought a common army stretcher and the pieces which had once formed the body of His Imperial Highness the Grand Duke Sergius Alexandrovich formed a very small pile, which disappeared altogether when a coat was thrown over the litter.

From the lawcourts where all the windows were shattered by the explosion and where a trial was in progress, an assistant prosecutor drove up in a cab. He made two or three feeble attempts to examine the smashed carriage, and then went on his way.

About this time Mlle. Hélène returned to the palace. When she reached the children's room she was breathless, hysterical, and almost out of her mind, her lips violet and her eyes staring. With immense difficulty she succeeded in conveying to the children that they must come out into the square. Trembling, the children put on their coats, and they would have gone running out if General Laiming, the Grand Duke's aide-de-camp, had not prevented them, saying he had received word from the Duchess that they must move away from the window and on no account enter the square.

At a quarter past three an honor guard of soldiers appeared. After roping off the place where the assassination had occurred, they carried the litter on their shoulders to the Monastery of the Miracle, where they laid it down gently before the altar. The monastery was next door to the Grand Duke's palace. Here shortly afterward came Count Shuvalov, the new governor-general of the city, himself to be assassinated a few months later by Kulikovsky who in this way proved to himself that he was still a member of the Terrorist Brigade. At last the Grand Duchess summoned the children, and long afterwards the Grand Duchess Maria remembered the frightened face of the priest, the ghostly light of the candles, the blood dripping from the litter and the strange hallucinated face of the Grand Duchess who knelt beside the litter in the candle-light, her sleeves still red with blood.

When Savinkov became a legend, the story was told that he was sitting in the Café Filipov when he heard the explosion, his face hidden behind a newspaper. Suddenly he rose, carefully folded the newspaper, slipped it in his pocket, remarked casually: "What terrible times we are living in!" and sauntered out. The story is almost certainly untrue. According to his own account he was still hurrying to meet Dora Brilliant at the pastry shop on the Kuznetsky Bridge when he heard a muffled roar, brief and not particularly loud. He paid no more attention to it; such a sound could have been made by a steam-engine or by the ice on the river. He hurried on, met Dora Brilliant and walked quickly back along the Tverskaya. A street urchin came running up, shouting: "The Grand Duke is dead! His head's blown off!" They went faster. At the Nikolsky Gate, which leads into the Kremlin, there was a huge crowd. All of Moscow seemed to be congregating there. Savinkov and Dora Brilliant tried to make their way through the crowd, but they were beaten back, and it was Moiseyenko, driving up in a sleigh, and pale as death, who shouted out to them that the Grand Duke was dead. They jumped onto the sleigh and drove off. Suddenly Dora Brilliant collapsed, her head fell on Savinkov's shoulders and she shook uncontrollably as she whispered over and over again: "I—I—I killed the Grand Duke."

Many others believed they had killed the Grand Duke. The Grand Duchess felt she was in some obscure way responsible. General Laiming, his aide-de-camp, tormented himself with the thought that the assassination would not have occurred if he had been in the carriage. Savinkov, who had planned the details, thought he was responsible. Behind Savinkov there was the infinitely sinister figure of

Evno Azev, the *agent-provocateur*. Behind Azev was Mikhail Gotz, the foreign representative of the terrorists, with
his bright eyes and superb intelligence, still lying on his
sick bed in Geneva.

It is possible, however, that none of these were as directly
responsible for the assassination as the Grand Duke himself.
He almost asked to be assassinated. Warned repeatedly
against making the journey between the Nicholas Palace
and the governor-general's headquarters on the Tverskaya
at the same hour and along the same route, he was too
proud to believe he would not survive an attack by the terrorists he despised, and too much in love with autocracy
to believe that autocracy was doomed. More than any of the
other Grand Dukes he urged the Czar to be uncompromising.
The journeys he made were useless. It was not necessary
that the son of an Emperor should take upon himself the
task of superintending the removal of furniture from one
palace to another. A bitter, proud man, he died unloved by
anyone except his wife. On the evening of the assassination
the young Grand Duke Dmitri stood by the window with
his sister, looking over the dark square. The ramparts and
roofs of the Kremlin were blue in the snow. The dark steeple
of St. Ivan's Cathedral stood out like a sombre black bar
against the sky. "What do you think?" asked Dmitri. "Will
we be happier now?"

During the following days flowers were heaped on the
place where the Grand Duke died, and a search was made
for remnants of his body. A finger with a gold ring still attached was found on the roof of one of the neighboring
houses. A piece of scorched and blood-stained cloth was
found on the other side of the square. Then the spring
rains came, and whatever fragments of him remained became part of the earth of Moscow.

Eleven years later, on December 29, 1916, the young
Grand Duke whose life Kaliayev had spared himself be-

came an assassin. In Prince Yusupov's palace facing the Neva three conspirators inveigled Grigory Rasputin to a feast. They gave him poisoned cakes, and when these failed to kill him, they shot him in the courtyard, sewed him up in a sack and dropped the body through a hole in the ice of the Neva. The three conspirators were the Grand Duke Dmitri, Prince Yusupov, and an obscure rightist member of the Duma. The wheel had turned full circle.

The Full Circle

The Grand Duchess Elizabeth Feodorovna was the grand-daughter of Queen Victoria and the daughter of Ludwig IV, Grand Duke of Hesse-Darmstadt. The Empress of All the Russias was her sister. Another sister was Princess Irene, the wife of Prince Henry of Prussia. A third sister was Princess Victoria of Battenberg. Tall and slender, with blond hair and gray-blue eyes, Elizabeth possessed to perfection the imperial manner of her ancestors. She loved the Grand Duke Sergius, always slept with him in the great double bed and seems never to have doubted that he was a pillar of strength to the empire. When he died, her life ended. Her remaining days were spent in the shadows, as the abbess of the Convent of Mary and Martha belonging to the order of the Sisters of Pity. Those who visited her found a strange, distracted, saintly woman who sometimes peered over their heads and muttered about ghosts.

Perhaps she had been muttering about ghosts from the very beginning. In the curiously-fabricated life of the Russian Imperial Court, the Grand Duchess seemed always slightly remote. She had no great affection for her sister, the Empress. She adored clothes and jewelry and spent long hours every afternoon interminably choosing among a thousand dresses the one she would wear in the evening. She liked gazing at herself in mirrors. She liked the glint of rubies and emeralds, which the Grand Duke bought for her in immense quantities. She hated familiarity; when the young Grand Duchess Maria once kissed her admiringly on the neck, the child was rewarded with a look so cold it chilled her. Childless, she could make nothing of the children who entered her household when the Grand Duke Paul married a commoner, though occasionally Maria would be allowed to hand her a piece of jewelry. She refused to recognize the Grand Duke Paul's marriage even when his wife, Olga Pistolkors, became ennobled and received the title of Countess Hohenfelsen, which was later changed to Princess Paley. She spoke Russian badly and read the language with difficulty. Once one of her ladies in waiting read to her Dostoyevsky's *The House of the Dead*. She ordered the doors to be closed, so that no one else in the palace would overhear the terrible, searching words. It is permissible to wonder what she made of the book. What did she say when she heard the words: "The man and the citizen disappear for ever in the tyrant," or: "The characteristics of the executioner appear in almost every modern man." She preferred English novels. French books with yellow covers she detested. She painted amateurishly, rode well, collected *bibelots* which she never read, and was never happier than when she was attending some court function which allowed her to wear the richly-brocaded costumes and jewelled head-dresses which were handed down to the Russian Court from the court of the emperors of Byzantium. Ice-cold, with a chaste, thin-lipped beauty, she seemed to have none of the instincts of a living woman but to have been carved out of some rare stone. But in the twenty-four hours which followed the assassination of the Grand Duke Sergius she twice showed there was a woman buried beneath the marble surface.

At six o'clock on the night of the murder she went to the hospital where Andrey Rudinkin, her husband's coachman, was dying of his wounds. There was little left of him and no hope of survival. His body had been gashed wide open, gangrene had set in, and he was barely conscious. She was afraid to frighten him, and so wore the same gay blue dress she had worn in the afternoon. When Rudinkin murmured: "How is the Grand Duke?" she answered bravely: "The Grand Duke sent me here himself to inquire after your health." Rudinkin died peacefully during the night.

On the evening of the next day, in deep mourning and driving in a carriage draped with crape, she visited Kaliayev in his cell. She asked to be left alone with him. The prison governor could only obey.

At first Kaliayev failed to recognize the woman who entered his cell, pale as chalk, dressed in black, with tears streaming down her face. She walked with slow shuffling steps, and suddenly she looked up, gazed straight into his eyes and said: "I am his wife." There was a moment of silence. She sat down on a chair. Her head was bent, and Kaliayev had the feeling she was gazing deliberately at his hands, those hands which had committed the assassination.

"Your Highness," said Kaliayev, "please do not weep."

There was a long silence. Kaliayev kept thinking: "It had to happen. Why come to me? What is she doing here?"

"You must have suffered so much to have done this terrible thing," the Grand Duchess said, and it was perhaps the worst thing she could have said at that moment. Kaliayev was furious. He seems to have thought she was being condescending, when it was more likely that she was showing a rare understanding.

"What does it matter whether I have suffered or not?" he replied sharply. "Yes, I have suffered! But I suffered with millions of other people. Altogether too much blood has been spilled, and we have no other means of protesting against a tyrannical government and a terrible war. Why do they come and talk to me only after I have committed the crime? Listen! When I was a boy, I thought of all the tears that are shed in the world, and all the lies that are told, and sometimes it seemed to me that if I could, I would shed enough tears for everyone, and then the evil would be destroyed! But what could I do? If I went to the Grand Duke and showed him all the evil he had done, the misery of the people, why, he would have sent me to a madhouse or —and this is much more likely—thrown me into prison, like thousands of others who have suffered for their convictions. Why didn't they let the people speak?"

Kaliayev was excited. It was the ultimate moment of revenge: the terrorist confronted with the royal house. He remembered afterward that he once waved his arms about in his overwhelming excitement, and once he paused sharply, as though daring the Grand Duchess to interrupt him.

The Grand Duchess said: "I'm sorry you did not come to us, and then we would have known you earlier."

Kaliayev was suddenly convinced she spoke out of her heart, without any concealed motives, but he remembered how the workers of St. Petersburg had set out along the Nevsky Prospekt from the miraculous Virgin of Kazan to offer a petition to the Czar. They had been shot down by the hundreds.

"So you think it is easy to go to you?" he went on. "Then look what happened on the 9th of January, when they tried to see the Czar. Do you really believe such things could go unpunished? Then there is this terrible war which the people hate so violently. Well, you have declared war on the people, and we have accepted the challenge! As for myself I would give a thousand lives, not one, if only Russia could be free!"

The Grand Duchess murmured impatiently: "You should think of the honor of our country—"

"Oh, the honor of our country!" Kaliayev replied ironically, and there was a long pause.

The Grand Duchess was baffled by the young prisoner. She

had expected to find him appalled by his crime; instead, he was jubilant. Dimly she saw that he regarded himself as the spearhead of the popular movement against the autocracy. He had talked about the Russo-Japanese War, about the suffering of the people, about his detestation of the autocracy. Now she reminded him that the autocrats also had their burdens. She said quietly: "You think you are the only ones to suffer. I assure you we suffer too, and we want only good things for the people."

Kaliayev was pitiless.

"Yes, you are suffering now," he answered, "but as for giving good things to the people, you give with one hand and take it back 'with the back of the knife.'"

The conversation was getting nowhere. Across abysses of history and custom they spoke to one another. For a while they were both silent. The Grand Duchess had taken a chair: in respect for her Kaliayev had remained standing. Now, as the Grand Duchess began to lose herself in memories of her husband, he sat down. She complained that the Grand Duke had not deserved death; he was powerless; he was no longer governor-general when he died; he was good to everyone.

"I beg you not to talk about the Grand Duke," Kaliayev answered. "I have absolutely no desire to talk about him. Everything I have to say will be said at the trial. I killed him with a full sense of responsibility—he was a man who played a powerful political role and knew exactly what he was doing."

"To me he never spoke about politics," she answered, and suddenly she seemed to be very calm and remote. "I came to tell you the Grand Duke forgives you," she went on, and from the folds of her gown she drew out a small ikon and presented it to her husband's murderer, saying: "I beg you to accept this little ikon in memory of him. Yes, and I shall pray for you."

Kaliayev accepted the gift of the ikon. In a way it was a symbol of his victory over the royal house.

"My conscience is clear," he said. "I am sorry I have caused you so great a sorrow. I acted with a deep sense of my responsibility, and if I had a thousand lives, I would give them all, not only one. And now again I will say how sorry I am for you, but still I did my duty and I'll do it again to the very end, whatever happens. Good-by. We shall never see each other again."

The Grand Duchess left the prison. On her return to the palace the children questioned her, but she said nothing. Years later the Grand Duchess Maria wrote that Elizabeth visited Kaliayev out of an impulse of Christian self-abnegation. More likely she went as one goes to a mystery and to look into Kaliayev's burning eyes.

Kaliayev himself was aware of the mystical character of their confrontation.

"I confess that we gazed at one another with a strange sense of mystery," he wrote. "We were like two mortal beings who have remained alive—I, by the accident of fate: she, because the organization had so willed it, because I had willed it, for we both desired to avoid unnecessary bloodshed. And I, gazing at the Grand Duchess, could not fail to see on her face an expression of gratitude, if not to me, then to that accident of fate by which she had escaped complete destruction."

For Kaliayev the intoxication was complete. Nothing could have given him greater joy. He almost certainly failed to understand why the Grand Duchess came to his cell. The autocracy was now humbled, and Kaliayev had achieved his purpose. In the few days that remained, he lived on the wave-crests. In a long poem written shortly after the meeting with the Grand Duchess, he wrote:

> *O joy and terror and torment and unrest!*
> *O storm of spirit and foaming stream!*

The air is filled with voices of anger.
True to my battle-vow, I with my hands
Was insolent and proud before the enemy.
I smiled at them, seeing their fear
And took revenge with my derisive speech.
The lightning plays upon my heart of storm,
And the wild echoes scream against the heavens.
My soul, intoxicated with purest wine,
Drinks from the sweet cup of victory . . .

In a more somber mood, and still in exultant happiness, he wrote to his friends:

I often think of the last moment; I should like to die immediately. It is an enviable fate. But there is a still greater happiness—to die on the scaffold. *Between the act and the scaffold there lies a whole eternity.* It is perhaps the supreme happiness of man. Only then does one know and feel the whole strength and beauty of the Idea. To commit the deed and later to die on the scaffold—it is like sacrificing one's life twice.

Between the act and the scaffold there lies a whole eternity! . . . No prisoner had ever been more eager for the hangman's noose. Yet outwardly Kaliayev showed little signs of his devouring excitement. The prison guards found him quiet and remarkably self-possessed. He wrote letters or sat over the books he received from outside. Taken to the Butyrky Prison, he was lodged in the Pugachov Tower, and this pleased him, for the great rebel Pugachov had been imprisoned there and it was a sign that the government feared an attempt to rescue him. To his friends he wrote that he would be faithful to them to death. The letters are written calmly in a mood which suggests that all his perplexities were at last resolved:

My dear friends and unforgettable comrades:
You know how I did everything I could on February 4 to bring about victory. And now within the confines of my own consciousness, I am happy in the knowledge that I have ful-

filled my duty towards Russia now lying in a pool of flowing blood.

You know how intensely I hold to my convictions and the strength of my feelings, and let no one grieve over my death.

I have given myself wholly to the fight for the freedom of working people, and for me there can never be any concession to autocracy. If in the end it should happen that my heart's aspirations have shown I am worthy to lead the protest of mankind against oppression, then let my death crown the cause I fought for with faith in the purity of an idea.

To die for one's convictions—what is this but a call to battle? Whatever the sacrifices needed to liquidate autocracy, I firmly believe that our generation will put an end to it forever . . . And this will be the great victory of socialism, throwing open the windows of a new life for the Russian people who have suffered so long under the yoke of Czarist oppression.

With all my heart I am with you, my beloved, dear and unforgettable ones. You held me up when times were hard: we shared together our joys and troubles; and when one day the people celebrate their triumph, then remember me, and let all my labors as a revolutionist be regarded as no more than the expression of inspired love for the people and profound respect for you. Take my work then as a tribute of deep devotion to the party, the bearer of the testament of *The People's Will* in all its immensity.

My whole life seems as strange as a fairy story, as though everything that ever happened to me was already foreseen in the days of my childhood, coming to birth within the secret recesses of my heart until it burst into a flame of hatred and revenge for all.

I should like to name for the last time all those who are close to my heart and infinitely dear to me, but let my last breath be my final greeting and a fierce clarion-call summoning you to victory.

I embrace and kiss you all.

A few days after the Grand Duchess' visit Kaliayev heard through the mysterious grapevine which operated throughout all Russian prisons that it was now widely believed he had sought the Grand Duchess' pardon, had knelt at her feet with tears in his eyes and begged her to intercede with the Czar for his life. Immediately Kaliayev wrote a letter to the Grand Duchess demanding an apology and a retraction. There was no reply. He wrote a second letter. There was still no reply, for the letters were intercepted by her family and never shown to her, and in any event it is unlikely that she would have answered them if she had seen them. The rumors about the original meeting were now widely believed, and in despair Kaliayev wrote a third letter to the Grand Duchess in the tones of an Emperor demanding the presence of one of his subjects. It is an unpleasant letter, full of the bitter taste of triumph, and it is entirely unlike anything else that Kaliayev ever wrote:

Grand Duchess!

Since the day of our meeting, I have twice asked to see you and both times I have failed to receive a reply. I shall not enter here into the motives of your refusal to see me, although I must be permitted to say that your refusal of a second meeting hardly recommends your intense desire to see me when you first visited my cell . . .

I believe it is the duty I owe to honor and conscience to explain in this letter all the reasons which have led me to demand another meeting with you.

Your visit on February 7 was completely unexpected. You came to me. You came to me with your sorrow and your tears, and I did not refuse you, I did not expel this visitor from the enemy's camp. You were so helpless in your grief. Perhaps it was the first time you had heard the screaming voice of terror which encompasses us all. You were so weak before the annihilation of all you held dear, in the face of destiny's torments.

For the first time a member of the royal dynasty has bowed her head before the vengeance of the people and acknowledged the crimes of the royal family.

Remember, if you had been in the carriage, you would have been destroyed. But it was not the intention of the Terrorist Brigade to deprive you of your life, and your death (as far as we are concerned) would have been a needless accident. It was in the interests of the brigade therefore that at the moment when I caught sight of you in the carriage, I should put aside all my detestation of the ruling house and "pray for you." But that you should remain alive—that, too, was my victory, a victory which after the death of the Grand Duke has filled me with overwhelming joy.

And surely you recognized all this at the moment when you came to visit me, wearing the aspect of perfect Christian humility, your soul lit with the earthly gleam of gratitude for the fate which has preserved your life . . . I did not ask you to come. You came to me of your own accord, and the responsibility for the consequences of the visit are entirely yours. Outwardly, at least, we can say that our meeting took place in an atmosphere of intimacy. It was not intended that it should be published to the skies, but for our own sakes alone. We met on neutral ground, as two human beings facing one another. And so you yourself defined it: we were both to enjoy the honor of incognito. How else am I to understand the disinterestedness of your Christian sentiments? I trusted in your nobility. I believed your exalted station and your honor would suffice to guard us against slander, and you are now yourself involved among the slanderous tongues. But you have not feared to be touched by those hands, and my confidence in you has not been justified by events. For there is no other way to explain what has happened: the slanders and the misinterpretations of what happened between us . . .

You may ask: who is guilty? For myself I can only say that my convictions and my attitude towards the ruling house remains unaltered. I myself have nothing in common with the superstitions of slaves and their hypocritical rulers.

I admit I was wrong. I should not have sympathized with you and I should have refused to speak with you. I behaved with kindness, momentarily suppressing the natural hatred I

felt for you. I have revealed the motives which moved me:
you have proven unworthy of my generosity. I cannot believe
otherwise than that you are yourself the source of the slanders
which have been published about me. How else could our
meeting have been made known? Who would have dared to
reveal what we said unless it was you? (The press reports are
inaccurate. I never said I was a believer. I never spoke about
repentance.)

Kaliayev seems to have regretted the letter shortly after
he wrote it. It was altogether too personal, too violent, with
too keen an edge of malice. There had been a strange
brightness in her eyes; he could not forget the long spatu-
late fingers, the widow's weeds, the hint of authority in her
tone. Shortly afterward he must have received a message
from the other members of the Terrorist Brigade, warning
him and explaining the vast damage which had occurred to
the Terrorist Brigade as a result of the newspaper reports
in which he was described as a repentant sinner. He wrote
to Savinkov:

I beg you to forgive me for any harm I have done. Nothing
can cause me greater pain than to know that you do not ap-
prove my conduct. Now that I stand on the edge of the grave,
I have only one consideration—my honor as a revolutionary.
This shall be my link with the Terrorist Brigade after my
death.

Within the four walls of my cell nothing is so difficult as to
distinguish between the significant and the insignificant things
of life. There are times when I fear that I shall be libeled
after my death. At such times I feel I would like to live on in
order to avenge myself against those who libel me.

I have balanced my accounts upon this earth. I loved you,
suffered with you, and prayed with you. Therefore defend my
honor. Perhaps I have been altogether too frank in talking
about my soul, but you know I am not a hypocrite. Farewell,
my dear, my only friend. Be happy! Be happy!

The trial which opened before the Court of the Senate on April 5, 1905, took place in an atmosphere of secrecy. The doors were locked. Only high government officials, magistrates, and police officers were allowed in the public galleries, though special permission was given to Kaliayev's mother to be present. The Grand Duchess, of course, was absent. She sent no one to represent her, and had long ago lost interest in the fate of Kaliayev. There was no doubt of his fate. Like Zhelyabov, he proposed to employ the few hours of his trial in a vigorous defense of his actions. Once again the government itself would be placed on trial.

The preliminaries were soon over. The witnesses testified to the fact of the Grand Duke Sergius' death. General-Major Zabudsky, an expert on high explosives, testified that the explosion had taken place inside the carriage: from thin splinters found on the scene of the crime he concluded that the bomb was contained in a tin canister, and from an examination of pieces of clothing from the bodies of the Grand Duke and the coachman he concluded that the bomb was packed with kieselguhr. Police officers described Kaliayev's arrest. At first he had refused to reveal his name, though he admitted that he belonged to the Terrorist Brigade. He was found to be carrying a passport in the name of a certain Andrey Shilnik, resident of Vitebsk. The passport was evidently false. He had shown no desire to conceal the fact that he had killed the Grand Duke; had shown indeed considerable satisfaction. Nothing was said about the visit of the Grand Duchess to his cell. There was a passing reference to the superficial wounds and scratches on the face of the prisoner at the time of his arrest. Then there was the testimony of the police officers who made the arrest. Shortly afterward the prosecutor launched on a panegyric in honor of the royal house, and once again there was heard in the Court of the Senate the strange, deep laughter of a prisoner already condemned to death.

Kaliayev was defended by the best lawyers of his time. Mikhail Bernshtam was Vice-President of the St. Petersburg Lawyers Association, a famous liberal and a man who was known to be in sympathy with many of the aspirations of the revolutionaries while at the same time receiving the respect of the official classes. He was ably assisted by Zhdanov, who made an impassioned plea for mercy. Bernshtam spoke more quietly. He went over Kaliayev's history: how he was arrested as a student, how he entered the party and was arrested for the second time in Silesia on the German border, only to be handed over to the secret police. He spoke of the "iron inevitability" which led young students to join the revolutionary organizations. Nothing could stop it. They were caught up in a wave of history; and must a swimmer be punished because he is swimming in an evil sea? But it was Kaliayev's speech in his own defense which was remembered afterward. Surprisingly, President Dreyer allowed him to read out a long speech in which he denounced the whole fabric of the trial, saying that he refused to recognize himself as a defendant—he was simply a prisoner, a man who had been arrested or captured by his enemies. They belonged to opposite camps. "Mountains of corpses divide us," he said. "Hundreds of thousands of broken lives and a whole sea of blood and tears flooding the nation in torrents of horror and resentment. You have declared war on the people, and we have accepted the challenge!"

Kaliayev's speech, very long and very carefully composed, was at once a vindication of his action in killing the Grand Duke and an attempt to vindicate himself in the eyes of the Terrorist Brigade. He refused to admit that "the gentlemen of the court draped in their senatorial togas" were worthy to judge him; the true judges were "the martyred people of Russia"; and he repeated the accusation which Zhelyabov flung in the teeth of the government: "You cannot judge because you are a party to the dispute." And he went on:

You dare to sit in judgment not only on what I have done, but also upon its moral significance. You do not call what I did an act of killing. You call it a crime, an evil thing. Who gave you this right? It comes strange from you, O most pious dignitaries, who have killed no one, but support your rule with bayonets, and with the force of the law, and with arguments of morality. There was a certain famous professor of the time of Napoleon III who was quite prepared to acknowledge the existence of two standards of morality. One was for ordinary mortals, and said: "Do not steal," "Do not kill." The other was for politicians, and this law permitted them to do anything they pleased. And you really believe you are above the law and no judgment will ever be passed on you!

Look around you! Everywhere there is blood and tears! War outside and war within the nation! Two worlds, uncompromisingly opposed to one another, have come into furious collision: the flowing waters of life and the stagnant wells, civilization and barbarism, brute force and freedom, absolutism and the people. And what is the result? The unheard-of shame of the defeat of our military strength, the financial and moral bankruptcy of the state, dissolution of the political foundations of the monarchy, the nations on the frontiers of our state each developing a passion for independence, and everywhere a rising discontent, the growth of opposition parties, open revolt of the working people ready to throw themselves into a prolonged revolution carried on in the name of socialism and freedom and—in the background of all this—acts of terrorism! What does it all mean?

It is the judgment of history upon you! It is a wave of new life arising out of the gathering storm—the death-agony of autocracy. And a revolutionary does not have to be an utopian to know what things are being dreamed of nowadays! He makes his summaries, seeks out a common denominator, gives expression to the awakening maturity of the new life around

him, and hurls his hatred into the enemy's teeth with a single
battle-cry: *I accuse!*

About this time the long-suffering President of the Court
suggested that Kaliayev should answer the direct question:
Was he guilty or not guilty of the murder of the Grand
Duke?

"I recognize that the death of the Grand Duke occurred
at my hands," Kaliayev answered, "but I do not therefore
regard myself as having committed a crime."

"Explain your statement," the President snapped; where-
upon Kaliayev explained the reasons why the Grand Duke
had to die:

The man we killed was a prominent leader of the reactionary party now ruling over Russia. The party dreams of a return to the dark days of Alexander III: his name has become a
cult. The influence of the Grand Duke Sergius has been felt
throughout the reign of Nicholas II, from the very beginning.
The terrible catastrophe on the Khodinskoye Polye* and Sergius' role in it were only the prelude to this unhappy reign.
In his investigation of the causes of the catastrophe Count
Pahlen said irresponsible people had no right to occupy responsible positions. And so the Terrorist Brigade of the Social Revolutionary Party was compelled to make the Grand
Duke, irresponsible in law, responsible before the people.

Of course, in making himself liable to revolutionary punish-

* The tragedy at the Khodinskoye Polye occurred just after the Corona-
tion of Nicholas II. On this immense plain on the outskirts of Moscow,
thousands waited at night to receive the gifts of painted porcelain cups
filled with sweets. There was a stampede at the moment when the gifts
were given out, and 1,400 men, women and children were trampled to
death. Sir Donald Mackenzie Wallace, who arrived on the scene the next
morning, said "it was a sight more horrible than a battlefield." Against the
advice of Trepov, the Grand Duke Sergius had ordered the police away;
Count Pahlen's strictures at the subsequent inquiry were widely believed
to be directed at the Grand Duke.

ment, the Grand Duke had to amass a whole heap of crimes. First, as governor-general of Moscow . . . he made the city his own feudal principality, interfered with all cultural work, suppressed educational organizations, tyrannized over poor Jews, attempted to pervert the workers, and prosecuted all the opponents of the existing order—I am mentioning only a few of the activities of the dead man, that little autocratic ruler over Moscow. Secondly, as one occupying a high position in the governmental machine, he stood at the head of the reactionary party, the inspirer of its most repressive measures, and the patron of the chief protagonists of a policy of violent suppression of all popular and social movements . . . Finally, there was his personal influence on the Czar. The "friend and uncle of the Czar" acted always as the most merciless and unbending upholder of the interests of the monarchy.

Against him the revolutionary organization decided to fight, and indeed it had no other alternative. The dynasty and its representatives had aroused the widespread hatred of the masses, and now at last the dynasty is paying its accounts. The deaths of three high officials—Bogolepov, Sipyagin*, and Von Plehve—provided the autocracy with three deliberate warnings, and the death of Sergius gives still greater point to the warnings already received . . .

My enterprise was successful. Against all the obstacles thrown against us, I know that my party will go forward, and crown itself with still greater victories. This I believe, and nothing will change my belief. Already I see the advancing hosts of freedom and the advent of a new Russia, the workers and the people all enjoying a new form of life. I am glad, I am proud to die for her in the consciousness of having done my duty.

So concluded Kaliayev's speech, but the President could not prevent himself from remarking ironically: "I am led to the conclusion that you regard yourself as an important

---

* Bogolepov, Minister of Education, was shot by Peter Karpovich in 1897. Sipyagin, Minister of the Interior, was shot by Stepan Balmashev in 1902. Both the assassins were young students.

member of this party you have spoken about. You are proud?"

"No," Kaliayev answered proudly. "As for myself, I have no importance."

"But you keep talking of your great accomplishment?"

"I did my duty, and I would do it again."

The prosecutor was Shcheglovitov, a lawyer with a reputation for liberalism who was to become Minister of Justice in the following year. He was a man who enjoyed power and conspiracy—in 1914 when the war was already three months old he presented a secret report to the Czar urging an immediate peace with Germany—and he enjoyed his role as defender of the dynasty. He urged that society could only protect itself against the terrorists by implacable vengeance, and demanded the death penalty.

When the judgment was handed down, separate penalties were awarded on the three charges on which Kaliayev had been arraigned. For belonging to a secret society determined to overthrow the dynasty: eight years' hard labor. For "bringing to an end the life of the Czar's cousin, His Imperial Highness the Grand Duke Sergius": deprivation of all rights together with the death penalty. For killing, even though by accident and without conscious deliberation, the driver Andrey Rudinkin: deprivation of all rights and imprisonment at hard labor for fifteen years. The sentence was announced at three o'clock in the afternoon. Kaliayev was asked if he had anything to say before sentence was passed on him.

"I rejoice at your verdict," he said. "I hope you will have the courage to carry it out as openly and publicly as I executed the sentence of the Social Revolutionary Party. Learn to look the advancing revolution straight in the eyes."

Then it was all over, and he was taken to his cell. Once, long ago, he had sung an old Polish song for Savinkov:

Niech pójdą dumni,
Niech wróca tlumni.

May they go forth proudly,
May they return triumphantly.

So it had happened, and the triumph was sweet to his taste. It had cost him so little. At the trial he had said that within ten years the revolutionary forces would overthrow the dynasty, "and not with secret weapons, but openly." And it pleased him that he had concealed nothing and spoken openly throughout.

In prison Kaliayev was haunted with the sense of glory which came to him every time he thought of offering his life for the revolution. It seemed to him at moments that he had many lives, and all of them were to be gladly given away. In a sense he had died when he murdered; he had died again under cross-examination; he would die finally on the scaffold. The thought of all these deaths freely offered captivated him, and of all the young revolutionaries he was the one who seemed most content in the death cell. He wrote a few days before his death an extraordinary poem in which he demonstrated that he had no regrets, only a towering delight in his achievement. It is a strange poem. In the original Russian it moves with the effect of hammer-beats, of a sustained and solemn grandeur:

Like a proud lion I waged this holy war:
The incorruptible testimony of the Ancients was by my side.
O terrible was my impetuous wrath!
I killed: the pompous enemy fell,
But fate returned the gift of life to me.
Then once again I, worthy of these chains,
Hurled at my enemy still another blow,
Quietly rejecting the life he offered me.
Then for the third time I summoned my enemy
To war with my incorruptible mind.

Now he trembles before his destiny
While I await in prison—an unassailable prisoner.

Kaliayev never made clear what he meant by "an unassailable prisoner." Perhaps he meant that he had survived
unharmed, and could never be harmed. Those who saw
him in prison were impressed by a strange quietness about
him. His death meant nothing to him. He would talk about
it as though it had already occurred. He seemed to be
saying that he belonged to the past, had already entered
history and saw no reason why anyone should be concerned
with his fate.

He refused to appeal. There was therefore nothing to
delay the execution. He remained in the Peter and Paul
Fortress until May 9, when orders were received to convey him by police launch to the Fortress of Schlusselburg
overlooking Lake Ladoga. He had already changed into the
black clothes prescribed for condemned prisoners. Handcuffed, his feet fettered, he was carried onto the motor-
launch and kept below decks. He was taken to a cell in the
fortress. Troops were stationed on the road leading to his
cell. Wherever he looked the windows were closed—orders
had been received that every window in the neighborhood
must be closed, and all the women and children in the place
must keep away from the streets.

His cell in the Schlusselburg was known ironically as "the
workroom." No one knew why this room had been set apart
for the last hours of prisoners condemned to death. It was
a small room, unfurnished except for a bed. Through the
windows he could look out on a wooden fence and on two
small flower-beds which were being tended by the prison
guards.

It was a cold day with a high blue sky and a great wind
whipping the ice on the lake. The guards paced outside
the "workroom" in the sunlight, but no sunlight fell into

Kaliayev's cell. After lunch he lay down on the bed and drew the thin prison blanket over himself. A guard stood watching him in the corner. Kaliayev saw the guard's half mocking smile and snapped: "You are quite wrong. I am not shivering with fear. I'm cold, and I would be glad if you would get me another blanket."

He rested for a little more than an hour and spent the afternoon writing. He wrote at great length, covering a large number of sheets of paper, but shortly before his death he crossed out everything he had written except a famous quotation from Peter the Great's speech before Poltava: "As for Peter, know that his life is not so dear to him as Russia's happiness." Visitors came to his cell. According to Chernov a last minute effort was made to make him sign an appeal for clemency. His own attorney entered the cell eight times, each time with some new reason why Kaliayev should throw himself on the mercy of the Emperor, and each time Kaliayev refused. He was asked whether there was anything he wanted. He answered that he would like hot tea and food, and for the rest wanted to be left alone with his thoughts. This wish was not granted. The celebrated Father Florinsky entered, saying he wanted to discuss religion with Kaliayev. Kaliayev answered that he had other things to think about. Around nine o'clock the prosecuting attorney, accompanied by the commander of the fortress, entered. Kaliayev was told he would be executed that night, just before dawn. Kaliayev showed no signs of emotion, asking only that his own attorney be allowed to witness the execution. For some reason this request was refused.

Around ten o'clock Father Florinsky again entered Kaliayev's cell, to receive his confession and administer the sacrament. Kaliayev explained patiently that he had no need of a priest, refused to recognize the ritual of the church, and was content to die. He had affirmed in court that he considered his death a supreme sacrifice in a world of blood and tears, and saw no reason to change his belief. There seems to have been a further effort to make him sign an appeal and it is possible that if he had signed, his sentence would have been commuted to life imprisonment, but there is no record that Father Florinsky spoke of anything except religious matters. Kaliayev was moved by the evident goodness of the priest and said: "Let me kiss you because you are a good man." They kissed and soon afterward the priest left the cell. They were to see one another again on the scaffold.

At midnight Kaliayev requested that the execution should take place immediately. This request was refused.

An hour later, sitting in his cell, Kaliayev wrote his last letter to his mother:

Dear, beloved Mother!
Soon I shall die. I am happy because I am in full control of myself, and so I shall remain to the end. Let your sorrow, Mother, Sisters, Brothers, overflow with the shining radiance of my triumphant spirit.
Farewell! Greetings to those who know and remember me. I beseech you all to preserve the purity of our Father's name. And never grieve nor cry. Once more—farewell! I am always with you!

At two o'clock in the morning the commandant of the fortress and the hangman entered the cell.

According to custom the hangman was dressed in red, with a red blouse, red breeches, a red cap. He wore a rope round his waist. From the rope hung a knout. The hangman was Alexander Filipiev, who had murdered seven people. He was reprieved upon his offer to act as hangman. Now as he entered the cell, he smelled strongly of vodka. He smiled good-humoredly and asked Kaliayev to hold his hands behind his back: then Filipiev quickly roped the hands together. The commandant looked more nervous than the prisoner or the hangman. Kaliayev was led into the courtyard, wearing a black suit, a black felt hat, no overcoat. The commandant went in front, Filipiev was in the rear. Only a few lamps shone; the gallows itself was veiled in darkness. As usual the scaffold was painted black and so was the small platform with the three steps leading up. In the courtyard were the privileged officials, a detachment of foot guards with fixed bayonets, and the commissioned officers who were free from prison duties.

Kaliayev stood motionless during the reading of the sentence. Father Florinsky held out a cross. Kaliayev refused to kiss it, and said: "I have already told you I have finished with life and I am prepared for death." The priest moved away.

The hangman approached, slipped the shroud over Kaliayev's head, threw the noose over his neck and then kicked the tabourette away, while the drummers in the small courtyard drowned any sounds made by the man who spun at the end of the thin rope. Hardly three minutes had passed since Kaliayev hurried across the courtyard.

The body dangled for thirty minutes before it was cut down. In the courtyard no one moved. The doctor pronounced that he was dead. As dawn came up at last, the body was placed in a wooden coffin, and the soldiers buried it outside the fortress walls, in the prisoners' burying ground between the mound that surrounds the fortress on one side of the lake and the King's tower. After the Bolshevik revolution, when an attempt was made to find the grave, they found only a wooden marker which had almost rotted away. The body itself seems to have slipped away into the lake water.

Kaliayev survived his own death. He was remembered as the handsomest, the most talented, and the most superbly dedicated of the small group of Russian revolutionaries who threatened the Czardom at the beginning of the century. Of them all, he alone had thrust cleanly, never plagued by doubts except when he saw the young children in the Grand Duke's carriage. Slight and fair-haired, speaking in a soft musical voice with a Polish accent, he brought to the revolution an idealism which seems to have vanished after his death. Once, talking with Savinkov on Vassily Island Kaliayev said: "Everything is beautiful. The stars and clouds and flowers and people and—death is beautiful, too." In a sense it had always been as simple as that.

For the Grand Duchess there were no simplicities—only a long agony. She attended her husband's funeral in the Monastery of the Miracle on the morning of February 23, and she must have observed that neither the Czar nor the Czarina had dared to attend. Of the many Grand Dukes who were invited only three had the courage to come. One was a distant cousin, another was the young Dmitri, the third was Dmitri's father, the Grand Duke Paul, who had received a special dispensation from the Czar permitting him to return from abroad. Others accepted the black-bordered invitations and at the last minute found excuses.

From the day when the remains of the Grand Duke Sergius were buried, the Grand Duchess gave herself to good works. She painted her bedroom, which was once mauve, in various shades of white, hung it with ikons and set up her own private chapel. When the First World War came she was still abbess of the Convent of Martha and Mary, and she still kept the small Nicholas Palace. It was as though she refused to be separated from the ghosts of the past.

By a strange turn of fate she was herself partly responsible for the death of Rasputin, who was believed by many to be responsible for the misfortunes of the war. The Grand Duke Dmitri had watched the growing power of Rasputin with horror. For some time he had been thinking of putting an end to the horror, but before committing himself he decided to seek his aunt's counsel. The Grand Duchess Eliza-

beth had no idea that Dmitri was about to take part in a
plot against Rasputin's life, but when he asked her whether
she considered he was a danger to the monarchy, Elizabeth
agreed only too fervently. She painted a dark picture of
Rasputin's influence over her sister, the Empress. She saw
no hope for Russia while Rasputin remained alive. Dmitri
returned to St. Petersburg. Within a few days Rasputin's
body was dropped into the ice of the Neva.

The Grand Duchess remained in Moscow throughout the
revolution. She was not interested in politics. She lived in
a world of her own. In June, 1918, she was arrested by the
Bolsheviks. She had hoped to be allowed to continue working in the hospital. She described herself as a simple abbess
whose only use in the world lay in her skill in tending the
wounded. But in a mood of violent hysteria and cynical
revenge, Lenin had given orders for the extermination of
the entire royal house. Had not Nechayev spoken of "terrible, total and merciless destruction"? Once, long ago,
someone had asked Nechayev which of the members of the
Imperial Family should be destroyed. Nechayev had answered immediately: "Why, the whole responsory!" meaning
all those members of the royal house for whom prayers were
said in the churches. Now the shadow of Nechayev fell over
the saintly Grand Duchess. For a few weeks she disappeared
from sight, then it was learned that she was living in the
obscure village of Alapaievsk in the government of Perm.
With her was Prince Vladimir Paley, the son of the Grand
Duke Paul by his morganatic wife. There were also the
three sons of the Grand Duke Constantine, Ivan, Constantine, and Igor, and the Grand Duke Serge Mikhailovich,
who had been given the responsibility of building up an air
force for the Czar. With Elizabeth was her maid Varvara.
They lived quietly. None of them knew what was in store.

On the night of July 16 the Czar and his whole family
were shot to death in the cellar of the house of the engineer

Ipatiev in Ekaterinburg. The bodies were then thrown on a truck and driven to a deserted mine shaft. Elizabeth was not so lucky. With the other members of the royal house at Alapaievsk she was driven to a mine shaft, shot and thrown into the mine. When voices were heard from the bottom of the mine, heavy stones were thrown down. It was said that their voices could be heard for a whole day; afterward there was silence. On April 24, 1920, a strange report appeared in newspapers all over the world:

PEKING IS MYSTIFIED BY RUSSIAN BURIALS

Seven bodies, four of them said to be members of the Russian Imperial Family, arrived in Peking from Harbin yesterday and were buried in the Russian cemetery, outside the city wall. The whole proceedings were surrounded with the greatest secrecy, even the Russian Legation receiving scant information of the circumstance.

The bodies were declared to be those of the Grand Duchess Elizabeth Feodorovna, the Grand Duke Serge Mikhailovich . . . It is alleged that they were killed and their bodies thrown into a coal mine near Perm.

The Mass Terror Begins

To the Bolsheviks the execution of the Royal Family was of such little importance that it was not even debated in council. When the report of the executions was received, Lenin made no comment. He announced quietly that the Czar was dead, and went on to discuss a new public health law.

But in Lenin's silence many things were said. The decision to kill the Czar and his entire family had been made many years before by Nechayev, who spoke of killing "the entire responsory." Nechayev's solution of the problem particularly pleased Lenin, who admired the young revolutionary's directness, unclouded by hesitations. Later he ordered the liquidation of the entire aristocracy, forgetting that among them there were men who possessed gifts useful to the state. Later still he ordered the liquidation of the one remaining revolutionary party bold enough to stand up against him. The Social Revolutionaries were mown down by the pistols of his secret police. With the aristocracy and the intelligentsia destroyed, he was free to attempt to bring about the new utopian state. With the ruthless exercise of force and the employment of mass terrorism, he was determined to make a heaven on earth.

When Lenin arrived at the Finland Station in April, 1917, he believed utopia would come about almost overnight. In this new state there would be no class differences, no army, no police, no need for punishment. The state would wither away, and the bureaucracy would simply perform the function of a general distribution agency, rewarding each man according to the work he performed. The armed peasants would seize the land, the armed workers would seize the factories, and the soldiers at the front would make peace with the enemy. It was to be as simple as that. As for capitalism, he was prepared to accept its abundant fruits. "Capitalism," he wrote in *State and Revolution,* "has already simplified to the utmost all the operations of bookkeeping and control, till they have become nothing more than an extraordinarily simple machine automatically controlling, recording, and issuing receipts, and this is now within the reach of anyone who can read and write and knows the first four arithmetical rules." The state, then, was to become a kind of benevolent adding machine, removed from the tragic momentum of politics, watching over the brotherhood of men, and in this brotherhood there would be no suffering and the age-old feuds of the human race would be resolved peacefully.

When Lenin arrived at the Finland Station, he was received with the honor which might have been accorded to a long-lost king returning to the throne of his ancestors. A cavalcade of armored cars brought him from the railway station to the palace of the Czar's mistress. Searchlights shone on the slow procession. There was a solemn beauty in his triumphal progress; and when he declared that the time had come for the peasants to take over the land and the workers to take over the factories, that everything was simple and the dawn of the socialist paradise had come, there was a long hush followed by a spontaneous acclamation. Standing there in the light of the searchlights he looked like the harbinger of peace which all Russians desired.

He was not yet however in complete charge of the situaion. Within a few weeks he was on the run, while Kerensky and Kornilov, with Savinkov as Minister of War, ruled over Russia. He escaped into hiding in Finland. There, he still dreamed of utopia. It was round the corner. Inevitably the revolution would succeed; inevitably it would bring peace and plenty. He emerged from his hiding place in October, to direct the Bolshevik shock troops against the newly-established government. Just before the seizure of power he wrote:

> The word must be: Power to the Soviets, land to the peasants, peace to the people, bread to the hungry. Victory is assured, and ten to one it will be bloodless.

There is no reason to believe the words were written cynically. A vast hope spread through the Russian people. Instinctively the people had chosen Lenin over the feeble dictatorship of Kerensky. The watchword was peace at any price. Talking to Bruce Lockhart, the British agent, Lenin spoke of passive resistance against all the enemies of his dictatorship. Russia would survive because the huge inertia of the peasants would absorb all blows. If the Germans continued their advance on Russia, the capital would be removed beyond the Urals, even to Siberia. All through January and February, 1918, the revolution seemed quiescent. Anti-Bolshevik newspapers continued to appear. Gorky, editing *Novaya Zhizn* (New Life) wrote bitterly against the Bolsheviks. But the Bolsheviks were in the saddle: the government consisted of eleven Bolsheviks and seven Left Social Revolutionaries. The acknowledged head of the Social Revolutionaries was Spiridonova, who had inherited the traditions represented by Sazonov and Kaliayev. March came, with the signing of the Brest-Litovsk treaty, and once again there was a vast hope for peace, with dreams of utopia round the corner.

We know the exact date, almost the exact hour and the

exact minute when Lenin launched his campaign of mass
terrorism against the terrorists themselves. The place where
it started was the German Embassy. There, for the last time
the Russian terrorist movement sought out and murdered
a man, this time the representative of the German Empire,
in the belief that he was actively supporting the Bolsheviks.
When the German ambassador was killed, Lenin threw the
whole weight of his power against the terrorists. Mass terror
had begun. It began a little after three o'clock in the afternoon of July 6, 1918.

On the previous day the Bolsheviks and the Social Revolutionaries were in conference in the Bolshoy Theatre in
Moscow. The Social Revolutionaries, led by Spiridonova,
bitterly denounced the Bolsheviks for signing the Brest-
Litovsk treaty with Germany, which they regarded as an
abject surrender. Lenin replied to their arguments sternly,
with cold precision and consummate mockery, but he did
not succeed in abolishing their arguments. Spiridonova accused him of outrageous crimes against humanity. Power
was being withdrawn from the workers' councils and the
village soviets; the death penalty was being re-introduced;
the people were being betrayed by the Revolution. The
Bolsheviks were establishing their position on the apex of
power without consulting the people and without a mandate
from the people. So the argument continued, and on the
following day there were only a handful of Bolsheviks at the
Bolshoy Theatre. Lenin had issued his order: there was to
be no more discussion. Determined to tame the power of
the Social Revolutionaries, he was searching for a pretext.

The pretext came in the afternoon. The German ambassador, Count von Mirbach-Harff, was sitting over lunch at the
Embassy. He was a Junker, with a small bullet-head and a
trim mustache and watery blue eyes. He held his slender
body stiffly, and moved with the curious jerking movements
common among Junkers from East Prussia. It was an-

nounced that two Russians, who said they came from secret police headquarters, wished to see him urgently. Count von Mirbach refused to see them, and sent Dr. Riesler, the Councillor of the Embassy, and a certain Lieutenant Müller, his military aide, to learn their business. Told that the matter was urgent, the Ambassador kept them waiting and telephoned to secret police headquarters. Shortly afterward he agreed to talk to the men, who had driven up together in an automobile and had had no difficulty in passing through the detachment of Bolshevik troops which guarded the Embassy. Dr. Riesler reported that the men brought news of an allied plot against the Ambassador. Their credentials were sound. They carried passes signed by Alexandrovich, the Social Revolutionary who acted in the coalition government as Vice President of the Cheka. They asked urgently for an interview. The Ambassador agreed to see the senior representative, a man called Blumkin. When Blumkin was introduced, the Ambassador stood at the head of a table. He seems to have guessed that he might be in danger, because he carefully arranged that Blumkin should stand with Riesler and Müller on either side of him. Blumkin laid on the table the documents which purported to prove an allied conspiracy against the Ambassador. Blumkin talked about the documents, stressing their importance, explaining at some length that they had only recently been discovered, but the Russian government was so concerned about the Ambassador's safety that it had been thought best to approach him before completing their inquiries.

"Then how," asked Count von Mirbach, "do you think they propose to assassinate me?"

"Like this," Blumkin replied, removing a Browning from his pocket, and jumping back so that he could take careful aim at the Ambassador.

The first shot was wild, and the Ambassador ran into the

next room, called the dancing-room. Blumkin caught up with
him. Standing at the door, he emptied his pistol into the
Ambassador. Then, breaking through a ground-floor window,
he lobbed a hand-grenade into the room to make doubly
sure he had killed the Ambassador, and escaped over a
fence. There was a sharp cry, and the sound of glass splin-
tering. The Ambassador was dying in a pool of blood, and
the whole room was black with smoke. Neither Blumkin nor
his accomplice, Andreyev, were ever caught: both escaped
abroad. By a quarter to three, on this warm summer afternoon, the Ambassador was dead.

The news was at once telephoned to Lenin. He immediately summoned Trotsky and Sverdlov to a conference.
"We should no longer regard ourselves as the Council of
People's Commissars," Lenin said. "We are now the Revolutionary Committee, and we must behave sternly." That
night Freiherr von Bothner, the head of the military mission, wrote in his diary after a long eulogy of Wilhelm
Maria Theodore Ernst Richard, Graf von Mirbach-Harff:
"This terrible act will cost many thousands of lives." Within
an hour of the outrage Lenin, Sverdlov, and Trotsky were
on their way to the Embassy to express their great grief.
The Social Revolutionaries were proscribed. Guns were
brought up against their headquarters, and though for a
brief while the Social Revolutionaries captured Dzezhinsky,
the head of the secret police, nearly all were arrested, many
of them as they sat in their places in the Bolshoy Theatre.

It was the beginning of the end. The next morning there
was an unusually heavy fog in the streets. Under cover of the
fog Lettish troops advanced and captured the headquarters
of the Social Revolutionaries. Only a handful survived, and
most of them were executed out of hand. Now there was no
longer a coalition government. An iron government, composed wholly of Bolsheviks, ruled over Russia. "Against the

weapon of individual terrorism," wrote Trotsky later, "we brought into being the far greater weapon of mass terrorism."

Years before, when the nihilists were talking glibly of progress and the advance of science and technology, Dostoyevsky had raised his hands in protest, demanding whether the revolutionaries themselves were aware of man's capacity for cruelty and depravity. Haunted by apocalyptic visions of wars and revolutions, disintegration and collapse, panic and chaos, he uttered his passionate warnings against the coming of the Nechayev monster, who would rule over men only to destroy them. He wrote in *The House of the Dead:* "Tyranny is a habit capable of being developed, and at last becomes a disease. The man and the citizen disappear forever in the tyrant." In *The Possessed,* which tells the story of the Nechayev conspiracy, though often violently distorting the course of events, Dostoyevsky makes Shigalyov say that he has prepared a blueprint for the millennium. Shigalyov himself is a little surprised by his blueprint, which calls for the division of mankind into two unequal parts, the minority, who enjoy "freedom of personality" and unlimited power over the majority, who surrender their individuality and live in innocence and bliss, happy toilers serving their masters. "It is very strange," says Shigalyov. "My system starts with the idea of achieving unlimited freedom, and ends in unlimited despotism."

Dostoyevsky never knew nor guessed how vast and powerful that despotism was to become. Under Stalin—a small thick-set man with a pock-marked face and a withered arm—mass terrorism, the murder of countless people for no reason except that they stood in the path of the dictator or appeared to stand in his path, became a commonplace of daily life in the Soviet Union. The *kulaks,* the middle-class peasantry, were destroyed root and branch. Whole nations were destroyed, and ethnic minorities were deported from the lands where they had lived since the beginning of history, to starve or perish in the wastes of Siberia. Whatever he could not dominate, Stalin attempted to destroy. Vain, suspicious, intolerant of the least sign of opposition, he used his power to stamp his name on the earth. He hated Lenin unyieldingly, and there are reasonable grounds for believing he was responsible for Lenin's death by poison. But this was the least of his crimes. His greatest crime was that he followed all the tortuous principles outlined in *The Revolutionary Catechism*, when he was in a position of supreme power.

Stalin was perfectly aware of his debt to Nechayev. Toward the end of 1926 he accused Zinoviev of attempting to impose the tyranny of party dictatorship on the Soviet Union. "Zinoviev," he said, "is trying to regiment the party to the highest possible degree. He intends to transform the party into an implacable machine, and within the party itself he wants to install a regime based on the principles of Nechayev." *

Dictators habitually accuse their enemies of the crimes they are themselves most guilty of. Stalin pretended to believe that the most terrible of all Zinoviev's crimes was a desire to impose "a regime based on the principles of Nechayev." In fact this was Stalin's greatest crime, and is the greatest crime of his successors.

The history of the Soviet Union under Stalin is the history of a senseless crime. Consumed by vanity, Stalin acted out the role of the conspirator when the revolution was already won. For him the real world possessed no existence; and seeing himself in the distorting mirrors of his own pride, he conjured up the ghosts of the ancient past and made war with them. Of himself he wrote: "Stalin never allowed his work to be marred by the slightest hint of

* *Speech at the Enlarged Plenum of the Executive Committee of the Comintern,* December 13, 1926.

vanity, conceit or self-adulation." In fact, vanity was the mainspring of his actions, and he was never happier than when consigning his imaginary enemies to their deaths. There is no evidence that he ever saw the execution of any of the countless men he sentenced to death. Like Hitler, he regarded the act of killing with distaste, but took vast pleasure in reading the reports of the N.K.V.D., with their tabulated lists of the executions of "enemies of the state." At the Twentieth Congress of the Communist Party held in Moscow on February 24, 1956, Nikita Khrushchev said of Stalin: "He abandoned the ideological struggle for that of administrative violence, mass repressions, and terror. Mass arrests and deportations of many thousands of people, executions without trial and without normal investigation created conditions of insecurity, fear, and even desperation." It was the salute of one terrorist to the greatest terrorist of all.

The terror continues. We have seen in Hungary that the habits of terror, practiced for so long by the Soviet Government, are not easily put aside. The terrible thesis which Nechayev drew up is still being fulfilled: "Our task is terrible, total, universal, and merciless destruction."

Bibliography

SERGEY NECHAYEV

The best introduction to Nechayev is to be found in Bakunin's correspondence, which has been published in Russian, German, and French. A brilliant but superficial account of Nechayev and his followers is given in V. P. Kozmin, *Nechayev i Nechayevtsi,* Moscow, 1931. More important work is to be found in special monographs which have appeared at various times in *Krasnii Arkhiv, Borba Klassov, Byloe,* and *Katorga i Ssylka,* four magazines devoted to revolutionary memoirs. I am especially indebted to P. Shchegolev's account of the Tula episode, which appeared in *Krasnii Arkhiv* at intervals between 1923 and 1926, and a series of articles on Nechayev in the Alexis Ravelin which appeared in *Byloe* in 1906. For an account of Nechayev's childhood I am indebted to N. C. Belchikov's brief monograph *S. G. Nechayev v sele Ivanove v 60-e gody,* which appeared in *Katorga i Ssylka* in 1925. There exists an excellent study of the *Revolutionary Catechism* in A. A. Shilov, *Katechesis revolutsionera k istorii nechayevskogo dela,* which appeared in *Borba Klassov* in 1924. I have based the present translation of the *Revolutionary Catechism* on the authoritative version printed by order of the Czarist government in *Pravitelstvenniye Vyestnik,* for July 11, 1871. Other issues of the newspaper give verbatim accounts of the trial of Nechayev's followers, from which it is possible to reconstruct the murder of Ivanov. I have delved into the memoirs of Herzen and Ralli-Arbore for details of Nechayev's visits to Switzerland, and I owe a particular debt to M. P. Sazhin's memoirs: *Vospominaniya, 1860-1880,* Moscow, 1925. For the rest it is only necessary to add that Nechayev dominated the thoughts of most of the terrorists who lived at the end of the last century, and nearly all of them have recorded minor details of his exploits.

ANDREY ZHELYABOV

The classic account of Zhelyabov's career is given in A. K. Voronsky, *Zhelyabov*, Moscow, 1925. Voronsky writes exceedingly well, and paints in the background with a consummate sense of artistry. A more extensive account of Zhelyabov's childhood and the early influences which formed his character in his student days is given in an article by V. N. Pisnaya, which appeared in *Byloe* in 1925 under the title *Studencheskie godi Zhelyabova*. David Footman's *Red Prelude* (Yale University Press, 1945), while largely based on Voronsky, contains considerable additional information and a good bibliography. A large number of accounts of the assassination of Alexander II are available. A well-informed four-column article on the deeds of the terrorists appeared in the *New York Times* for March 15, 1881, immediately after the assassination.

YEGOR SAZONOV

The source of most of our present knowledge of Sazonov is contained in an extensive collection of his letters edited by B. P. Kozmin and I. I. Rakitinkov under the title *Pisma Yegora Sazonova k rodnim 1895-1910*. The account of his years in Siberia is derived from two articles which appeared in *Katorga i Ssylka* in 1921 and 1922 by V. Pirogov. I have also used the brief sketch which appears in *Vyestnik russkoi revolutsii*, Geneva, 1905. A brief but informative account of Sazonov, dealing particularly with his last years, is to be found in I. Steinberg, *Spiridonova: Revolutionary Terrorist*, London, 1935. Like Nechayev and Zhelyabov, Sazonov became a legend in his own lifetime, and many brief and illuminating references to him can be found in the revolutionary memoirs of the period.

IVAN KALIAYEV

I have relied largely on Savinkov's memoirs and the brief memorial volume *Ivan Platonovich Kaliayev* published by the Social Revolutionaries in Switzerland in 1905. This book, no more than a slender, closely-printed pamphlet, contains most of Kaliayev's verses and nearly all his surviving letters together with an account of his execution, a summary of his life and some excellent photographs. I have also used the article on him which appeared in *Byloe* in 1908, and I have occasionally consulted Savinkov's novels which describe, sometimes incisively, but nearly always with a curious diffusiveness, the workings of the terrorists' minds. I am also indebted to Boris Nikolajewsky's study of Azev, which illuminates many dark corners of these tragic times.

GENERAL

ARBORE-RALLI, ZEMPHYR. *Sergey Gennadievich Nechayev* (*iz moikh vospominanii*). In *Byloe.*

BAEDEKER, KARL. *La Russie.* Paris: Paul Ollendorff, 1902.

BAKOUNINE, MICHEL. *Correspondance de.* Paris: Perrin et Cie., 1896.

BIENSTOCK, J. *Un Précurseur des Bolsheviks: Nétchaiev.* In *La Mercure de France.* tom. 137, pp. 5-27. Paris, 1920.

BREITFUS, ANDREI. *Iz vospominanii o kazni 3-go Aprela 1881 goda.* In *Byloe* (No. 25), 1924.

BRESHKOVSKAIA, KATERINA. Hidden Springs of the Russian Revolution. Stanford University Press, 1931.

BRUFORD, W. H. Chekhov and his Russia. New York: Oxford University Press, 1947.

CARR, E. H. The Romantic Exiles. Harmondsworth: Penguin Books, 1949.

CHALIAPIN, FEODOR. Man and Mask. New York: Garden City Publishing Co., 1932.

CHERNOV, VIKTOR. *Pered burei.* New York: Chekhov Publishing House, 1953.

COQUART, ARMAND. Dmitri Pisarev. Paris: Institut d'Etudes Slaves, 1946.

DOSTOYEVSKY, AIMÉE. Fyodor Dostoyevsky: A Study. New Haven: Yale University Press, 1922.

FIELD, CECIL. The Great Cossack. London: Herbert Jenkins. (n.d.)

FIGNER, VERA. Memoirs of a Revolutionist. New York: International Publishers, 1927.

FOOTMAN, DAVID. Red Prelude. New Haven: Yale University Press, 1945.

GOTZ, MIKHAIL. *I.V. Kaliayev* (*iz vospominanii*). In *Byloe* (No. 7), 1908.

KOROLENKO, VLADIMIR. *Istoriya moevo sovremennika*. Moscow: Isdatelstvo Vozrozhdeniye, 1922.

KOZMIN, B. P. *Nechayev i Nechayevtsi, Sbornik materyalov*. Moscow: Gosudarstvennoye Sotsialno-economicheskoye Izdatelstvo, 1931.

KROPOTKIN, PRINCE PETER. Memoirs of a Revolutionist. Boston: Houghton Mifflin Co., 1899.

LAFERTÉ, VICTOR. *Alexandre II. Détails Inédits sur sa Vie Intime et sa Mort*. Basle, 1882.

MARIE, GRAND DUCHESS OF RUSSIA. Education of a Princess. Blue Ribbon Books, 1930.

MAYNARD, SIR JOHN. Russia in Flux. New York: The Macmillan Company, 1948.

NIKOLAJEWSKY, BORIS. Azeff the Spy. New York: Doubleday, Doran and Co., 1934.

NOMAD, MAX. Apostles of Revolution. Boston: Little, Brown and Co., 1939.

PERRIS, G. H. Russia in Revolution. New York, 1905.

PISNAYA, V. N. *Studencheskii godi Zhelyabova*. In *Byloe* (No. 32), 1925.

RAMBAUD, ALFRED. *Histoire de la Russie*. Paris: Librairie Hatchette et Cie., 1918.

SACK, A. J. The Birth of Russian Democracy. New York: Russian Information Bureau, 1918.

SAVINKOV, BORIS. Memoirs of a Terrorist. New York: Albert and Charles Boni, 1931.

SAVINKOV, BORIS. *Iz vospominanii ob Ivane Kaliayeve*. In *Byloe* (No. 7), 1908.

SEMENYUTA, P. *Iz vospominanii ob A. I. Zhelyabove*. In *Byloe* (No. 8), 1906.

SEREBRENNIKOV, SEMEON. *L'Arrestation de S. Sérébrénikoff par la Police de Genève*. Geneva, 1870.

SHCHEGOLEV, P. *S. G. Nechayev v Alekseyevskom Raveline* (1873-1883). In *Krasnii Arkhiv*, 1923-1926.

SHUB, DAVID. Lenin: A Study. New York: Doubleday and Co., 1948.

SIMMONS, ERNEST J. Dostoevski: The Making of a Novelist. New York: Oxford University Press, 1940.

SLONIM, MARC. *Le Précurseur de Lenine*. In *Revue Universelle*, tom. 62, pp. 684-705, 1935.

STEINBERG, I. Spiridonova: Revolutionary Terrorist. London: Methuen and Co., 1935.

STEPNIAK (KRAVCHINSKI). Nihilism as it is. London: T. Fisher Unwin. (n.d.)

STEPNIAK (KRAVCHINSKI). Underground Russia: Revolutionary Profiles and Sketches. New York, 1883.

VENTURI, FRANCO. Il Populismo Russo. Rome: 1952. (two vols.)

WALLACE, SIR DONALD MACKENZIE. Russia. New York: Henry Holt and Co., 1905.

WILSON, EDMUND. To the Finland Station. New York: Doubleday and Co., 1940.

YAROSLAVSKY, E. History of Anarchism in Russia. London: Lawrence and Wishart. (n.d.)

Index